How to Get Out of Iraq with Integrity

Other Books and Collections by Brendan O'Leary

Authored/Coauthored

The Northern Ireland Conflict: Consociational Engagements
Policing Northern Ireland: Proposals for a New Start
The Politics of Antagonism: Understanding Northern Ireland
Explaining Northern Ireland: Broken Images
Northern Ireland: Sharing Authority
The Asiatic Mode of Production: Oriental Despotism, Historical Materialism,
    and Indian History
Theories of the State: The Politics of Liberal Democracy

Edited/Coedited

The Kurdistan Region: Invest in the Future: An Official Publication
    of the Kurdistan Regional Government
Terror, Insurgency, and the State: Ending Protracted Conflicts
The Future of Kurdistan in Iraq
Right-Sizing the State: The Politics of Moving Borders
State of Truce: Northern Ireland After Twenty-Five Years of War
The Politics of Ethnic Conflict Regulation: Case Studies
    of Protracted Ethnic Conflicts
Prime Minister, Cabinet, and Core Executive
The Future of Northern Ireland
Jack Watson's Success in World History Since 1945

How to Get Out of Iraq with Integrity

Brendan O'Leary

PENN

University of Pennsylvania Press
Philadelphia

Published by
University of Pennsylvania Press
Philadelphia, Pennsylvania 19104-4112

Printed in the United States of America on acid-free paper

10 9 8 7 6 5 4 3 2 1

Library of Congress Cataloging-in-Publication Data
O'Leary, Brendan.
  How to get out of Iraq with integrity / Brendan O'Leary.
      p.   cm.
  Includes bibliographical references and index.
  ISBN 978-0-8122-4201-0 (alk. paper)
    1. Iraq—Politics and government—2003– 2. Iraq War, 2003—Causes. 3. Postwar reconstruction—Iraq. 4. Constitutional law—Iraq. 5. Federal government—Iraq. 6. Territory, National—Iraq. 7. United States—Armed Forces—Iraq. 8. United States—Foreign relations—Iraq. 9. Iraq—Foreign relations—United States. 10. United States—Foreign relations—21st century. I. Title.
DS79.769.O44   2009
956.7044'3—dc22   2008048162

ISBN 978-0-8122-4201-0

For Khaled Salih, Kurdish nationalist and Iraqi federalist
For Lori Salem
     and
For Anna O'Leary, my daughter

The ones who deserve to be praised are those who, after succumbing to human nature by ruling over others, are more just than they have to be in view of their strength.

    —*Thucydides, from the speech of the Athenian ambassadors to Sparta*

Contents

Preface

In August 2005, I was just below one of the peaks in the Safeen Mountains in Kurdistan. Saddam Hussein's army had occupied it when the dictator's regime was at the peak of its power. Kurdish soldiers, the Peshmerga, now patrolled it, and I had special permission to visit this restricted site. A long way beneath stretched the pretty village of Shaqlawa, inhabited by Kurdish Christians and Kurdish Muslims and a small number of Arab tourists. Its natural ice-cold springs have made it richly endowed agriculturally and a destination for those seeking relief from the parching heat of the plains of Erbil.

Shaqlawa was looking slightly burnt in the fierce summer sun. But despite the heat and the glare, no training in generalship was required to understand the military significance of the Safeen Mountains. They prompt flashbacks in anyone with a historical education. Sargon, Cyrus, Alexander, Crassus, Trajan, Suleiman, or their subordinates looked out from these commanding heights before they descended to take Mesopotamia, or before they ascended into the Zagros Mountains in the vain hopes of permanently subduing their long-time inhabitants, the Kurds, known to Xenophon and the ancient Greeks as the "Karduchis" and as the "Guti" to the inhabitants of ancient Babylon (the Kurds themselves say they are the descendants of the ancient Medes).

I was in Kurdistan as a member of an international constitutional advisory team, working for the Kurdistan Regional Government.[1] My Kurdish friend Khaled Salih was in Baghdad. He had just rung me by cell phone to say, "We have a constitution." "Or rather," he corrected himself, "Iraq has a constitution." I looked forward to celebrating with Khaled on his return. I knew that the final text of the Constitution met all of Kurdistan's critical negotiating "red lines," namely, the recognition of (1) the Kurdistan Region's right to make its own laws on all domestic issues other than the management of Iraq's currency; (2) its Peshmerga, the name of the lawful army of Kurdistan, which translates as "Those who face death"[2]; (3) its rights over its unexploited oil and gas resources; and (4) its right to reunify with Kirkuk and other "disputed territories," through either a referendum or a lawful process of new boundary demarcation.

Once the Constitution was ratified, I knew that on paper Kurdistan would be freer within Iraq than any member state within the European Union. After all, each new member state of the European Union has to accept nearly 100,000 pages of European law. Kurdistan would have its own flag, army, and police. It would have full veto power over changes to Iraq's Constitution that affected the region's powers. It would have a proportionate share of Iraq's oil revenues from currently exploited oil fields. It would have the right to have international missions and representation within Iraq's embassies on all regional policy questions—that is, most questions in Iraq's decentralized federation. And, not least, by virtue of Iraq's proportional representation electoral law and other provisions in the new Constitution, Kurdistan's parties and leaders would be key players in the Iraqi federal government—if they wanted to play that role.

I turned to the Peshmerga with whom I was drinking hot tea, a wise drink in hot weather. I asked them what they thought of the constitutional negotiations taking place in Baghdad. I know only a small number of words in Kurdish and Arabic and so the conversation took place through a guide, whom I will not name because he now works in dangerous places. A small, wiry, and rather wizened Peshmerga looked up, smiled, and spoke quietly before the others laughed loudly. The translation came next: "We trust President Barzani to negotiate on our behalf. We even trust General Talabani for now. But most of all we trust our weapons. We will read the Constitution, but we will polish our weapons."

This book is not being written to persuade the Peshmerga that they no longer need to polish their weapons. They and their leaders need no lessons from anyone in geopolitics. They need no reminders of the ruthlessness and amoral amnesia that characterize the diplomacy, military interventions, and military withdrawals of the Great Powers. They are taught, truthfully, that the British promised them autonomy but failed to deliver it. They are taught, accurately, that Presidents Woodrow Wilson, Richard Nixon, Gerald Ford, and George H. W. Bush betrayed the Kurds of Iraq when it was expedient to do so. They have not forgotten that Saddam's Baath party and an Iraqi army executed genocide and ethnic expulsion against them. Just 20 years ago the Anfal campaign was in full operation, gassing Kurds, bulldozing 4,000 of their villages, incarcerating them in detention centers, and separating out the males of all ages for execution.[3] Kurds are fully aware that substantial American withdrawal from Iraq will happen. They know that self-help and self-reliance remain critical to their survival. They will be vigilant. They will polish their weapons but not rely on their weapons alone.

This book is written for those Americans who are willing to listen to a proposal on how to get out of Iraq with integrity. It seeks to define and defend the limits to feasible withdrawal. With integrity means with honesty. There is no reason why America's withdrawal from Iraq should be as dishonest as its intervention has been judged to be. But many of those who want America to withdraw from Iraq make dishonest arguments, and these arguments are confronted here. Integrity also refers to the "integrity" of Iraq. Iraq is not a gift or a work of nature. It is a product of British imperialism. And it has been a catastrophe for most of its citizens since at least 1968. But that does not mean that it would be prudent to partition Iraq into independent states. Kurdistan has every moral right to seek independence for its region, but its leaders and its citizens appreciate that prudence counsels otherwise. They have endorsed Iraq's federal Constitution in a voluntary union, and are trying to make it work in good faith. America's role should be to assist in the implementation of that Constitution rather than to persist in futile efforts to reverse it—or ignore it.

The Iraqi Constitution, endorsed by four out of five of Iraq's voters in October 2005, still offers the best framework for stability, democracy, and a pluralist federation. But to preserve the territorial integrity of Iraq does not mean that any rational person should support a significantly recentralized Iraq. Honesty, realism, and morality point toward the same story: a centralized Iraq was a disaster. And it is not coming back. It is not coming back because most citizens of Iraq do not want it to come back or are not prepared to pay the price of bringing it back. Efforts to recentralize Iraq will only reproduce the past repertoire of horrors.

Integrity requires the recognition that the greatest dangers to Iraq after a substantial American withdrawal will come from its neighbors: Turkey, Iran, and the Sunni Arab-dominated states of Syria, Jordan, and Saudi Arabia. By contrast, the rich minnows of the Gulf pose only positive possibilities. America must have an open military and diplomatic policy in place to prevent the dangerous neighboring powers from invading Iraq or from provisioning insurgents and terrorists within it. That policy will have to be negotiated and maintained with the European Union, which will be vital in managing Iraq's relations with Turkey and Iran.

Iran is the greatest external beneficiary of the U.S. decision to remove Saddam's regime from power. Instead of bemoaning that fact, or seeking to reverse it, American policymakers need to think about how to take advantage of it. The Turkish state is the neighboring country rendered most fearful by America's intervention in Iraq. Some of its fears are foolish, ideological, and cloudy. Instead of appeasing these fears, a wise American policy will defend Iraq's Kurdish experiment and facilitate the efforts of a fully reformed, liberalized, and democratized Turkey to join the European Union. Skeptics should read on.

Recognizing Iraq's external realities must be matched by a realistic understanding of its internal realities and a commitment to explain them to American and European citizens, as well as to the citizens of Iraq. Whether Iraq has a democratic future or not, its Sunni Arab minority will never again politically dominate the country from Baghdad. It is dishonest to hold out to their leaders the promise of any other vista—one in which America supports a recentralized Iraq in order "to balance against Iran." The Sunni Arabs' loss of power within Iraq may be cushioned, but it cannot be recovered. They can and should have a fair share—no more, no less.

Honesty warrants unblinking and unblinkered recognition of the fact that the Shia Arabs are the winners from democratization because they are a demographic and electoral majority of Iraq's population. They are a fractured and internally divided majority, but America lacks the resources to divide them in order to rule them, and lacks the skill to pursue any such Machiavellian policy—as the evidence to date suggests. A thoughtful American administration will work with a Shia Arab-led Iraq, and not against it. A thoughtful America will see that the Kurdistan Region is an ally, and a resource, useful for American soft and hard power in the Middle East. It should act as if the Kurdistan Region were a beneficial resource, and not a political embarrassment or moral burden. Considered carefully, the Kurdistan Region should be the kernel of a feasible democracy-promotion policy.

There are two components to the argument proposed in the title of this book: the case for withdrawal, and the case for withdrawal with integrity. But before these are considered, it is necessary to evaluate America's goals in its intervention. These goals were articulated by President George W. Bush. Congressional leaders sought to modify them. Critics of the intervention, on the political right and on the left, have suggested that the official goals were not what drove the intervention. Knowing how to withdraw with honesty requires us to know why we are where we are.

Part I
Evaluating the U.S.-Led Intervention in Iraq

In the battle of Iraq, the United States and our allies have prevailed. (Applause.) And now our coalition is engaged in securing and reconstructing that country.

—President George W. Bush, May 2, 2003

In the end, how we leave and what we leave behind will be more important than how we came.

—Ryan Crocker, U.S. Ambassador to Iraq, April 8, 2008

Before one leaves a place that belongs to others, it is wise to look behind carefully. The current orthodoxy holds that the Iraq war is lost, and that it was lost some time ago. Depending on the exponent's view, it was lost when the United States and its allies chose to enter Iraq, or when no weapons of mass destruction were found after May 2003, or after the tempo of the Sunni Arab-dominated insurgency increased in 2004, or after the revelation of the shame of American-organized torture at Abu Ghraib, or amid the shambles of the governance of the Coalition Provisional Authority, or during the mass slaughter and expulsions of 2005–7. But the orthodoxy, whatever the chosen definitive moment of loss, shows signs of needing revision. Indeed, the dominant trend in informed U.S. public debate is shifting. The key argument may soon focus on whether the future U.S. withdrawal from Iraq will amount to a substantive victory, or, instead, be deemed the termination of a series of Pyrrhic victories. The resolution of that argument will depend on who successfully defines what constitutes victory.

The United States and its dwindling number of international allies have not yet, however, lost the Iraq war: too many commentators have rushed to judgment on these matters.[1] Indeed, the United States and its allies have nearly won one of the Iraq wars, namely, the war against al-Qaeda in Iraq, even though that has hardly been quite the war intended.[2] And the United States may still be able to resolve another war, namely, the war of succession to Saddam, in favor of the elected federal government of Iraq and its ally, the Kurdistan Regional Government. But, it will be strategically better to do that as part of a policy of substantive but coherent military withdrawal.

When the next U.S. president does withdraw most or all American troops from Iraq, it need not be registered as a formal defeat. But an irresponsible, poorly organized, and hasty withdrawal will certainly be perceived as a major military, diplomatic, and political debacle for the world's superpower. Humiliation would be added to ignomi800. The stunning incompetence of the occupation after the successful six weeks of combat operations against Saddam's armed forces, and the equally badly handled two years after the end of the formal occupation of Iraq, would then be theatrically matched by the incompetence of a strategy-free exit. This unfolding of events must be avoided, in the interests of Iraqis as well as Americans.

Wars, with their bombs and bullets, are bloody instruments, but for the moderately rational among us they are means, not ends. They must be judged not just by the horrors they inflict, or halt, but by the political goals they are supposed to serve. How should we judge the attainment of American goals in its latest involvement in wars in and over Iraq?

There are three ways we might do so. We could judge them, first, by the Bush administration's declared goals at the outset of its intervention; second, by the goals of mainstream Republican congressional leaders, such as Senator Richard Lugar (the ranking Republican on the Senate Foreign Relations Committee) and the mainstream Democrats who endorsed the findings of the Iraq Study Group (known as the Baker-Hamilton report); or, last, by the hidden goals attributed, accurately or otherwise, to the Bush administration by its numerous critics, inside and outside the United States.

Chapter 1
The Bush Administration's Formal Goals

> Mr. President, it is natural to man to indulge in the illusions of hope.
> We are apt to shut our eyes against a painful truth....For my part,
> whatever anguish of spirit it may cost, I am willing to know the whole
> truth; to know the worst and to provide for it.
>
> —Patrick Henry, Speech to the Virginia Convention, March 23, 1775

At a January 1, 2003, White House press briefing, the Bush administration defined its goals for Iraq as follows: "To disarm the country, dismantle the terrorist infrastructure, and liberate the Iraqi people."[1] These three objectives would become the official tasks of the U.S. intervention, and measured by them the performance of the Bush administration has been excoriated, often rightly.

Disarming: The Evidence, 2003–7

In the months after the American intervention on March 19, 2003, the Baathist regime was officially disarmed. Neither nuclear weapons nor substantive programs to try to make them were found by U.S. inspection teams, to the surprise of very many.[2] (It is often conveniently forgotten that in the run-up to the war, both the Bush administration and many of its critics publicly shared the premise that Saddam was at least trying to obtain weapons of mass destruction.)[3] The United Nations weapons inspectors had done a far better job than even they supposed.[4] Equally, no significant evidence of programs to manufacture biological or chemical weapons was found after 2003.[5] There had been such programs, and the regime had used chemical weapons both against Iranian soldiers and Kurdish civilians in the 1980s; therefore suspicions were amply justified though not confirmed as fact. Controversies over the extent to which the Bush administration and the government of British Prime Minister Tony Blair manipulated intelligence to make the case for intervention continue to this day; that there was media-spinning, no one denies.[6]

Formally, we may conclude that Iraq no longer possesses weapons of mass destruction. Moreover, Iraq's 2005 Constitution commits the country both to its international treaty commitments, which include binding non-proliferation pledges, and to a non-nuclear defense policy.[7] Iraq, in this sense, is "disarmed" according to the original war goals of the Bush administration, though hardly in the manner expected, and at the expense of conventional international law, which outlaws preemptive war without UN Security Council authorization.[8]

But, by any other standards of armament, Iraq is now heavily remilitarized. And it has become the site of one of the bloodiest conflicts of this century.[9] More than 4,100 U.S. soldiers have been killed in Iraq since March 19, 2003, and some 30,000 have been wounded. There is no reliable estimate of the numbers of Iraqi combatants, government troops, jihadists, or militia killed in action, or seriously injured. On August 5, 2008, the independent and careful web site *Iraq Body Count* reported that between 86,000 and 94,000 civilians had died violently in Iraq since March 2003.[10] The median of these figures is 90,000, which means that in an average month approximately 1,400 civilians have been killed. Put differently, the civilian death toll at present approximates 30 massacres on the scale of New York's 9/11. According to these figures, the civilian death toll is still well below the lowest estimates of the genocidal massacres carried out by the Baathists by more than a factor of three. That, however, is small comfort to the survivors of the victims of the wars since 2003, or to the supporters of the U.S.-led intervention, who had hoped for a quick closure of conflict after the removal of Saddam.

The U.S. intervention got off to a poor start by deploying insufficient troops to police post-Saddam Iraq, despite prior and appropriate warnings of what was required. General Eric Shinseki, in testimony before the Senate Armed Services Committee, suggested on February 25, 2003, that several hundred thousand soldiers would be required for the intervention and occupation, figures which both Defense Secretary Donald Rumsfeld and his deputy, Paul Wolfowitz, publicly repudiated two days later. In consequence, Baghdad's liberation became a riot of looting and criminality. The same happened in many other cities in Arab Iraq, although not within the Kurdistan Region. Saddam's release of ordinary criminals before the U.S. intervention added to the chaos and mass criminality that ensued from the collapse of the Baathist order in Arab majority provinces. Insufficient troops and aircraft also left Iraq's borders open to fleeing Baathists and to arriving Salafi jihadists and Iranian agents.

The key institutions of the genocidal regime, the organizations that executed state terrorism against its citizens, were outlawed by the U.S. occupation government: the Baath party itself, and the military, police, and intelligence organizations that supported its tenure. But the disarmament of these institutions was disastrously ill-managed. Simplistic critics blame the Coalition Provisional Authority (CPA), established as Iraq's occupation authority in 2003, for disbanding Iraq's army and for excluding Baathists from public life. They thereby hold the CPA—known even to many of its own officials as "Can't Provide Anything"—responsible for fueling a Sunni Arab-dominated insurgency. It would be more accurate to say that managing the dissolved army, which had never formally surrendered and had simply walked away from its posts, was mishandled—with insufficient incentives offered to soldiers and officers to demobilize in an organized manner, through monitored surrendering of weapons and materiel in return for substantive benefits.[11]

Disbanding rather than reconstructing an army that had committed genocide against Kurds in the north and Shia Arabs in the south was essential if the new Iraq was to have the support of a majority of its population. But the chosen process, especially in the absence of sufficient Coalition forces, was thoughtless. It left numerous skilled Iraqi officers available to organize the insurgency and even more numerous and unpaid soldiers available for bloody retaliation. The reconstruction of the police, equally, might have been better organized, although a moral cleansing was certainly required. Likewise, de-Baathification should have been handled with more forethought. Dissolving the Baath party, which had become a totalitarian party, and a crucial component of Saddam's regime of mass destruction, was absolutely necessary for any humane reconstruction of Iraq. Kurds, Shia Arabs, and others were rightly fearful of its bloodthirsty record. In January 2005, Muhammed Abdullah al-Shawani, the first director of the new Iraqi National Intelligence Agency, maintained that the Baathists were the dominant force in the insurgency. The party once had 2 million members, and "if 20 percent still remain, that is a substantial number to lead the insurgency."[12] A better policy would have found means to avoid alienating the entirety of the party's active cadres (many of whom had joined as the sole means to achieve a professional career), which had reasons to be opposed to the new Iraq as well as the United States. Some senior Baathists could have been temporarily co-opted, and some junior Baathists could have been provided with opportunities to be rehabilitated in public life, policies that were eventually adopted under the pressure of the Sunni Arab-dominated insurgency.[13]

Between the fall of 2003 and the fall of 2007, especially in the Sunni Arab-dominated center and west of the country,[14] in Baghdad, and in some of the cities of the Shia Arab-dominated south, major conventional rearmament of Iraqis took place outside of any formal government authorization. Insurgents and militia organizations proliferated, initially made up of former Baathists and former Iraqi soldiers in central and western Iraq. The Sunni Arabs fought better once they were "deprived" of the enforced leadership of the Hussein family.[15] The predominantly Sunni Arab insurgents were soon joined in a holy or unholy alliance by foreign jihadists. Analysts counted at least 56 organizations and small factions that claimed to be involved in organized insurgency, self-defense, or jihad in the new Iraq.[16] By 2006, "consistent claims of responsibility for operations narrowed substantially to about eight groups": the Islamic Army of Iraq, the Mujahideen Shura Council (which included al-Qaeda in Iraq), Ansar al-Sunna, the al-Rashidin Army, the 1920 Revolutionary Brigades of the Islamic Resistance Movement, the Salah al-Din al-Ayoubi Brigades of the Islamic Front for Iraqi Resistance, the Mujahideen Army in Iraq, and the General Command of the Mujahideen of the Armed Forces (Baathists).[17]

The most infamous would be organized under al-Qaeda in Mesopotamia, led by Abu Musab al-Zarqawi.[18] He would mastermind a deliberate strategy of attacking Shia Arab civilians—apostates in his view. His goal was to provoke a civil war that would render Iraq ungovernable, and thereby prompt an American withdrawal. His most spectacular method was multiple suicide bombings at mosques, marketplaces, bus stations, and any public places where Shia Arabs predominated. Processions of peaceful Shia pilgrims were frequently targeted. When Zarqawi and his associates organized the bombing of the sacred Shia mosque in Samarra in February 2006, they provoked intercommunal strife on such a scale that only pedants and the Bush administration denied that Arab Iraq was in civil war.

By the spring of 2004, Shia Arabs were multiply reorganized with their own militias. The long-established Shia parties, whose leaders had been in exile in Iran and Western Europe, especially Da'wa and the Supreme

Council for the Islamic Revolution in Iraq (SCIRI), reemerged in Iraq with significant strength. SCIRI, which later renamed itself the Iraqi Supreme Islamic Council, or ISCI, had its own military organization, the Badr Brigades, many of whose leading members subsequently enrolled in the new police and army.

Within SCIRI the al-Hakim family is preeminent. It suffered an early blow when its leader, Ayatollah Mohammed Bakr al-Hakim, was killed in a car bombing in August 2003. His brother Abd al-Aziz al-Hakim immediately replaced him. The Badr Brigades had been launched and trained in Iran during the long war between Iraq and Iran that Saddam had initiated in 1980. They participated in the overthrow of the Baathist regime and would later bloodily avenge their Shia brethren, both against known or suspected Baathists and in retaliation for the attacks made by Sunni insurgents against civilian Shias. They would be renamed the Badr Organization in 2003 in nominal compliance with the U.S. wish to disband party militias.

The biggest surprise to external analysts was the emergence of the Sadr movement and its paramilitary wing, the Jaish al-Mahdi (or the Mahdi Army), centered on Muqtada al-Sadr, the surviving son of the Grand Ayatollah Mohammed Sadiq al-Sadr (known as Sadr II), who had been murdered along with his other sons by Saddam's regime in 1999.[19] The young Muqtada would prove an effective communal leader who became idolized by the poorer urban Shia population. The Mahdi Army fought running battles with the U.S. Army in April 2004, after an ill-judged effort by L. Paul Bremer to close the Sadrist newspaper, *Al-Hawza al Natiqa* (roughly *The Voice of the Islamic University*), and to arrest Muqtada on charges of organizing the murder of a leading Shia cleric, just when the U.S. Marines were intent on retaking and pacifying the Sunni city of Fallujah with extreme force. Bremer's decisions led to Sunni and Shia Arabs' briefly attacking U.S. forces on two fronts. The episode culminated in a siege in the holy city of Najaf. After mediation Muqtada emerged unscathed and uncharged, a hero to many Shia for standing up to the Americans.[20]

The Sadrists and numerous other local Shia militia groups, some of which were tribal, entrenched themselves in numerous cities in the south, as well as in what had been Saddam City in the Baghdad metropolis but is now renamed Sadr City.[21] Without strongly centralized leadership, the Sadrists, who were Iraqi nationalists as well as Shia communal contenders, intermittently attacked U.S. and British forces. They also spearheaded revenge killings by Shia after the bombing of the Samarra Mosque and played a major role in sectarian killings and expulsions in Baghdad during 2006–7.

The failure to establish a monopoly of publicly organized force by legitimate authorities meant that large swathes of Iraq entered a Hobbesian state of nature. Some remain there. But Hobbes was not quite right. When the state collapses, a war of all against all, or of person against person, does not ensue. Rather, when a repressive state collapses, people seek security through more traditional organizations—through their religious, ethnic, or tribal institutions. Criminals and thugs may also exploit these identifications. Today there are still heavily armed Sunni Arab insurgents intent on overthrowing the federal Iraqi government as well as forcing the Americans to withdraw. And there are armed Shia communal contenders battling for influence within the Shia majority bloc, and in Iraq as a whole. The major rival sectarian militias have killed one another's respective civilians in huge numbers. In short, a fragmented Arab Iraq has undergone a major communal civil war, pitting the formerly dominant minority of Sunni Arabs against the newly ascendant majority of Shia Arabs. Some of the blame for this must be attached to the poor administration of the American occupation, especially the failure to supply sufficient troops and police to maintain order while organizing regime replacement. It failed in its moral and legal duties—as an internationally recognized occupation authority until June 2004—to protect Iraqi lives and limbs.

It is true that the Baathist regime and its precursors, through deliberately discriminatory policies, had created the huge gulf between Sunni and Shia Arabs in Iraq, building upon centuries of manifest and latent religious antagonism and upon the privileged position carved out by Sunni Arab elites during the British imperial occupation and its aftermath. It is also true that any termination of the "psychotic" rule of the Hussein family[22] and the Tikriti clan at the head of the Baath party would likely eventually have led to some explosion of tensions between Sunni and Shia Arabs. But to say that not all the blame for the Iraqi civil war lies with the Bush administration is all that can be said in its favor.

By contrast with Arab Iraq, the Kurdistan Region is under the control of its lawfully elected government and the trained Peshmerga forces who make up the constitutionally authorized army of the region. The U.S. intervention in Iraq has had the opposite effect in Kurdistan to that in Arab Iraq. It prompted the major Kurdish parties to form a pan-national alliance, to unify what had become separate administrations, and to heal the civil war that its parties had fought in the mid-1990s. It should be the goal of a responsible American administration to help make the rest of Iraq resemble the Kurdistan Region, "the other Iraq," which has had no significant U.S. military presence since 2003 (except in the form of soldiers on vacation).

Demolishing or Breeding Terrorist Infrastructures?

The second formal war goal of the Bush administration was to destroy terrorist infrastructures. The efforts of the Bush administration to link Saddam Hussein directly to al-Qaeda, and thereby directly to the events of 9/11, are not now accepted by any authoritative researcher, intelligence analyst, or public commentator. (The links were, however, successfully established in American public opinion polls before and after the American intervention in Iraq, and therefore served the administration's purposes.) A standard criticism of the Bush administration is that it fought the wrong war (against Saddam, instead of making a greater commitment to reconstruction in Afghanistan) and that it fought it with perverse results. Al-Qaeda came to thrive in Iraq. Iraq became a magnet for foreign Salafi terrorists, and the place where terrorists, defined as organized groups that deliberately kill civilians for political purposes, killed more people than anywhere else on the planet. This movement inspired self-starting al-Qaeda cells in Western Europe, leading to greater numbers of terrorist attacks in established democracies.[23] The global war on terror (GWOT) became a global exercise in remarkably crazy crusading (GERCC).

More temperate analysis that avoids the partisan political debate in the United States is possible.[24] Saddam Hussein's regime was state terrorist—it killed civilians, unlawfully, for political purposes, on a mass scale. It also supported and was linked to organizations that used terrorist methods. It was a champion of pan-Arab and anti-Israeli causes, including violent Palestinian organizations. The regime paid rewards to the families of Palestinian suicide bombers in a deliberate riposte to Israeli collective punishments of such families. The regime indirectly supported Kurdish Islamists, notably those organized in Ansar al-Islam. They did so because Ansar al-Islam attacked the major secular Kurdish nationalist parties, the Kurdistan Democratic Party, and the Patriotic Union of Kurdistan. Ansar al-Islam included veterans of the Afghan jihad and therefore had personnel linkages to Osama bin Laden, and it would welcome Zarqawi and others to Kurdistan when they fled Afghanistan. These linkages illustrated mutual convergence of interests between Islamists and Baathists against nationalist Kurdish interests. But from Saddam's point of view such links were maintained from an Iraqi perspective. He resented loss of control over Kurdistan; he was not supporting any global jihad.

Therefore there were indirect links between Saddam and al-Qaeda, but they were not as portrayed by the Bush administration, and it was never accurate to link Saddam to 9/11, although he was foolish not to condemn the massacres of that day. "He openly mocked America's grief, taunted its power," maintains the Arab-American intellectual Fouad Ajami, who has also argued that "a war of deterrence had to be waged against Arab radicalism. Baghdad was the proper return address...notice was served on the purveyors of terror that a price would be paid by those who aid and abet it."[25]

It would be presumptuous to claim it possible to provide an accurate assessment of the state of organizations prepared to use terrorism in Iraq today. But it seems clear that a significant number of Sunni Arab insurgents, especially in Anbar province, turned on al-Qaeda in Iraq, especially in 2007. The Anbar Awakening Council, composed of Sunni Arab tribal leaders and former insurgents, preferred to make a bargain with the American government and go on its payroll—both to weaken al-Qaeda, which had destroyed its own reputation by its form of local government over the Sunnis, and to avoid a complete victory for the Shia-led Baghdad government and the Shia militias in Iraq's civil wars. The Sunni insurgents may therefore be counted as down, but not out, and, of these, al-Qaeda is now looking like a spent force.[26] Shia militias are another matter. The Mahdi Army, which is under the control of a bevy of local commanders and in some cases indistinguishable from extortion rackets, is also down, but not out. Officially it has recognized a cease-fire since October 2007, rather than being engaged in decommissioning its weapons and disbanding. But the Shia of Iraq have never been international terrorists. They are not Salafists —the latter are a Sunni phenomenon, and they treat Shia as apostates, deserving of death. The Shia may be much closer to Iran than the United States wants, but that was an almost inevitable outcome of replacing the Baath regime.

The U.S. objective of defeating al-Qaeda in Iraq is formally on the way to being met. This goal was met not through good planning and execution—except for the extinction of Ansar al-Islam by the Kurds and U.S. forces, and the belatedly more sensitive counterinsurgency policies in Sunni Arab Iraq. Arguably, the U.S. intervention temporarily attracted and radically increased the numbers willing to join al-Qaeda in Iraq, but that does not gainsay that it has now been effectively repressed by fellow Sunni Arabs.

Liberation Through Bloody Luck?

The liberation of the Iraqi people was the third goal proclaimed by the Bush administration. It certainly removed the regime quickly. The defeat of the Baath government in formal war took just six weeks, and contrary to many expectations and subsequent claims, involved significant care to avoid lethal or serious damage to civilians, a welcome contrast to the first Gulf War. Traveling around Kurdistan and northern Iraq in 2003 and 2004, I saw with my own eyes that U.S. smart bombs had successfully targeted the regime's key institutions—military targets, police barracks, and Baath party and intelligence centers. But, infamously, the Bush administration had no settled postwar plan. It had been good at regime removal but would prove utterly disorganized and ineffective at regime transformation, admittedly a more difficult task.

The State Department and the Defense Department were engaged in deeply personalized turf wars, with the latter temporarily in the ascendancy. Defense Secretary Donald Rumsfeld wanted a rapid military withdrawal after the rapid formal military victory, and failed to recognize the development of an insurgency in the summer of 2003, treating it merely as the activity of regime "dead-enders." General Jay Garner, who had done so much to organize relief for Kurdish refugees in Operation Iraqi Comfort in 1991–92, was appointed to head the Office of Reconstruction and Humanitarian Affairs on a ninety-day contract. But he was soon replaced by L. Paul Bremer III, of Kissinger Associates, and a former U.S. Ambassador to the Netherlands, who headed a UN-recognized occupation under the Coalition Provisional Authority. Instead of a rapid hand-over to a transitional Iraqi-led government, there would be a formal occupation. Bremer and his associates went through multiple plans for organizing regime transformation while appointing an Iraqi Governing Council, which was granted no significant powers. His complex plans to organize an indirect (s)election of Iraqis to draft a transitional constitution (to be crafted by American lawyers and advisors) and to head a potential transitional government were halted in their tracks.

Liberated Shia Arabs, who made up a majority of the country's population, took novel political steps to thwart Bremer. They had initially welcomed Saddam's removal but had been very cautious in their responses to the American occupation. Seared in their recent memories was the recollection that President George H. W. Bush had averted his eyes during Saddam's repression of the Shia intifada of 1991 after the Gulf War. He did so on the advice of James Baker, then Secretary of State, Brent Scowcroft, then National Security Advisor, and Dick Cheney, then Defense Secretary. The first president Bush even denied that he had called upon the Shia to rebel. Many Shia Arabs also blamed the Americans for their hardships during the UN-authorized sanctions against Saddam's regime. Most were, however, utterly delighted at the removal of the Baathist regime, apart from collaborators and informers whose lives were now in danger from the relatives of their victims. Aside from the secular Shia, who rallied to Iyad Allawi's Iraqi National Accord and to Ahmed Chalabi's Iraqi National Congress, it was soon apparent that there were stronger and more popular sources of authority among the Shia, all of them religiously based. There were, first, the long-established Shia religious parties, Da'wa and SCIRI, whose level of commitment to Iranian styles of governance was initially unknown, but it would soon become clear that they were not committed to a Khomein-ist theocracy of Islamic jurists. Then there was the Sadrist movement, led by the junior cleric Muqtada. It was clear it was populist, Iraqi national-ist, and a voice for the poor segment of the Shia. Its rabid sectarianism would become more obvious. The Sadr movement opposed the U.S. occupation but it was not at all clear whether it was democratic, and some of its members had been co-opted by the Bathists. The Fadila Islamist Shia party would also emerge in the south as an intermittent partner of the Sadrists. And last, there were the senior ayatollahs and the Shia clerical institution, the Hawza al-Marja'iyya. The most distinguished and most widely regarded cleric was the Iranian-born Grand Ayatollah Ali al-Sistani.[27]

Despite being a quietist by disposition, Sistani put the Shia behind the banner of immediate democratization. He was also, formally, remarkably solicitous of the interests and rights of minority religions and nationalities. He rejected all of Bremer's plans to have either a constitution, transitional or permanent, or an Iraqi government, transitional or otherwise, without Iraqis voting to decide the matter. He refused to meet directly with Bremer and resisted entreaties to endorse the government of what he called the "guests." Soon most Shia, secular or religious, rallied behind Sistani's opinions or *fatwas* in late 2003 and early 2004. Understanding democracy as a system of majority rule, the Shia appreciated that rapid democratization would not only put Iraqis in charge of their own fate, but also put the Shia themselves in charge, and end the hated tyranny of the formerly dominant minority of Sunni Arabs. Rallying behind Sistani, the Shia successfully used demonstrations and solicitations to force Bremer to concede that a permanent Iraqi constitution would be drafted by an elected Iraqi parliament and obliged him to bring in the United Nations to advise on the prospects for holding elections in Iraq. The democratization of Iraq, problematic as it has been, therefore owes more to Sistani and Shia pressure than to the Bush administration's planning. Had Bremer and his colleagues had their way, there would have been a much longer and controlled transitional government, and a constitution without any legitimacy before the first federation-wide elections.

What happened during the constitution-making process in post-Saddam Iraq? The Iraqi Governing Council—composed of thirteen Shia Arabs, five Sunni Arabs, five Kurds, one Turkoman, and one Christian—under Bremer's supervision and direction, negotiated the Law of Administration for the State of Iraq for the Transitional Period (the Transitional Administrative Law, or TAL) in February and March of 2004.[28] Initially intended as an interim constitution,[29] the first drafts showed the Coalition Provisional Authority advisors' ambitions for Iraq. They wanted a centralized federation, based on the eighteen governorates (provinces) established under Saddam's Iraq (see Map 1), and they plainly thought of Iraq as an Arab nation and composed of just one nation. But the final text was not what Bremer's advisors had in mind. The text of the TAL was modified significantly by Shia pressure for immediate democratization, which also meant recognizing Islam's constitutional status in a way that Sistani and others could accept. A liberal recognition of Islam's status acceptable to all the negotiators was achieved.[30] The Shia negotiators, especially in SCIRI, also expressed interest in being able to aggregate the southern governorates into larger regions. Provision was made for that, though no more than three governorates were to be allowed to aggregate, and Kirkuk and Baghdad were excluded. Democratization also meant that the United Nations would be entrusted with consulting and subsequently advising on an electoral and party law, advice that Bremer accepted.

The TAL was also significantly affected by Kurdistan's negotiators. They insisted that Iraq be a democratic federation and that it should recognize the existing Kurdistan Region within its current borders (see Map 2) with very significant autonomy, and that it should provide a fair process for resolving the status of Kirkuk and other disputed territories. The de facto powers and de jure laws of the Kurdistan Region and Kurdistan National Assembly respectively exercised after 1992 were recognized. Kurdish was to be treated as an official language along with Arabic. Kurds successfully insisted that Iraq should be proclaimed a pluralist federation composed of

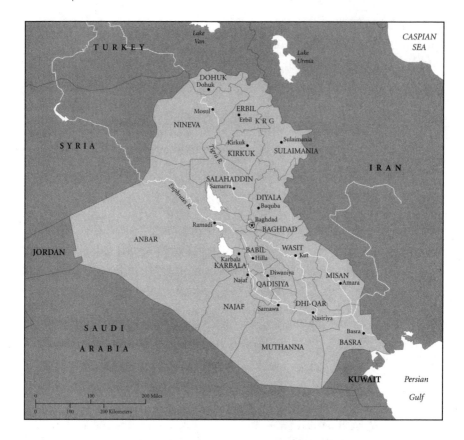

Map 1. The eighteen governorates (provinces) of Iraq in 2003.

multiple nationalities. Bremer refused Kurdistan's demand to control its own natural resources and sought to centralize all security arrangements in Iraq. Kurds, however, successfully won the right to control internal security within the Kurdistan Region.

The major point of controversy in the making of the TAL arose over the procedures for making and ratifying the permanent Constitution. The Shia Arabs preferred majority decision making within the elected convention, and ratification by a simple majority of Iraqi votes in a referendum. Kurdistan sought a separate right of ratification—that is, to establish a federal method of ratifying the Constitution. A compromise was reached. The draft Constitution would require the support of a majority in the new National Assembly, but the Constitution was to be ratified by a qualified majority. Ratification would require a simple majority of Iraqi voters in favor but it

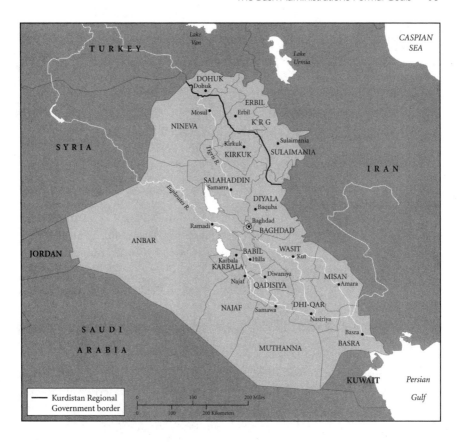

Map 2. Existing borders of the Kurdistan Region.

was also specified that no three provinces would vote against the Constitution by a two-thirds majority. Since the existing Kurdistan Region encapsu-
lated most of three governorates (Dohuk, Erbil, and Sulaimania), it had
won a de facto separate right of ratification. But the text of the TAL did
not require the governorates to be contiguous, which was deliberate. The
de facto veto was also intended to protect Sunni Arabs. It was presumed
that Sunni Arabs, especially if they made any alliances, might have a similar capacity to block any draft constitution that they did not approve. They
appeared to have such prospects in four governorates: Anbar, Ninevah,
Salahaddin, and Diyala. (But at this time many Sunni Arabs suffered from
demographic delusions of grandeur, believing that they were the demographic majority not simply the historically dominant group in Iraq.) This
compromise, eventually accepted by Shia Arabs, would eventually give

Kurdistan's negotiators a pivotal role in the making of the permanent Constitution in 2005.[31] Therefore neither Bremer nor his liberal Arab counselors were directly responsible for enabling Iraqis to remake their country as a pluralist federation.

The United States and the United Kingdom dissolved the Coalition Provisional Authority at the end of June 2004. The United Nations recognized the restoration of Iraq's sovereignty. The multinational forces under U.S. command are to remain, under a treaty with the transitional government and under UN Charter Section 7, until 2009. The expanding and eventually huge new U.S. Embassy in Baghdad took on many of the staff, mindsets, and legacies of the discredited CPA. Bremer appointed Iyad Allawi, a secular Shia, former Baathist, former Western intelligence asset, and head of the Iraqi National Accord to be the transitional prime minister. He also appointed a Sunni Arab of the Shammar tribe, Ghazi al-Yawar, as president. The Kurds were outraged that a Kurd had not been selected for one of the top two positions and by Allawi's refusal to legislate to make the TAL the interim law of the land (the United Nations had remained silent on the TAL, implicitly suggesting a constitution made under occupation was legally void). Allawi eventually agreed to comply with the timetable and the constitution-making protocols laid down in the TAL, and the Kurds then agreed to support the transitional government.

During the fall of 2004, Sunni Arab-led insurgents increased their attacks on U.S. forces, new Iraqi security forces, and the transitional government. The insurgents thought Iraq was still under occupation, and the transitional government was merely an American puppet. For similar reasons, many Sunni Arab organizations and parties, including the Association of Muslim Scholars, urged a boycott of Iraq's forthcoming free and fair universal suffrage elections supervised by an independent Electoral Commission and the United Nations Electoral Assistance Unit. The elections were held at the end of January 2005. They were boycotted by a very high proportion of Sunni Arabs, but Kurds, Shia Arabs, and others turned out in extraordinarily high numbers, and the United Nations judged the contest free and fair.

The electoral system was an Iraq-wide proportional representation list. Iraqis in exile, disproportionally Shia Arabs and Kurds, were entitled to vote. The Shia voted overwhelmingly for a coalition of religious parties, the United Iraqi Alliance, blessed by Ayatollah Sistani. It took 48 percent of the vote and 140 of the 275 of the seats in the Iraqi National Assembly, which was authorized to write the Constitution. The Kurds voted even more overwhelmingly for the Kurdistan Alliance, taking 26 percent of the vote and

75 seats. Outgoing Prime Minister Iyad Allawi's secular Iraqi list, supported by middle-class Sunni and Shia, trailed in third place with 14 percent of the vote, and 40 seats. Ghazi al-Yawar's "The Iraqis" was the sole Sunni Arab list to achieve significant representation, albeit with less than 2 percent of the vote and five seats.

The citizens of Iraq had had their first taste of meaningful formal democratization since the removal of the Baathists. They had voted out of office the American chosen and backed prime minister and his party. They had also demonstrated that there were no significant Iraq-wide parties. Kurds had voted as nationalists for the Kurdistan Alliance; the Shia had voted for their coalition of religious parties throughout the south and center of Arab Iraq; and the Sunni Arabs (and some Turkomen) had mostly boycotted the elections in central, western, and northwestern Iraq.[32] Allawi's grouping had some cross-sectarian support among Arabs, and among Christians.

The election ensured that the transitional elected Iraqi government that would control the drafting of the Constitution would be dominated by Saddam's principal victims, namely, the Shia Arabs and the Kurds. The new Prime Minister Ibrahim al-Ja'afari of Da'wa was nominated by the United Iraqi Alliance after Jalal Talabani of the Patriotic Union of Kurdistan had been elected President. Despite Ja'afari's allocation of eight cabinet ministries to Sunni Arabs (one more than was allocated to Kurds), Sunni Arabs were determined to be alienated. Rich or poor, many of them remained racial and religious supremacists toward Kurds and Shia Arabs. "For them, de-Baathification was synonymous with de-Sunnification."[33] Their postures, truculence, and general unreasonableness, aggravated by the threats posed to their security by extremist insurgents within their own ranks, would cost Sunni Arabs dearly in the negotiation of the Constitution in the summer of 2005. Some of their leaders claimed to be intent on meaningful negotiations, but many more hoped to derail the Constitution-making timetable through obstructionist tactics and to have fresh Iraq-wide elections if the Constitution failed to be drafted on time or to vote down any draft composed by the Shia Arabs and the Kurds.

The Kurdish and Shia Arab party leaders surprised many by successfully negotiating a constitutional text to near completion in August 2005. Subsequent emendations and modifications to allay what were treated as legitimate Sunni Arab anxieties continued up until just before the date for the referendum to validate the Constitution, October 15, 2005. The Constitution of Iraq of 2005 provides for a highly decentralized and pluralist federation, which recognizes Iraq as a land of many nationalities and religions. The Kurdistan Region's autonomy, previously established in the TAL, was not only confirmed but extended. The Kurdistan National Assembly obtained powers over currently unexploited natural resources, the recognition of the Peshmerga as the lawful security forces of the region, the right to veto the application of any federal legislation outside of the very limited exclusive competencies of the federal government, the ability to veto any future constitutional amendments, and the right to diplomatic representation in all of Iraq's embassies and missions on all matters within its jurisdiction.[34] Vitally, it obtained regional legal supremacy on all matters not within the exclusive powers of the federal government.

In the TAL the Kurdistan Region had been exceptional. In the permanent Constitution, by contrast, all governorates (except Baghdad and Kirkuk) could unify to create regions with powers as extensive as those of Kurdistan. They could also choose to opt for fewer powers or to remain as governorates. The text was a radical victory for a decentralized federation precisely because the exclusive powers of the federal government were so few and so limited. They did not even include the independent power to tax where a region existed. The provisions on natural resources, which many later falsely held to be ambiguous, did not define, unlike the TAL, oil and gas resources to be an exclusive purview of the federal government. Therefore, where regions would form, they would have legal supremacy over such resources. The Constitution also declared that the revenues from all currently exploited fields would be distributed across Iraq as a whole provided that provisions were made to rectify historical and deliberate underspending in some regions and to aid regions that had suffered at the hands of the Baathists.[35]

The Constitution provided a similar status for Islam to that agreed to in the TAL. It provided for a federal parliament, headed by a prime minister and council of ministers. It made provision for the subsequent creation of a federal second chamber and of a federal supreme court—the enactment of both would require the support of two-thirds of the representatives in parliament to be valid. It also made provision for a transitional Presidency Council that would enable a Shia Arab, a Sunni Arab, and a Kurd to share power and jointly exercise a partial legislative veto without requiring quotas.

The Constitution, like the TAL, was not what the Bush administration's officials had sought. They had wanted a more centralized Iraq, for their own geopolitical reasons. They had wanted a Constitution more appealing to the absent Sunnis, who had boycotted the National Assembly elections. They had also wanted a reduction in the severity of the de-Baathification law but merely won the constitutional possibility of such changes.

The Kurdish and Shia Arab negotiators proved to be representative of their voters: four out of five Iraqi voters endorsed the Constitution, and the independent Electoral Commission and the United Nations endorsed the results. Sunni Arab Iraq overwhelmingly voted "no," this time deciding that turning out was in their interests. A majority of "no" votes was delivered in three governorates, but only two had the two-thirds of the total required to restart the constitutional negotiations.

Shortly after, in December 2005, fresh elections to the new Council of Representatives were held. Because the Sunni Arabs participated, the number of seats held by the United Iraqi Alliance was cut back to 128 out of the 275 in the new Council of Representatives. The Kurdistan Alliance's share of seats fell to fifty-three (five seats were won by the Kurdistan Islamic Union after it ran on an independent platform).[36] The Iraqi Consensus Front, a coalition of Sunni religious and tribal alliances, won forty-four seats, and the secular neo-Baathists in the Iraqi National Dialogue won eleven seats. Talabani was reelected president, but Ja'afari's reelection was unacceptable to Kurds and Sunni Arabs.[37] A new prime minister, again from Da'wa, Nouri al-Malaki, emerged. Thus in two elections, spanning just a year, Iraqis had voted for assemblies that changed the incumbent prime minister and in which their votes decided the general composition of the federal executive.

Iraq at the federal level thus meets many standard minimal definitions of democracy: competitive elections and consecutive turnovers in the office of chief executive. Provincial elections were held in January 2005, and debate now focuses on when the next set will be. There is therefore a decent prospect of the routinization of democracy in Iraq. That is not to suggest that the rule of law, civil rights, human rights, and clean government are the hallmarks of the new Baghdad government or of all its provincial governments. That would be absurd. The embers of civil war are still burning. There are still militias in Arab Iraq without legal authorization. Foreign forces remain on Iraqi soil, assisting the federal government to restore basic order in Arab Iraq. But a decisive regime shift has taken place, and it is reasonable to suggest that the new regime is being stabilized. There has been a liberation of Iraqis—albeit one soaked in blood, occasioned by the old regime's die-hards and new religious communal contenders as well as by the new security forces and the U.S.-led Coalition forces and by meddling by Iraq's neighbors.

Let me complete this rapid survey of controversial and contestable evidence to set against the original war goals of the Bush administration. If it is broadly correct, it necessitates a more nuanced assessment than has been typical in global and American mass media commentary. In the summer of 2008, the formal goals of the Bush administration in Iraq are closer to being met than at any time since May 1, 2003, when President Bush announced that major combat operations in Iraq had ceased. That does not mean the administration merits much praise. This has mostly been no thanks to intentional American policy and management, with the debatable exception of "the surge" that started in 2007 and that will be examined in due course. But the broad picture needs to be appreciated.

- Iraq poses no immediate threat of becoming a state that uses weapons of mass destruction, either against its regional neighbors or its own citizens. By the standard of the Bush administration's original goal, Iraq is disarmed. The new Iraq has no nuclear, chemical, or biological weapons, and it is constitutionally mandated to remain that way.
- Iraq's new federal government, despite its extremely shaky and chaotic beginnings, is restoring order in Arab Iraq. Together with the United States, Iraqi forces have dismantled much of the new terrorist infrastructure created by the Sunni Arab insurgents, and they are on the verge of compelling the Sadrists to choose between constitutional politics or being outlawed. The Kurdistan Region is free of bases run by Ansar al-Islam and its successors. The depleted numbers of Arab, Kurdish, and Turkomen Sunni jihadists are now concentrated in Arab Mosul, Diyala, and in the border region where Iran meets Kurdistan. Progress overall is, of course, fragile. The United States has in effect placed the Sunni tribes of Anbar and elsewhere on its payroll, and their formal incorporation into Iraqi security structures has not been resolved.
- Iraq since October 2005 has had a new Constitution, ratified by its voters and underpinned by overwhelming endorsement by the major communal victims of Saddam, namely, Shia Arabs and Kurds. It has democratic institutions that determine who holds power at federal, regional, and provincial levels. After fierce but eventually ineffective resistance, Sunni Arabs, however truculently, are negotiating their inclusion within the institutions of the new Constitution. They want the constitutional order modified but, so far, most are working to change it within its rules. If the Constitution holds and even roughly describes the rules within which politicians operate in the future, then Iraqis will have been liberated both from Baathism and from the authoritarian imposition of either a Sunni or Shia theocracy. Progress here, of course, is slow and fragile. The federal government has not met its obligations to resolve the status of the territories disputed between Kurdistan and Arab Iraq, especially

in Kirkuk. Sunni Arabs are likely to be disappointed at what constitutional amendments if any are likely to be feasible. Iraqis still contest the meanings of the Constitution of 2005 and have not delivered on many of their institutional obligations.

Judged by the Bush administration's formal war goals, the United States stands on the verge of a partial success but after horrific and unnecessary losses of life and after four years of ill-advised and brutally repressive policies for which Defense Secretary Donald Rumsfeld and Vice President Dick Cheney are rightly held chiefly responsible.[38] Such costly success may alone be sufficient to suggest that it may be time to go—to declare victory and leave. But for success to be complete with respect to these formal war goals requires that two currently elusive objectives be met: an Iraqi security settlement that will survive a substantive U.S. withdrawal and a matching Iraqi political settlement within the framework of the 2005 Constitution in which Sunni Arabs can play their role as equal citizens. I will assess these prospects in Parts II and III of this book, but I now turn to the goals of the mainstream congressional supporters of the war, especially those goals which they retrospectively established for the intervention.

Chapter 2
The Bipartisan
Congressional Goals for Iraq

In politics, what begins in fear usually ends in folly.
—Attributed to Samuel Taylor Coleridge

The American intervention in Iraq was not just George Bush's doing. His decisions were underpinned by support from both parties and had congressional authorization from both the House and the Senate. American public opinion supported the intervention as it began and in its initial phases. Moreover, the United States constructed a significant but limited international coalition that supported enforcing UN resolutions that called for Iraq's unambiguous disarmament after the first Gulf War.[1]

Therefore a second way to assess whether U.S. war goals have been met is to evaluate them alongside the wishes of major mainstream Republican and Democratic congressional leaders. War aims change shape during a conflict—it is rare for any war to be successfully conducted and won according to plan—and these aims are not identical to the original public goals of the White House that Congress supported. Senator Richard Lugar, the senior Republican on the Senate Foreign Relations Committee, may be taken as a representative figure here. In a widely discussed speech in June 2007, he identified America as having "four primary objectives" in Iraq:

1. "Preventing Iraq or any piece of its territory from being used as a safe haven or training ground for terrorists or as a repository or assembly point for weapons of mass destruction";
2. "Preventing the disorder and sectarian violence in Iraq from upsetting wider regional stability";

3. "Preventing Iranian domination of the region"; and
4. "Limiting the loss of U.S. credibility."[2]

Senator Lugar's speech foreshadowed the Warner-Lugar amendment proposed in July 2007 to the National Defense Authorization Act, which was subsequently vetoed by President Bush.[3] The four goals cited may be fairly described as a coherent distillation of the most rational goals of the Iraq Study Group Report of 2006, also known as the Baker-Hamilton Report, but without the latter's manifest contradictions.[4] (The Baker-Hamilton Report, organized by James Baker, the Secretary of State under the first President Bush, may be fairly said to represent the bipartisan consensus of congressional critics of the Bush administration's intervention in Iraq.)

The first goal specified by Senator Lugar is part of the Bush administration's formal agenda. As we saw in Chapter 1, the key question is how this goal of preventing Iraq from becoming (or remaining) a terrorist safe haven can best be satisfied through a substantive U.S. withdrawal or without one. The other goals, by contrast, are much farther from realization.

Regional Stabilization

The second goal merely aspires toward containment—that is, preventing internal conflict within Iraq from destabilizing the wider region. But this destabilization has already occurred. In 2007, at the peak of sectarian violence, there were estimates from the UN High Commissioner for Refugees, António Guterres, that 4 million Iraqis had been displaced: 2 million internally and 2 million as refugees in foreign countries, mostly in neighboring states.[5] That is perhaps one in seven Iraqis. Refugees cause instability in the places where they go—they are an unexpected burden on local budgets and they may generate a nativist reaction. Refugees also occasion instability for the places from which they have fled—they may want to return in force, and they may finance, support, or join violent diaspora organizations. The United States will have to have a long-term commitment to facilitate the return of refugees from Iraq.

Iraq's regional neighborhood, to understate matters, has not always sought to stabilize the new government of Iraq, and the conflicting interests of the neighboring powers render such a helpful convergence very difficult. Iran, having been publicly—and misleadingly—defined by the United States as part of an "axis of evil" in January 2002, has had significant strategic reasons to make life bloodily awkward for America in Iraq. Syria's Baathist government has had equally powerful strategic reasons for

fear of the U.S. presence in Iraq, especially when American neoconservatives talked excitedly of making "a left turn" to Damascus after the U.S.
military took Baghdad. Iraq's Syrian, Saudi, and Jordanian borders have
often been porous. Traditional lands of Sunni Arab tribes straddle them
all. Their governments have not been especially concerned to stop their
local jihadists from volunteering to fight for Sunni organizations in Iraq.
They prefer them to cause trouble outside of their own countries, and they
fear a Shia-dominated Iraq. In these three countries the joke is that their
governments give militant Islamists a one-way ticket to Iraq—they are not
allowed to come home.

Senator Lugar, along with former Secretary of State James Baker, Representative Lee Hamilton, and bipartisan congressional opinion in general, does not want conflict in Iraq to destabilize America's allies in Iraq's
immediate neighborhood, such as Turkey, Jordan, Saudi Arabia, Kuwait,
and the Gulf states. But how is that to be achieved? Turkey, for example,
wants a settlement of the Kurdish question in Iraq that does not destabilize its territory or security. Turkey is unhappy with the Kurdistan Regional
Government's management and alleged appeasement of the Kurdistan
Workers' Party (known by its Kurdish acronym, PKK). The latter fought a
major insurgent war of secession against Turkey in the 1990s and it intermittently strikes military and civilian targets in Turkey. According to Turkish authorities, it does so from remote sites within the Kandil Mountains
inside the Kurdistan Region of Iraq.[6] Turkey opposed the federalization
of Iraq because it did not want a strong Kurdistan Region to emerge. Now
that it has, Turkey's officials do not want the Kurdistan Region to expand,
as it may do lawfully under Article 140 of Iraq's Constitution, which mandates the holding of a referendum—yet to be held—to determine the territorial status of Kirkuk governorate.

Jordan, Saudi Arabia, and Syria[7] have Sunni Muslim majority populations, which mostly sympathize with Iraq's Sunni Muslims. Their governments opposed the replacement of Saddam's regime, both because they
are Arab nationalists, and in the case of Jordan and Saudi Arabia, because they feared that its removal would strengthen the Shia in Iraq and
Iranian power. Their regimes, unlike their populations, share a strong interest in the successful defeat of al-Qaeda in Iraq (even though many volunteer jihadists have come from their lands). The smaller Gulf states, such
as Kuwait, the Arab Emirates, and Bahrain, comprise Sunni Muslim rulers presiding over significant or majority Shia populations. They, too, fear
a Shia takeover. That is why they supported Saddam Hussein's Iraq against
Iran, as the United States did during 1980–88. Their fate must also be con-

sidered in any rational appraisal of the prospects for regional stabilization, with or without a substantive U.S. withdrawal.

Preventing Iranian Domination?

The third goal of mainstream U.S. political leaders is to prevent Iranian domination of the region. But it is a bit late for that thought. "Thanks to George W. Bush...Iraq is now the Arab world's first Shiite-ruled state."[8] Since its 1979 revolution Iran has been both a champion of international Islam and Shia Islam. After the fall of the Shah of Iran, the enemies of Iran had good reason to fear that Ayatollah Khomeini's revolution might spread to the Shia-populated lands that extend from Iran through central and southern Iraq, eastern Saudi Arabia, through to Bahrain, that is, the fabled Shia demographic crescent that hovers over the world's largest known oil and gas fields. That is one reason why Saddam Hussein went to war against Iran and one reason why he was backed by the Reagan administration.

In politics, as in life, the enemy of my enemy may be my friend. The Iranian government hated no government more than Saddam's. It had more reason to fear Saddam's apparent determination to hold or develop weapons of mass destruction than anyone apart from the Kurds. When the United States defeated Saddam in the first Gulf War, Tehran was delighted. When the United States overthrew the Taliban regime in Afghanistan, Iran's leaders were equally pleased. The Taliban, Sunni extremists par excellence, had crushed the Afghan Shia population and murdered Iranian diplomats. Both the first Gulf War and the displacement of the Taliban had shown the enormous capabilities of U.S. power and diplomacy. In the fall of 2001, Iran cooperated with the U.S. intervention in Afghanistan, shared intelligence on al-Qaeda, and refused admission to fleeing al-Qaeda and Taliban operatives. Given this pattern, a strategically astute U.S. administration would have at least sought Iran's cooperation in the overthrow of Iraq's Baathists. Both the United States and Iran would have stood to gain. Iran would not have had any reason to destabilize an Iraq in which the Shia majority, whose leaders it had supported in exile, would come to power. The United States would have had Iranian cooperation while regime replacement took place in Baghdad.

Instead, the Bush administration did its unintentional best to look like the Great Satan of Khomeini's imagination. In January 2002, in his State of the Union address, President Bush condemned an "axis of evil" linking Iraq, Iran, and North Korea. Whatever their shades of evil, these three countries were not allies and were not a geometric or geographic axis. Bush was publicly describing them as a coalition of rogue states, equally likely to develop and use weapons of mass destruction and to supply such to terrorists. The Iranian government had not had any official diplomatic contact with the United States since the Tehran hostage crisis that had started at the end of President's Carter's term. The message they received from Bush's speech was unambiguous. After Saddam, Iran's regime would be the next target of American power.

The Iranians responded with much greater strategic astuteness than Saddam. Having witnessed his fall, they supported their allies in Iraq, Da'wa and SCIRI, in their bid for power through the democratization of that country. But they diversified their political investments. They also supported the Sadrists with money, materiel, and advisors from their Revolutionary Guards to harass U.S. and UK troops in central and southern Iraq. They may have also been sufficiently Machiavellian to assist some of the Sunni insurgent groups. Iranians, according to Kurdish intelligence sources, certainly gave lists of individual Sunni Iraqis to be eliminated by Shia militias because of their role in the Iraq-Iran war.

The atmosphere generated by America's apparently enormous ambitions for the Middle East probably aided the election—or selection if you prefer—of hard-line President Mahmoud Ahmadinijad. Iran's guardians decided they would develop their nuclear capabilities—as a rational deterrent against American ambition. In January 2006, amid severe U.S. difficulties in Iraq, the Iranian government publicly proclaimed it would enrich uranium—the type that can be deployed in nuclear weaponry. The U.S. intervention to dismantle Saddam's weapons of mass destruction has therefore encouraged Iran to develop weapons of mass destruction, while the U.S. military presence in Iraq exposes U.S. troops to any retaliation Iran might consider in the event of a U.S. or U.S.-supported attack on Iranian nuclear facilities.

In short, the U.S. intervention in Iraq has, inevitably, made the Iranians far more dominant in the region than they were before 2003. Iraq and Iran are formally at peace. The new Iraqi federal government has acknowledged Saddam's responsibility for starting the Iran-Iraq war. U.S. threats have encouraged the Iranians to go nuclear—or to bluff that they are going nuclear—faster than they might otherwise have done. Before the U.S. intervention, Paul Wolfowitz and others thought that the Shia of Iraq were Arabs (or Iraqis) first and Shia second in their identifications. They reasoned that as Iraqi nationalists the democratic leadership of the Shia would oppose Iran's theocracy. The Bush administration, however, did little to encourage such a possibility. The formal occupation and the reluctance to democratize in 2003–4 suggested that the United States was determined to prevent the Shia from winning their democratic ascendancy.

In their public statements, if not always in their conduct, the Shia of Iraq, so far, have proved to be more democratic than theocratic, or at least to be as democratic as they are theocratic—liberalism and democracy are not synonyms. But given the response of Sunni Arabs to their displacement from power and the support rendered to Sunni Arab insurgents by states with Sunni Arab majority populations, the Shia Arabs have reacted with strategic intelligence. They have mostly backed their own religious parties and organizations and have sought to have Iran as a friendly ally rather than a nationalist enemy. Their mainstream leaders in Da'wa and ISCI find themselves in the stretched position of trying to act as allies of the United States and Iran. Their potential role as mediators in U.S.-Iranian relations has been completely unexploited.

There are only two obvious ways for the United States to bring an end to the Iranian domination of the region brought about by its victory over Saddam. One way is through escalation: to follow up the Iraq wars with armed intervention against Iran's nuclear ambitions. That would be most unwise, as I shall argue in Chapter 8. The other way is to back an Iraqi government that is anti-Iranian. Since Da'wa, ISCI, and the Sadrists are not going to become vigorously anti-Iranian any time soon, that would require the United States to bring back to power an undemocratic Sunni Arab-dominated government. That would not merely be unwise and immoral but an incredible about-face. In short, America's mainstream congressional opinion must look at the world as it is and not as they would like it to be. The United States has to adapt to and try to steer Iranian domination of the region. Directly trying to end that domination is not feasible and would only end in more tears, wasted lives, and lost treasure. It was once U.S. policy to support a strong Iran, before 1979. Thirty years later, it may well become sensible U.S. policy to build détente with Iran, which is what I shall maintain in Chapter 8.

Limiting Losses of U.S. Credibility?

Credibility, unlike currency, cannot be easily measured, but it is like currency in that it can be inflated or deflated. When mainstream congressional leaders refer to losses in U.S. credibility since March 2003, it is not clear what they have in mind. Guesses are not hazardous. They have in mind America's conception of itself as the leader of the world's democratic states, committed to international law and human rights. They have in mind the idea of the United States as a reliable ally, which does what it says it will do. They have in mind the idea of the United States as a skilled user of all modes of power—diplomatic, financial, organizational, communicative, and military. They would like these conceptions to be credible and widely believed. They think that they were credible before March 2003. By contrast, they believe that the U.S. intervention in Iraq has created an unhelpful image of the United States in international relations. It is now seen as a swaggering bully rather than an alliance builder. It is portrayed as a hammer that does not recognize when a word would be more useful than a blow, as a destroyer rather than an architect, and as a global bungler and burglar rather than a global manager and strategist. Ethically it is seen as placing an inordinately larger value on American lives than on the lives of others.

The Pew Global Attitudes Project tracks international public opinion on the United States and on Americans. Between 2002 and 2007, the number of people with a favorable view of the United States fell in twenty-six countries out of the thirty-three where trend data are available. Andrew Kohut and Richard Wike of Pew comment: "Ratings of the United States are disturbingly low among many of our longtime European allies, and they have dipped in Latin America and other parts of the world as well. The findings are especially dismal in Muslim nations."[9] The severe dent in the global brand-image of the United States is not entirely a linear function of global views on the U.S. intervention in Iraq. Among other sources of resentment are the Bush administration's general foreign policy, America's perceived partiality toward Israel, and America's general global dominance. But there is little doubt that the intervention in Iraq has not resonated on balance in favor of the standing and prestige of the United States. A well-organized substantive U.S. withdrawal will therefore restore some of the lost U.S. credibility, both among governments and mass publics.

In contrast with the original formal war goals proclaimed by the Bush administration, the objectives of mainstream congressional opinion are therefore much farther from realization. Al-Qaeda in Iraq is likely defeated, but Iraq remains a site of struggle with those who would want to use parts of its soil against U.S. personnel and interests. Regional stabilization is some way off. Iran's regional domination probably cannot be avoided without suicidal costs. U.S. global credibility is probably lower than at any time since the latter part of the U.S. war against Vietnamese nationalism. Will a well-organized and substantive U.S. withdrawal meet each of these four objectives more successfully than existing policy? That is the test we might expect the next Congress to pose, and we shall incorporate that test into Parts 2 and 3 of this book. But we must now turn to wider and more critical conceptions of the U.S. agenda in Iraq.

Chapter 3
The Imputed Goals of the
Bush Administration

When people are least sure, they are often most dogmatic.
—John Kenneth Galbraith, *The Great Crash*

Critics of the Bush administration—a large, vocal, and insistent group—offer a third perspective through which to view U.S. goals in Iraq. This is a very large conglomerate—to which this author belongs—but it is by no means a grouping with one voice. Nevertheless, conservative American realists and European leftists converge on key matters when appraising the ulterior agenda of the Bush administration.

The critics include realists, such as John Mearsheimer of the University of Chicago, who has condemned the Bush administration for idealistic over-reach, overcommitting the United States to what he sees as the quixotic venture of democratizing Iraq let alone the wider Middle East, and for believing that other governments in the world, awed by American military power in Iraq, would rush to comply with U.S. wishes.[1] The Bush administration's neoconservatives not only underestimated Iraqi nationalism, but its actions, in his view, have locked it into a losing occupation and have led others to form alliances, tacit and overt, and to take measures to protect themselves against the United States. For example, Iran and North Korea's pursuit of nuclear weapons seemingly accelerated when they were named as members of an "axis of evil" along with Saddam's Iraq in 2002.

The realists on the American and European right generally criticize the Bush administration for hubris and overweening ambition. The strategist Edward Luttwak has suggested that rather than trying to hold the ring in

Iraq after its intervention, the United States should have stood to one side, with a partial disengagement. It should have allowed Iraq to have its civil war escalate and burn out as a necessary precursor to future peace.[2] (Ironically, some critics maintain that the United States did exactly that, though they debate whether it did so deliberately.)

The columnist Daniel Pipes, who is normally outrageous though never dull—and who is convinced that Arabs and Muslims are generally culturally authoritarian[3]—has proposed ending U.S. support for the current democratically elected federal government in Baghdad and backing a strongman who would eventually facilitate democratization.[4] Nikolas Gvosdev, the former editor of the *National Interest,* and Ray Takeyh of the Council on Foreign Relations, by contrast, maintain that the United States should have backed the Shia Arabs because they were likely to win the civil war. Gvosdev and Takeyh have also argued that "the Iraq war is already over," with the United States defeated not militarily "but in its inability to shape political outcomes."[5]

West European and North American leftists match their right-wing realist counterparts when it comes to criticizing the Bush administration for its hubris and overambition. But they generally see the hard-headed interests of American capitalism behind the actions of the Bush administration and generally treat with contempt the notion that democratizing Iraq, or any other part of the Middle East, was ever part of the game plan of the president and his neoconservative advisers.[6] Prominent leftists writing on Iraq include the former student radical and member of the International Marxist Group, Tariq Ali, a British citizen of Pakistani origin, who quickly attacked Bush for attempting the recolonization of Iraq.[7] He unambiguously led the *New Left Review,* the premier journal of the international left in the English language, to support the insurgents against the U.S. occupation. A notorious editorial written by his partner, Susan Watkins, compared the transitional Iraqi government to France's Vichy regime.[8] The Salafists, Wahhabists, jihadists, and Baathists (and the Sadrists), by contrast, were heroically compared to the Maquis who fought for the liberation of Algeria from French rule. French intellectual Emmanuel Todd spoke for many when he wrote that, "When they denounce the evil ones, these people are not speaking about rogue states and terrorists, they are talking about themselves. They have after all turned the 9/11 tragedy into an opportunity for external aggression; they have lied to the world, obviously with a certain amount of relish.... We must therefore consider the possibility that they are in fact 'evil.'"[9]

From the U.S. left, Noam Chomsky has argued that the U.S. administration's current overt agenda—to win "permanent military installations" and "to guarantee U.S. control over the oil-resources of Iraq"—confirms what in his estimation were the covert reasons for America's intervention in the first place.[10] Canada's Naomi Klein has a different emphasis. She places America's Iraq policy within her portrait of a new political world in which disasters, natural and policy-induced, are used as coercive pretexts for free-market transformations that the relevant public would normally reject.[11]

Rashid Khalidi, the holder of the Edward Said Chair in Arab Studies at Columbia University, has penned perhaps the most succinct elaboration of the hidden agenda imputed to the Bush administration's intervention in Iraq. In *Resurrecting Empire: Western Footprints and America's Perilous Footpath in the Middle East,* he synthesizes "several, largely unacknowledged, war aims." Each element in this imputed agenda may be found among both right-wing and left-wing critics of the U.S. intervention in Iraq, though each would individually phrase and emphasize matters differently. Khalidi's theses are, in abbreviated form, that

> this was a war fought firstly to demonstrate that it was possible to free the United States from subordination to international law or the U.N. Charter, ...and from the constraints of operating within alliances.... [I]t was...fought because its planners wanted to free the greatest power in history from these Lilliputian bonds, and saw the tragedy of 9/11 as a golden opportunity to achieve this long-cherished goal.... [T]his was a war of choice, and Iraq was a suitable guinea pig for a new hyperunilateral American approach that would "shock and awe" the rest of the world. The Iraq war was fought secondly with the aim of establishing long-term military bases in a key country in the heart of the Middle East... [as] replacements for the increasingly contested bases established in Saudi Arabia in the wake of the 1991 Gulf War. It was a war fought thirdly to destroy one of the last of the third world dictatorships that had at times defied the United States and its allies (notably Israel) ...creating in its place a pliable client regime. It was a war fought finally to reshape along the radical free-market lines so dear to the Bush administration's ideologues, the economy of a country with the world's second-largest proven resources of oil.... Bush [along with Cheney and Rice] ...had all been intimately involved with the oil business. All these things—the demonstration effect of a unilateral, "preemptive" war, military bases, a client regime, and access to oil—were seen as vital to fending off potential twenty-first-century great-power rivals.[12]

Khalidi's summary—imperial demonstration; military bases; a client state; access to oil and gas—captures the presumptions of many non-Americans, especially of Middle Easterners and Arabs who opposed the U.S. intervention both before and after it took place. There is one major exception. Arab Iraqis, especially Baathists, are far more likely to emphasize Israeli interests than does Khalidi's nuanced phrasing, in which Israeli interests are a subdued theme.[13] Iraqis, especially insurgent Sunni Arabs and

Sadrists, are more likely to emphasize the Jewish provenance of many U.S. neoconservatives as weighty causes in the U.S. intervention.[14]

Let us assume for the sake of argument that the imputed agenda outlined by Khalidi and the hidden Israeli interests emphasized by others provided the real agenda of the Bush administration. If these were its five major goals, it makes sense to ask how well they have been met over five years since the intervention.

Demonstrating the Enormous Power of an Imperial Uncle Sam?

Intervening in Iraq demonstrated that the United States could, with minimal help from its allies and without explicit sanction from the United Nations, fight a foreign war against a repressive state on the other side of the globe with initially commanding effectiveness and with remarkable precision, using a range of new technologies that could cripple institutions and their communications. Saddam's Baathist regime was shocked and awed into retreat and collapse. Saddam's sons and heirs-apparent were killed in combat shortly after the intervention and their father subsequently arrested, tried, and executed. Most leading Baathists have been killed or incarcerated. The United States proved that it could fight two wars—in Iraq and Afghanistan—in two theaters, in rapid succession, with initially minimal losses in manpower. The massacres of 9/11 made large swathes of Americans willing to sustain significant losses of their soldiers. What was soon called the "war on terror" was held to have put the "Vietnam syndrome" in the trashbin of history. Most Americans who opposed the intervention in Iraq continued to support the war in Afghanistan and the hunt for Osama bin Laden.

But there was no wider domino effect, either within the "axis of evil" or among other Middle Eastern countries. The Arab countries did not experience a rerun of the 1989 democratization of Eastern Europe, with one regime tumbling after the other into well-deserved oblivion. The Sunni Arab majority states were partially cowed, notably Libya. But many of Iraq's neighbors—Syria, Saudi Arabia, and even Jordan—did little to help the United States, and in some cases turned blind eyes to their own jihadist expeditions to kill U.S. soldiers. Egypt's government remained disaffected and undemocratic—and openly justified itself as an alternative to Western democracy, which it suggested would only encourage throat-slitting civil war and jihadist theocrats. All the Arab majority states berated U.S. partiality in the conflict between Israel and the Palestinians. Turkey, another neighbor and a long-funded U.S. ally during and after the Cold War, was offered an enormous bribe to facilitate a northern front in Operation Iraqi Freedom. Variously estimated at between $70 and $90 billion, the funds were alleged to cover the potential costs of the war to Turkey—although they would have been subject to U.S. congressional authorization. But the Turkish Parliament, after complex maneuvers, followed Turkish public opinion in saying "no."

Regimes that opposed the United States may have learned two strategic lessons from the Iraq intervention. These lessons have unsettling implications. First, the fact that the United States, in the end, bypassed the United Nations may encourage "rogue states" to go nuclear, precisely to deter the United States from organizing a preemptive intervention—the logic which many think is being pursued by Iran. Second, regimes that experience an armed U.S. intervention should make no effort at formal engagement of the enemy on the battlefield in conventional war. Instead, after firing their nuclear weapons at their targets, they should prepare exclusively to conduct guerrilla and terrorist operations in their cities and in rough terrain— that is, adopt a scorched earth and societal collapse policy to deter any long-term occupation or reconstruction.

The United States, contrary to the now stylized renderings of the Iraq intervention, did try to win a UN Security Council authorization to disarm Saddam's regime—at the prompting of both Secretary of State Colin Powell and British Prime Minister Tony Blair. The United States failed in this multilateral effort, partly because it was obviously half-hearted in its public relations and diplomatic intensity, partly because Saddam Hussein surprisingly allowed the UN weapons inspectors to return after the passage of UN Security Council Resolution 1441 in November 2002, and partly because this last surprising move on Saddam's part enabled the French government to argue that there was no imminent threat and therefore no case for a preemptive war.[15]

The Iraq intervention is perhaps too easily presumed to demonstrate that it is more effective and cheaper for the United States to fight foreign wars with large-scale multilateral endorsements and that any interventions to execute regime changes will likely fare better if they have multilateral support.[16] The difficulty with this conclusion is that it suggests that the intervention in Afghanistan should by now have been a greater success than that in Iraq. But that is a very hazardous assumption—even when one allows that U.S. resource and troop commitments to Iraq have subtracted from those potentially available to Afghanistan. Yet only the last stranded platoons of neoconservatives code the Iraq war as a success for what Khalidi calls "hyper-unilateralism." Uncle Sam is a more humble power than in 2002.

Military Bases?

The United States now has large-scale military bases in Iraq as a consequence of its intervention, its occupation, and its continuing commitment to the new Iraqi government. I have seen some of them. Their social milieu is that of the American heartland (all that is missing are the children's amusement arcades of Hershey Park). They are also obviously foreign fortresses in Iraqi soil, denials of Iraq's recovery of full sovereignty. There is some evidence that before 2003, a few Pentagon planners and Washington think tanks extolled the virtues of bases in Iraq on a permanent basis, especially to replace those in Saudi Arabia and the Gulf states, and to be in a position to launch attacks against Iran and hot spots in central Asia, including Pakistan's tribal zones.[17] But, contra Chomsky, it is not clear that these aspirations directly shaped policy immediately before the intervention in Iraq. Rather, the bases are best understood as the byproducts of an intervention fought for other reasons.

If, however, for the sake of argument, we concede that the bases were a latent war goal of the U.S. administration, then the goal may seem to have been met. The bases are not tent cities. U.S. forces currently operate within Iraq under a treaty, authorized by the UN, although it expires in 2009. But it is equally possible to argue that if bases were a covert goal, then their accomplishment is being eroded, and that overtly trying to maintain permanent bases will act against long-term U.S. interests. In place of the existing treaty, the federal government of Iraq, including its Kurdish foreign minister, wants a new agreement, not a treaty, that places limitations on the operations of American troops within Iraq and that makes clear the temporary status of any U.S. military bases.

The obtrusive British military and advisor presence in Iraq, both after 1932 when Iraq obtained its formal independence as a state and after World War II, animated intense nationalist and postcolonial resentment, especially among Arab Iraqis. What they remembered was a British reentry into Baghdad in 1941—to depose Rashid Ali's pro-German military government—and a subsequent occupation. The treaties of 1930 (the Anglo-Iraq Treaty) and 1948 (the Portsmouth Treaty) were seen as intrusions on Iraq's sovereignty.[18] Resentment of British bases and neocolonial control contributed to Iraq's decisive tilt away from the Western powers after 1958. Informed

U.S. policymakers know that formal efforts to entrench permanent military bases will undermine the legitimacy of any Iraqi government on which they are enforced. Without such legitimacy, the bases and their personnel will be political and terrorist targets—exactly analogous to the situation Pentagon planners found themselves facing in Saudi Arabia after 1991. The voluntary retention of a limited number of bases with training personnel to aid those of Iraq's governments that have security powers—that is, federal and regional governments—is the absolute limit of America's intervention and is only likely to be welcomed in the Kurdistan Region.

Client Regime?

Among the expressions typically and repeatedly trotted out to characterize the new federal government in Baghdad by critics of the U.S. intervention are that it is a client regime, a vassal state, a dependency, or a protectorate. The Kurds and their leaders are also treated as needy servants in these evaluations. It is equally typical in critical commentary to treat the new political leadership in Iraq as a government of American-backed former exiles—an observation that ignores the Kurds (who are, after all, supposed to be Iraqis). How accurate are these portraits?

The Baathist regime in Arab Iraq was removed almost entirely by American efforts; that is true. SCIRI's Badr Organization and Ahmed Chalabi's Iraqi National Congress made limited military contributions in the south. In the north, however, the Kurds made decisive contributions to the defeat of Saddam's front lines in Kirkuk and Mosul in 2003. Many Peshmerga lost their lives and Mas'ud Barzani's brother was severely injured.

The seven person Iraqi Leadership Council (ILC) and the Iraqi Governing Council (IGC) were respectively recognized and appointed by Paul Bremer, the head of the U.S. and UK occupation administration. The ILC had been elected in December 2002 by Iraqi opposition parties in a conference held in London. In 2005 in the two Iraq-wide elections, the parties of the ILC won 90 percent and then 75 percent of the votes (the difference is accounted for by the Sunni Arab boycott in January and the Sunni Arab turnout in December).[19] No better proof of the representativeness of the so-called exiles can be found than their overwhelming endorsement by the electorate. Bremer created the IGC: he appointed representatives from the parties on the ILC to it, but he asked them to expand its membership beyond their ranks. They deliberately failed to act. They knew they represented Iraqi public opinion better than Bremer. Bremer then unilaterally added eighteen representatives to the original members of the ILC to create the Governing Council—without meaningful governmental powers. These eighteen appointees won less than 3 percent of the vote in January and even less in December 2005. The point is that the ILC and the parties embedded in it have genuine support within Iraq and had such support in 2003. They were not U.S. lackeys or out-of-touch exiles.

In the course of winding down the CPA, Bremer appointed Iyad Allawi as the interim Iraqi prime minister—and supported him vigorously as a strongman. Being seen as America's puppet, together with his own inclinations toward ill-targeted repression, doomed Allawi's prospects of success as his party trailed third behind the coalition of Shia religious parties and the coalition of Kurdish nationalists. Iraqis, not Americans, chose the next two prime ministers.[20] Within the Kurdistan Region, the January 2005 elections put in power an alliance led by the two major nationalist parties, the Kurdistan Democratic Party and the Patriotic Union of Kurdistan, with a mandate of nearly 95 percent of the vote. These leaders were freely chosen; they were not U.S. clients.

The most talked-about Iraqi exile in the Anglosphere, Ahmed Chalabi, who was invariably described as the Pentagon's favorite Iraqi, was neither imposed on Iraqis as prime minister nor did he remain regarded as a loyal ally. Threatened with arrest by the United States, he decamped to Iran before returning to Iraq as a temporary ally of the Sadrists. America therefore lost whatever controls it might have hoped to exert in shaping Iraqi leadership selection—as, of course, is appropriate in a democratic and sovereign state. But the Iraqi federal government has remained highly dependent militarily upon the U.S.-led Coalition for support. As the Kurdistan extraregional affairs Minister Mohammed Ihsan put it to me, "When I quarreled with the Prime Minister [of Iraq] I would remind him that for now he was the Mayor of the Green Zone; he was not even the Mayor of Baghdad."[21] It is also true that the Iraqi federal government has been heavily dependent upon American help in its limited reconstruction efforts.

There are signs, however, that both Iraq's military and economic dependencies are drawing to an end. Iraqi cabinet leaders are negotiating with the intent to achieve a dated withdrawal of U.S. combat troops and rejecting permanent military bases. The Iraqi Treasury is accumulating huge unspent balances from rising oil prices. There will shortly be a simple test of whether the new regime in Baghdad is a client or a self-standing entity: if and when its elected leaders request the United States to withdraw its military and civilian commitment to Iraq by a specified date. It is my judgment that the request will be made and that any such request will be met. America has two unexpected alliances in contemporary Baghdad—a unified Kurdish nationalist leadership and Shia religious parties historically succored in Iran. It does not have subservient clients.

For Oil and Gas?

Oil and gas should be consumed and discussed with sobriety. During 2002–4, materialistic explanations abounded of the American intervention against Saddam. Michael Moore's film *Fahrenheit 9/11* even suggested that George W. Bush was a front for the interests of the Houston oil capitalists and their chief clients, the Saudi royal family. The evidence is a bit more complicated. Conspiracy theories about the House of Saud and the House of Bush do not tell us all we need to know.

Former U.S. Secretary of State James Baker III is close to the Saudis and played a major role in the elections of both Presidents Bush and in the court battles that culminated in *Bush v. Gore* in 2000. But Baker had opposed extending Gulf War 1 to remove Saddam and also rejected a regime change in 2002–3. He later coauthored the Baker-Hamilton Report of November 2006, which condemned Bush the son's policy in Iraq. Baker's stance lent credence to a diametrically opposed theory, expressed in 2002 by a former British Labour Minister, Dr. Marjorie Mowlam: "The real goal is the seizure of Saudi oil. Iraq is no threat. Bush wants war to keep U.S. control of the region.... Under cover of the war on terrorism, the war to secure oil supplies [is to be] waged."[22] Mowlam speculated that the planned removal of Saddam was a deliberate distraction. It would cause mayhem, the unreliable House of Saud would fall to its Arab street, but the United States would have what it wanted: its armies deployed to seize the Arabian oil fields.

No one doubts that Iraq's oil fields made its territory and Saddam's regime geopolitically pivotal. In 2002 Iraq had 11 percent of the world's proven oil reserves and one quarter of the world's oil supplies came from the Persian Gulf region. Oil-fueled revenue growth had enabled a massive expansion of the Iraqi state under the Baath regime. It had also financed the huge expansion of the Iraqi military after 1968. The Iraqi rentier state was soon rich enough to co-opt significant numbers of Shia Arabs and some Kurds with extensive government patronage. When Saddam formally came to power in 1979, he directed a prosperous Iraq toward aggressive expansion. He went to war against Iran in 1980, in part to seize prime oil and gas fields near the Iraq border. The Reagan administration tilted toward him in that eight-year war because Ayatollah Khomeini's Iran was judged a greater threat to U.S. energy security interests in the Persian Gulf. In 1990 the dictator from Tikrit accused the Kuwaitis of stealing from Iraq's reservoirs through their drilling positions. That became a pretext for conquest. He also maintained that Kuwait was Iraq's "lost 19th province," although Iraq had not had eighteen provinces when British imperialists created Kuwait. Saddam's attempted conquest was motivated both by the prize of Kuwait's oil wealth and the need to pay off Iraq's crippling debts from the war with Iran. The prospect of Saddam controlling Iraqi and Kuwaiti oil supplies and the Gulf of Hormuz could not be tolerated by the Western powers. The United Nations agreed that conquest should not be part of normal international relations, so the first Gulf War was nominally fought to protect the territorial integrity of Kuwait. Primarily, however, it was fought to prevent any monopoly or strategic choke point being established over American and European oil imports.

Critics and supporters of the Bush administration can agree on the above historical analysis. It is much more difficult to identify the oil-based motivations behind the U.S. intervention of 2003, or to trace the impact of such alleged motivations on formal occupation policy, and on policy outcomes. Was it a U.S. policy goal to control the Iraq oil fields, denationalize them, and hand over ownership and control to U.S. corporations? There were policy papers floated to that effect, notably by Ariel Cohen of the Heritage Foundation,[23] which argued that increased oil production by Iraqi private owners could break OPEC and the power of Saudi Arabia. But Bremer's CPA neither dismantled nor privatized Iraq's nationalized oil corporation. The preference of the U.S. president and vice president, judging by policy decisions and some papers that sketched similar proposals from the James A. Baker III Institute and the Council on Foreign Relations, was to maintain an Iraqi state oil company that could make agreements with international oil companies and that would operate within OPEC rather than try to destroy it. A French critic of the Bush administration also points out that "the oil giants were noncommittal before the intervention... [whereas] the service companies and the civil engineering sector... were very much for it."[24]

It has consistently been U.S. policy since 2003, as I shall later elaborate, to try to recreate a centralized Iraq, in which a strong Baghdad government owns and directs Iraq's oil resources. That is one reason why Bremer, during the making of the Transitional Administrative Law, blocked Kurdistan's proposals for regional ownership of natural resources. It is also why U.S. Ambassador to Iraq Zalmay Khalilzad tried to resist proposals along the same lines during the negotiation of Iraq's Constitution in 2005 and why subsequent American ambassadors have consistently supported a federal hydrocarbons law that would give preeminence to the Iraqi federal government in licensing, exploration, management, marketing, and pricing policies. In short, U.S. policymakers have allowed their geopolitical security preference (for a recentralized Iraq) to prevail over other policies on oil and natural gas that might have been more in keeping with a right-wing capitalist agenda, such as promoting large-scale privatization or encouraging regional ownership and control that would have enabled American companies to have profitable relations with Shia in the south and Kurds in the north.

The United States did secure Iraq's Oil Ministry in Baghdad in April 2003, but it had no intention of outright seizure of Iraq's oil fields and transferring them to U.S. corporations. The Bush administration's preferred global energy policy emphasized freedom of the market. In 2002–3, obtaining lower prices for oil on world markets was not a major U.S. priority—and the war to remove Saddam threatened to send prices higher (because of the anticipated damage to Iraq's oil wells in combat or though a possible scorched earth policy, modeled on Saddam's exit from Kuwait). Iraqi production was significantly less than 3 million barrels a day before the intervention. That output would be halved in the worst moments of intercommunal conflict in 2006–7.

The Iraq wars since 2004 have had no obviously dramatic effect on the globalized oil and gas market. That is partly because in Saddam's last phase in power, during the UN-authorized sanctions, Iraq's share of global exports fell to marginal importance, the result of underinvestment, isolation following sanctions, and Saddam's own decisions. (Kurds and Shia Arabs suspect that Saddam deliberately did not develop the promising sites in Kurdistan and the south to prevent these regions from developing at the expense of the Sunni Arab heartlands in western and northwestern Iraq).

The tightening of the global oil market after 2003 owed little to Iraqi supply failures (or to insurgents' attacks) and much more to the increases in demand from newly industrialized countries like China. Saddam's regime had eroded the caliber of Iraq's extraction infrastructure—a fact known to the world before March 2003.[25] Any prospective enhancement of Iraq's production under a new government was therefore known to be likely to be gradual at best. It would take even more time before any major impact on global exports could materialize.[26] In 2008 Iraqi oil revenues began to benefit dramatically from increased global oil prices, but this outcome was not the result of major increases in production or of deliberate policy in Iraq by either the United States or the Iraqi government. The surge in Iraqi oil revenues that Paul Wolfowitz had expected would ensure that the reconstruction of Iraq self-financing has come too late for the fulfillment of his hopes.

A grander materialist explanation of America's intervention in Iraq would seek to portray it as a far-sighted endeavor, intended to diversify the number of countries and friendly regimes from which American and European oil supplies could be secured. This may be called the Greenspan presumption, and it goes beyond Khalidi's analysis. In 2007, Alan Greenspan, the former chairman of the U.S. Federal Reserve Board, argued in *The Age of Turbulence* that he was "saddened that it is politically inconvenient to acknowledge what everyone knows: the Iraq war is largely about oil."[27] This typically oracular statement provides no causal account of decision making to support what we all allegedly know. The Greenspan presumption fits poorly with the overwhelming evidence that the toppling of Saddam was a hastily improvised decision taken in the aftermath of the tragedy of 9/11. It embedded many goals and fantasies. Calculated reflection on the management of America's needs for black gold does not seem to have been one of them. It is true that an Iraq that is friendly toward the United States will secure and diversify the sources of western and American energy supplies, but it is not clear that this consideration was a central part of the Bush administration's decision making.

Israeli Interests?

We have now appraised the key elements in Khalidi's account of the ulterior agenda of the Bush administration. A minor place in Khalidi's account was given to Israeli interests. Others have expanded on this theme to a much greater extent. In a famous article published in the *London Review of Books* in 2006, John Mearsheimer of the University of Chicago joined with Harvard University's Stephen Walt to launch another argument about the U.S. intervention in Iraq, one grounded in a larger thesis: that the Israeli lobby in the United States is so powerful that it has caused successive U.S. presidents and Congresses to advance the interests of another state at the expense of America's national interests.[28] The article documented the power of the American-Israel Public Affairs Committee (AIPAC) as well as a range of other pro-Israeli interest groups, think tanks, intellectuals, and policies influential in the shaping of U.S. foreign policy. They claimed that "pressure from Israel and the lobby was not the only factor behind the decision to attack Iraq in March 2003, but it was critical...the war was motivated in good part by a desire to make Israel more secure." They also maintained that "apart from Kuwait, which Saddam invaded in 1990, Israel was the only country in the world where both politicians and the public both favored war," and that "within the U.S., the main driving force behind the war was a small band of neoconservatives, many with ties to Likud," the rightist Israeli party. It was, they argued, wrong, however, to blame the war in Iraq on "Jewish influence" because American Jews were less supportive of the Iraq war than other Americans.

For the sake of argument, let us accept the entirety of Mearsheimer and Walt's arguments. The relevant question for our purposes is whether Israeli interests have been met by the U.S. intervention in Iraq. Saddam's regime was anti-Israeli, pro-Palestinian, had attacked Israel during the first Gulf War with missiles, and Israelis feared its potential to develop weapons of mass destruction. To that extent Israel's strategic interests have been met by the regime replacement. But the newly democratic Iraq is in general a pro-Palestinian Iraq. Both Sunni and Shia Arabs generally favor Palestinian as opposed to Israeli interests—Sunni Arabs strongly so. Kurds and Shia Arabs are more ambiguous, partly because Saddam employed Palestinians in his repressive security institutions. Kurds have observed how Arabs support Palestinian rights to self-determination but rarely those of the Kurds. For that reason there are reservoirs of empathy for Israel in Kurdistan, partly on the principle that they have a common foe in aggressive Arab nationalism and partly in recollection of Israel's support for the elder Barzani against the Baathists. (Arabs also tend to portray Kurdistan as a second Israel in "Arab lands.") The newly democratic Iraq may also attract U.S. materiel support for many years to come, thereby potentially lessening the resources available to Israel, and it will certainly oblige the United States to choose between its democratic allies in the region in the future.[29]

Regionally, the U.S. intervention in Iraq has made Iran into the strongest power in the Persian Gulf. It is now apparently wholly determined to obtain nuclear weapons and achieve the same nuclear status as Israel. The survival of the new Iraq restrains U.S. policy toward Iran; it also puts constraints on Israel's independent ability to carry out an offensive policy toward Iran.

Tehran's potential ability to make southern Iraq ungovernable is matched by its ability to support Hezbollah in Lebanon and Hamas in Gaza and the West Bank. Iran has been able to make life difficult for Israel through these organizations, which are not its simple proxies, but which it can strongly influence.[30] The U.S. intervention has certainly not led, as yet, to the democratization and reform of the wider Middle East, earnestly hoped for both by U.S. neoconservatives and the Israeli intellectual and former Soviet dissident Natan Sharansky.[31] Israel is now more isolated in the Middle East than ever and yet must unavoidably address its Palestinian questions. U.S. officials can no longer claim the road to Jerusalem (peace) lies through Baghdad (regime change). The U.S. intervention in Iraq has arguably provided an instructive lesson to Washington policymakers. Unconditional support for Israel handicaps the U.S. ability to be flexible and to win alliances in the wider Arab world. So, even if the Iraq intervention served some policymakers' conceptions of Israeli interests, it may not have met them.

The agenda imputed to the Bush administration, both by its right-wing and left-wing critics, obliges us to address considerations wider than those glossed over in the official goals of the administration and the objectives of mainstream congressional leaders. The United States is no longer the same colossus it was after the end of the Cold War. It is certainly weaker in international public opinion, at least where reliable polls can be held, than it was in 2003. To date it has lost both the public diplomacy and the public relations battle over Iraq globally. Its prestige, honor, and self-assessment are dented by the Iraq experience. Whether there will be bases in Iraq, and on what terms, will shortly be decided, appropriately, by Iraqis rather than Americans. America does not have a client-government in the new Iraq but rather faces an emergent power eager to demonstrate its independence—through visiting Iran or condemning Israeli actions. Iraq has no completed federal hydrocarbons law that dramatically improves U.S. energy supplies, although Iraqis and Americans stand to gain from a rational settlement, as I shall argue. Israel, like the Kurds, Shia Arabs, non-Baathist Iraqis, and Iran, has benefited from the end of Saddam's regime. But whether Israel accrues long-term net gains remains to be seen. It also remains to be seen what the net long-term gains are for the United States once it withdraws from a Saddam-free Iraq. It is with that question in mind that we turn now to the arguments for an American withdrawal from Iraq—bearing in mind the goals of the Bush administration, mainstream congressional leaders, and those suggested by the right- and left-wing critics of the U.S. intervention.

Part II
The Case for a
Substantive Withdrawal

And yet it is not nightfall that has descended on Iraq, but a savage and uncertain dawn.

—Fouad Ajami, April 2007

What might an American withdrawal from Iraq mean? The air is thick with efforts to condition how we will subsequently think. For a patriotic Iraqi it will mark the restoration of sovereignty. For a Kurd it might arouse intense anxiety. For a patriotic U.S. Marine it might suggest an ignominious martial defeat.[1] For a jihadist it may be seen as a glorious victory over the infidel, the retaking of the land between two rivers won by Mohammed's immediate successors, the rightly guided caliphs, as well as the defeat of America's effort "to guarantee security for its Israeli protégé."[2] For a Western leftist[3] or an Iraqi nationalist of Baathist disposition, it will be celebrated as an enforced decolonization after a failed conquest—or as a defeat for the "new military humanism," the discourse in which recent American and British interventions have been justified.[4] For a French-European liberal it may suggest that America's failed "menacing unilateral behavior has accelerated the integration of Europe and moved the rapprochement between Europe and Russia irreversibly forward."[5] Withdrawal from Iraq would confirm for some the thesis that "there will be no such thing as an American Empire in the future" and that "the invasion of Iraq" was an irrational "war of aggression," conducted without the requisite economic, military, or ideological resources, "a stupid and bloody war … that produced only negative effects in terms of American power."[6]

Andrew Greeley, the liberal Irish-American Catholic priest and multitalented intellectual, has already made up his mind on the meaning of what he, too, calls "a stupid" but also an unjust and criminal war:

> The ultimate mistake of the Bush administration was not reliance on slanted intelligence, not the failure to consider postwar problems in Iraq, not the incompetents chosen to administer postwar Iraq, not ignorance of the religious conflicts in the country, not the pretense that the situation was improving when it was not, not the naiveté about the ability of the American armed forces to win the war. The most fundamental failure was the adoption of the theory of preemptive war, a failure both moral and strategic.[7]

More cautious estimations than these are possible, and they may eventually prove more judicious. A well-organized and substantive U.S. withdrawal, executed by a new U.S. administration with a fresh electoral mandate, may temper the credibility of most of the foregoing claims. That is partly because it may shortly be possible to proclaim a preliminary but extremely costly victory based on some of the original war aims, both real and imputed. Fantasies of a rapid democratic revolution throughout the Arab majority world or the wider Middle East have not been realized, but a democratizing and constitutionalized Iraq may have been won after too much spilling of blood. Al-Qaeda in Iraq will likely be defeated in its last holdout positions in the city of Mosul and the province of Diyala. Iraq is and will remain Muslim, but it may not become Islamist—though constitutional Islamists, both Sunni and Shia, and religious parties will be key players in its politics. A withdrawal of most U.S. combat troops to their bases, followed by the withdrawal of most of those bases from Iraq, will replace the vestiges of occupation by a free alliance between Iraq and the United States. (Indeed, the United States may be able to sustain two new strategic allies, the federal government of Iraq and the government of the Kurdistan Region.) Any U.S. military bases that remain in Iraq should be there because the federal government of Iraq, and its regions, and a majority of their voters want them. Those in the Bush administration who favored installing a new client government did not succeed in shaping policy. For that reason the new Iraq is not a neocolonial vassal state, although it nearly became a failed state. Iraq's oil and gas reserves may soon be developed under a federal power-sharing agreement in a manner that benefits all Iraqis first instead of the elite of a fascistic and sectarian regime or outside powers.

The wider and long-term consequences of the intervention in Iraq may soon be left for subsequent consideration and evaluation. The reestablished consensus may indeed be, as Greeley hopes, to condemn the doctrine of preemptive war and unilateral interventions. But we might also learn to recognize that genocidal regimes are and should remain international outlaws. They should not be protected by international law on the grounds that they are not at present committing genocide. A law of peoples that allows governments to destroy peoples as long as they get away with it is not a law worthy of the name.

Chapter 4
Costs, Sunk Costs, and Potential Benefits

The cost of liberty is less than the price of repression.
—W. E. B. Du Bois, *John Brown* (1909)

The case for a U.S. withdrawal from Iraq must rest both on calculations of presumed benefits and costs for Americans and Iraqis and on sincere efforts to establish the considered preferences of Americans and Iraqis. Although I first examine the costs and benefits of withdrawal from an American perspective, Iraqis of all nationalities, religions, and sects (and none) have every right to insist that their interests and preferences should count first, both morally and politically. It is their federation.

The Human Costs

Let us begin with lost lives. These are, as economists call them, sunk costs—that is, they cannot be recovered.[1] Over 4,100 U.S. military personnel have been killed in combat in Iraq, and at least 30,000 have been wounded.[2] Returned soldiers are showing significant incidence of post-traumatic stress disorder. The additional psychological and material damage to the families and friends of the dead and injured veterans cannot intelligibly be put in indices or dollars.

Whether America stays in Iraq or withdraws, lost lives cannot be recovered. Injured limbs, bodies, and brains can only be partly rehabilitated. To argue against any substantive withdrawal because these deaths and injuries will be rendered worthless rests on hidden assumptions. One might be that no substantive withdrawal in the near future can meet original U.S. war goals. Yet some of the arguments advanced in Part I of this book suggest otherwise. A second assumption might be that "staying the course" will make the existing losses of soldiers more bearable or meaningful. Perhaps that is what President Bush meant in 2005 when he declared in Salt Lake City at the national convention of the Veterans of Foreign Wars that "We will finish the task that they gave their lives for. We will honor their sacrifice by staying on the offensive against the terrorists."[3] That makes sense only if "staying on the offensive" is better on balance for living Americans (and Iraqis) than a well-organized withdrawal from Iraq. Otherwise, it suggests that no commander-in-chief or officer should ever order a retreat to fight better later or on another day. A third premise might be that only the president or U.S. military commanders in the field can make such a decision, and can only do so if they render soldiers' sacrifices worthwhile, both for their own sake and for future American wars. The president and Congress are the joint constitutional authorities to make such decisions for Americans. They should make them bearing in mind the future morale of the American military, which matters for American security and that of America's allies. But it would be futile to waste additional lives and resources just to render earlier sacrifices somehow "nobler." The dead cannot speak, and the surviving injured rarely favor adding more to the stock of violent deaths to improve how they feel about their disabled bodies.

Iraqis, minimally, must be treated as full partners on the pace and scale of a U.S. withdrawal. The Iraqi government should have the final say on whether there is an American presence in Iraq beyond that of normal diplomatic and commercial ties. Since 2003 Iraqis have suffered by several orders of magnitude more deaths and physical and psychological damage than have American soldiers. The web site *Iraq Body Count*, www.iraqbodycount.org (cited earlier and discussed further in Appendix 1), suggests that upwards of 100,000 Iraqi civilians have died violently in criminal and political killings since the U.S. intervention. The injured most likely number in the vicinity of 1 million. The human costs of regime replacement have therefore been enormous in Arab Iraq (the Kurdistan Region bore its worst losses earlier).

It should, however, be kept in mind that the Baathists under Saddam are estimated to have killed, at a minimum, 300,000 people in internal genocidal acts and repression between 1979 and 2003.[4] These estimates exclude those killed in wars between the Baathists and Kurdish insurgents before 1979 and those killed in Saddam's wars with Iran and Kuwait, which led to at least 1 million dead (soldiers and civilians). Peter Sluglett, a historian of contemporary Iraq, estimates that up to 300,000 people may have been killed in Saddam's counterattack against Kurdish rebels and in the Shia intifada in the spring of 1991.[5] The Kurdistan Regional Government officially estimates 182,000 deaths from Saddam's "Anfal campaign" of 1987–88— so-named after a verse in the Quran in which Mohammed commends the spoliation of unbelievers.[6] Baathist genocidal killings because of people's presumed racial, ethnic, or religious origins continued after 2003. They were resisting the loss of their regime and animated by resentment at the lost preeminence of Sunni Arabs. There are, however, no existing reliable estimates of the killings we can directly attribute to Baathists after 2003.

Since the U.S. intervention, Iraqis have also borne huge costs in human displacement—although some of this may be reversible. But at least such displacement has not been either U.S. or Iraqi government policy. By contrast, large-scale ethnic and sectarian expulsions were part of the Baathist regime's practices. In its early stages of consolidation the regime expelled Kurds (and Turkomen) from the city of Kirkuk and other territories that were in dispute between Kurdish autonomists and the Baathists, creating as many as 200,000 internally displaced persons after 1976. In the regime's last stages the Baathists drained the habitat of the Shia Marsh Arabs, again causing huge internal displacements. A favored tactic was to blow up villages and then sow mines in the water before the villagers left. The ecosystem completely collapsed, turning millennia-old wetlands into a wasteland of dried-out and salinated earth. Military conquest and repression of Kurdish and Shia Arab rebellions led millions of Iraqis to flee, before and after 1991, and to seek refugee status in neighboring countries and beyond.[7]

After the U.S. intervention, Christians fled from Baghdad in large numbers after suffering intimidation by Sunni Arabs. Baghdad became the major site of intercommunal provocations, largely but not exclusively initiated by Sunni Arabs from Zarqawi's al-Qaeda. These provocations eventually led to massive retaliation by Shia Arabs and horrific sectarian expulsions of both Sunni and Shia Arabs. These expulsions occurred especially in the mixed districts of central Iraqi cities. Peak estimates suggest there are now 2 million internally displaced persons (IDPs) and 2 million refugees from Iraq—although it is not possible reliably to separate the numbers of IDPs created before and after 2003. But the trend line is definitely down. The Brookings Institution's Iraq Index of July 31, 2008, reported that newly displaced persons fell below 10,000 per month from January 2008 by comparison with estimates of 90,000 a month in the first quarter of 2007.[8]

The quantitative estimates of violent deaths in Iraq, both before and after 2003, are neither clear nor uncontested. The same applies to estimates of the numbers of IDPs and refugees. However, despite all the horrors, the March 2003 intervention and the war over the succession to Saddam have still cost far fewer lives than the Baathists took while seizing, consolidating, and losing power.[9] We should all agree that whatever their exact scale, the postintervention violent deaths, injuries, and expulsions suffered by Iraqis have been enormous and unnecessarily so. As the formal occupation power until June 28, 2004, the United States bore a trustee's responsibility to protect Iraqi lives. As the primary agent of regime replacement, it was responsible for upholding order with better planning and greater resource commitments. There was extensive knowledge of what Saddam's Baath party had done to Iraqis—through atomization, retribalization, and deliberate manipulation of ethnic and sectarian antagonisms. Saddam's legacy meant that large-scale disorder was likely after the fall of the regime, even if the Sunni Arab-led insurgency had been avoided. Qubad Talabani, the Kurdistan Regional Government's representative in the United States, was not joking when he told me just after the intervention that Iraq did not simply require more troops to establish order and prevent looting but thousands of psychiatrists to deal with the sick society created by Saddam. His father, now the first elected president of Iraq, Jalal Talabani, presciently warned Americans of the dangers of looting but, sadly, to no avail.

Who is responsible for the violence that Iraq has experienced since March 2003? At least seven groups can be identified as the dominant initiators and users of violence and force, although amid the mayhem it has been extraordinarily difficult to assess their individual as well as total responsibility for causing deaths and injuries. First, Sunni Arab-dominated insurgent organizations have attacked Coalition troops, Iraqi soldiers, and police, and their alleged civilian collaborators. They have deliberately targeted (mostly Shia Arab) civilians or shown callous disregard for those killed as byproducts of their actions. Second, Coalition and Iraqi forces have attacked Sunni Arab insurgents and Shia Arab militias. These attacks have led to significant numbers of civilian casualties caused both as "collateral damage" and through brutal lack of restraint on the part of the troops and police before more measured counterinsurgency strategies came into full effect in 2007. Third, Shia Arab militias have also attacked Coalition forces and Sunni Arab civilians. They have been prime agents of sectarian cleansing, admittedly often in response to provocations. They have less often engaged in direct combat with new Iraqi security forces. Fourth, militias that have penetrated the new state organizations (mostly, it appears, Shia Arab) have deliberately engaged in "representative killings" of young men, either in retaliation or in deliberate acts of provocation.[10] Fifth, foreign jihadists, especially al-Qaeda in Iraq, have deliberately targeted Shia Arab civilians to provoke mayhem and encourage a U.S. withdrawal. They have been the primary deployers of suicide bombers against civilians and Coalition and Iraqi forces. Sixth, there have been numerous intrafactional disputes leading to deaths, injuries, and flight among the Sunni Arab insurgents (and their foreign allies) and among the Shia militias. Last, criminals have killed and kidnapped for profit on a large scale, confident that the police are otherwise preoccupied.

I have had in-depth conversations with Kurds, mostly from the major nationalist parties, and with Shia Arabs, mostly SCIRI (now ISCI) representatives.[11] They generally say that Saddam's repression was worse in magnitude and longevity than the recent anarchic chaos and civil wars and still judge his violent removal as both necessary and worth the costs, although they unanimously lament it was not done better—and earlier. They agree with a widely cited Iraqi woman, Dr. Lina Ziyad, who said that under Saddam everyone lived in a big prison, and though they now they live in a wilderness, she prefers that wilderness. Or they would consent to the assessment made by the current Iraqi ambassador to Canada, Howar Ziad, who maintains that a messy democracy is preferable to the stability of tyrants. "When asked if, despite the absence of weapons of mass destruction, the persistence of the terrorist insurgency and the resulting death and instability, the campaign to topple Saddam Hussein was justified, Ziad's answer is categorical and emphatic. 'Absolutely. To put this question to the average Iraqi is ridiculous and probably insulting. That regime enslaved people and caused genocide, wars, and breached every human right.'"[12] Sunni Arabs and Turkomen, many of whom voted for the neo-Baathist Iraqi National Dialogue that won 11 of the 275 seats in Iraq's December 2005 parliamentary elections, are the least likely to accept this judgment. But some of their public representatives whom I met in Kirkuk in 2004 and 2005 were as likely to blame fellow Iraqis, especially Shia Arabs and Kurds, for violence in postintervention Iraq as they were to blame the Americans.

The eventual judgment of historical demographers on the absolute numbers of dead before and after 2003 and the precise assignments of responsibility for violent deaths after 2003 remain to be definitively made. What matters immediately for current Iraqi and U.S. policymakers is whether the human losses of Iraqis and Americans will be made worse or better by the organized withdrawal of U.S. combat forces. That will depend on whether a stable security settlement is emerging, which is discussed in the next chapter, and whether it is underpinned by a stable political settlement, also discussed in the following chapter.

The Financial and Economic Costs

With *The Three Trillion Dollar War*, the Nobel-prize winning economist Joseph Stiglitz and his coauthor, Linda Bilmes, have established a figure for what the subtitle of their book calls *The True Costs of the Iraq Conflict*.[13] That is their estimate of the costs to Americans.[14] They speculate that the total costs to the rest of the world—including Iraq and the United Kingdom— will be approximately double that: $6 trillion.

Stiglitz and Bilmes base their calculation of the financial costs to the United States by adding together the "socio-economic costs" and the "budgetary costs" of the Iraq and Afghanistan wars. It is not always clear how they separate out the two. The socioeconomic costs are roughly those that the federal government does not pay—for example, the economic costs of lost soldiers' lives (net of death payments), injuries, familial, medical, and societal expenses (less standard disability benefits), and other social costs. The budgetary costs are those borne by taxpayers, past and projected operational military costs, future veterans' costs, and other military costs and adjustments. They estimate the budgetary costs to lie between $1.7 and $2.7 trillion in today's dollars, without counting interest costs. The socioeconomic costs they estimate in the range of $300 to $400 billion. They claim that in the best-case scenario, the total direct costs to the United States will be $2 trillion but reckon that $3 trillion is more realistic.

They should, however, have called their book *The Four Trillion Dollar War*, because they also calculate the cost to the American economy of the presumed Iraq effect of the cost of higher oil prices and of the macroeconomic budgetary impact of the Iraq intervention. They suggest that these items will add another $1 trillion in costs, although the manner in which they fuse the macroeconomic costs of the Iraq and Afghan wars makes their presentation confusing.[15] A trillion here, a trillion there, and pretty soon we are talking about serious money.

Some of the claims made by Stiglitz and Bilmes are highly contestable. Economic and financial data and calculations are interpretations, not hard empirical facts.[16] Right-wing critics have suggested that "the military will not disappear, even if the Iraq war does. Whether or not we retain forces in Iraq, they will have to be equipped, housed, and trained somewhere. Attributing these costs to the Iraq War is disingenuousness."[17] Moreover, Stiglitz and Bilmes devote no significant attention to the costs of the previous policy toward Saddam: containment. This policy, which operated between 1992 and 2003, required the presence of significant U.S. military forces in southern Turkey and the Persian Gulf, roughly 30,000 troops, 200 military aircraft, and 30 naval vessels. Three University of Chicago economists have suggested that these items cost about $14.5 billion per year.[18] Absent the intervention to remove Saddam, and based on reasonable estimates of its likely duration, these economists have estimated the continuing costs of containment to an expected present value of 300 billion in 2006 dollars—on the assumption that the policy would have been effective.

Most of the estimates in *The Three Trillion Dollar War* appear to depend on operational and other direct costs extending through to 2017. In estimating many costs, such as the impact of the Iraq intervention on the global price of oil, the authors rely on guesses, or, if you prefer, they display remarkable confidence in their counterfactual analyses (that is, of what would have happened if there had not been a U.S. intervention in Iraq).[19] Many of these guesses appear vulnerable to present-day shifts in events. How quickly, for example, will current increases in Iraqi oil production and increases in Iraqi oil revenues upset their assumptions on these matters, which, within a year, have come to look pessimistic rather than realistic?[20] They engage in a lengthy analysis of the presumed costs to the American economy of the rise in the price of oil (owed they assume, in significant part, to the intervention in Iraq). Yet not once do they consider whether higher oil prices might benefit the U.S. economy in the longer run through making non-oil-based and more energy-efficient investments more worthwhile and urgent and thereby reducing U.S. security exposure in the Middle East. They proceed as they do because they presume that obtaining a lower oil price (or preventing a rise in the global oil price) was a key goal of the Bush administration, which is a moot point. Stiglitz and Bilmes are, in the end, more or less determined to deny that the Iraq intervention might have had any significant economic benefits, which makes their analysis seem partial.

Their approach to the economics of war is highly contestable.[21] John Maynard Keynes and Michal Kalecki famously argued that wars could be beneficial for the relevant macroeconomy if they raised effective demand, especially if war expenditures were largely incurred in the relevant government's domestic economy. Stiglitz and Bilmes claim, however, that "no serious economist holds the view that war is good for the economy."[22] That may mean that they do not regard the most famous neo-Keynesian in the

United States, Paul Krugman of Princeton, who publishes regularly in what is widely regarded as America's most authoritative newspaper, as a serious economist. In a recent posting Krugman writes,

> One thing I get asked fairly often is whether the Iraq war is responsible for our economic difficulties. The answer (with slight qualifications) is no. Just to be clear: I yield to nobody in my outrage over the way we were lied into a disastrous, unnecessary war. But economics isn't a morality play, in which evil deeds are always punished and good deeds rewarded. The fact is that war is, in general, expansionary for the economy, at least in the short run.... The $10 billion or so we're spending each month in Iraq mainly goes to U.S.-produced goods and services, which means that the war is actually supporting demand. Yes, there would be infinitely better ways to spend the money. But at a time when a shortfall of demand is the problem, the Iraq war nonetheless acts [to] support...employment directly and indirectly. There is one caveat: high oil prices are a drag on the economy, and the war has some—but probably not too much—responsibility for pricey oil. Mainly high-priced oil is the result of rising demand from China and other emerging economies, colliding with sluggish supply as the world gradually runs out of the stuff. But Iraq would be exporting more oil now if we hadn't invaded—a million barrels a day?— and that would have kept prices down somewhat. Overall, though, the story of America's [current] economic difficulties is about the bursting housing bubble, not the war.[23]

Krugman is entitled to his views on lies and disasters. His economic analysis is different and more convincing than that of Stiglitz and Bilmes, however. But like them, he assumes that Iraqi oil production would have been higher if not for the U.S. intervention. However. this assumption glosses over the decay of the Iraqi infrastructure under Saddam and what might have been the impact of continuing or reimposed UN-authorized sanctions (which was the most likely alternative to the U.S.-led intervention).

Stiglitz, Bilmes, Krugman, and the right-wing activist Grover Norquist agree on one matter. The best way to consider the costs of the Iraq intervention is through an appraisal of its "opportunity costs"—what could otherwise have been done with the expenditures incurred as a result of the March 2003 intervention, and, I would add, what could have been achieved had resources been better allocated during the intervention. For Stiglitz, Bilmes, and Krugman, the resources would have been better allocated to universal health care, for Norquist to tax cuts.[24] However they may have been allocated, these lost resources are now sunk costs.

The intervention in Iraq has had beneficial macroeconomic effects for the United States, which its critics have been reluctant to acknowledge; however, the idea that monies might be better spent in future no one can dispute. The U.S. military will have to "reset" to replace much of its lost capital equipment. So although withdrawal will relieve the U.S. military of the direct costs of aiding the new Iraqi authorities in combat operations, immediate savings on the defense budget cannot be expected to be huge unless it becomes U.S. policy to cut back defense expenditures more generally. How much U.S. economic resources can be freed from Iraq for other civilian as opposed to military uses is unclear. The next president is committed to high defense expenditures.

We can, however, presume that there will be some budgetary benefits to the U.S. taxpayer from a well-organized withdrawal through a reduction in government borrowing, a reallocation of fiscal resources and other federal expenditures, or tax cuts, that is, if we presume no catastrophic outcome from the U.S. withdrawal from Iraq, such as as a renewed and deeper civil war with multiple military interventions by the neighboring powers that ends up obliterating Iraqi oil production and exports. It is possible to avoid that catastrophic outcome, although not cheaply—the United States will still have strategic commitments in the general area, which will be costly. If a substantive withdrawal incorporates a period in which there are extensive numbers of U.S. military trainers deployed to assist Iraqi security forces and extensive U.S. aerial and ground-force deployments to protect Iraq's territorial integrity, then the direct operational costs of the intervention will continue to be extensive and budgetary relief will be limited.

What have been the financial and economic costs to Iraqis of the U.S. intervention? To answer that question, we need to look at the state of the Iraqi economy before the intervention. Under Saddam, Iraq suffered under UN-authorized sanctions and heavy government debts (incurred from Saddam's wars against Iran and Kuwait). Oil revenues did not increase because of the country's decaying oil infrastructure, which restricted its contributions to the global oil supply. The Kurdistan Region suffered from double sanctions. It was hit, as part of Iraq, by the UN-authorized sanctions regime and, secondly, was completely cut off from all of Iraq's oil revenues and public services by Saddam when he abruptly downsized and withdrew all Iraqi administration and services from the region in the hope of bringing the Kurds to heel and dividing their parties. Kurdistan eventually became the limited beneficiary of the UN "oil-for-food" program, through which it received a less than properly proportional share of permitted Iraqi oil sales.

The modification of sanctions took place under international public pressure because the regime had passed on the costs of sanctions to its subjects, especially children. Saddam's calculated responses to the sanctions regime led to short- and long-run crises in health-care provision, sanitation, and other public services. Illiteracy and infant mortality rose sharply while Saddam built palaces and encouraged the building of mosques to display his newfound Islamic credentials. Corruption and smuggling were rife throughout Iraq, partly aggravated by the sanctions regime.

I paint this story quickly to encourage readers to make the right comparison. Iraq in 2003 was not the Iraq of 1979, before Saddam, nor was it the Iraq of 1990, before the invasion of Kuwait. Saddam's despotism had wasted much of Iraq's oil-revenue bonanza on losing wars and expensive repression. Its nominal Arab socialism oversaw a rentier state. The potential development of a vigorous mixed economy, underpinned by significant increases in education in the years following World War II, was stalled and reversed by the regime's direction after 1979. Stiglitz and Bilmes estimate that its gross domestic product in 2001 was a quarter less than in had been ten years earlier.[25] University of Chicago economists Steven Davis, Kevin Murphy, and Robert Topel estimate that real per capita income fell roughly by three quarters as a result of Saddam's misrule.[26]

After Saddam's overthrow, the UN-authorized sanctions regime was completely dismantled, and the scale of Western and Eastern corruption (including that of the United Nations) in the oil-for-food program became apparent. The clearest benefits (or cost savings) to Iraqis came from the end of sanctions and the end of Saddam's killings of Iraqis. Davis, Murphy, and Topel estimate that sanctions cost about $13 billion per annum.[27] Updating that suggests that Iraqis have so far saved $65 billion in 2003 dollars (about one year of current oil revenues). They also estimate that Saddam was responsible for an average of 10,000 to 30,000 killings annually, which suggests that by 2008, some 50,000 to 150,000 lives have been saved by the intervention (to be offset against those lost since the U.S.-led intervention). Under the CPA, the American government was successful in organizing extensive debt relief for Iraq, which at least lifted the drag on the economy created by Saddam's military aggression. (It is not easy to establish the exact figure, but it appears to have been of the order of $30 billion.) It is perhaps the best economic measure the United States has taken on behalf of the Iraqis. It also introduced an independent central bank and a new currency. The Kurdistan Region, freed from sanctions, responded best to the regime shift, largely because it was already autonomous, and its institutions did not collapse during the collapse of Baathist Iraq. It used its share of Iraqi oil revenues—still below what they should have been on a per capita allocation and often received late, either from the CPA or its successor governments in Baghdad—to organize large-scale construction and infrastructure booms. Having had a decade to adjust to the withdrawal of the Baathist control economy, Kurds found it much easier to adapt after

2003. Having their own political institutions and security, enhanced by the administrative unification of the region in 2006, has put the Kurds of Iraq into their most prosperous period, ever. It is not an accident that the Kurdistan Region now advertises itself under the heading "The Other Iraq."

In 2007 the author of this book edited *The Kurdistan Region: Invest in the Future*.[28] Editing such a publication for Iraq as a whole in 2007, and especially for Iraq outside of Kurdistan, would have been an act of a ludicrously ambitious "boosterism," wishful thinking at best. That is because Iraq outside of the Kurdistan Region has had a dreadful economic performance since March 2003. The program of economic shock therapy administered by the CPA was both heartless and deeply damaging in its consequences. Heartless, because much of the population had become state-dependent, and without security and a well-organized stimulation of Iraq's private sector, many ended up unemployed. Deeply damaging, because the seismic shift from a controlled to a market economy enhanced the grievances amid which Sunni Arab men set forth on their insurgency. Iraq-wide unemployment rates between January 2004 and November 2004 were never less than 30 percent and were as high as 45 percent; from November 2005 the lower-bound estimate has been 25 percent, the higher one 40 percent.[29] The shock therapy also made most Iraqis outside the Kurdistan Region—Sunni, Shia, others, and secular—less enamored of regime replacement, however much they were glad to see the back of Saddam.

The shock therapy may not have been motivated by Naomi Klein's caricature of "disaster capitalism," but it certainly provides her with multiple anecdotes. An early calculation of the costs of the U.S. intervention to Iraq's gross domestic product was carried out by Colin Rowat of the University of Birmingham, who put them at least at $24 billion, a per capita loss of $900 for each Iraqi in 2005.[30] But as he readily acknowledges, his estimates depend on guessing how the Iraqi economy might have performed without the U.S. intervention and on assuming that Iraq would have been an unambiguous gainer from the rise in the world price of oil after 2003. Davis, Murphy, and Topel of the University of Chicago estimate, by contrast, that "If, over the course of a generation, Iraqis recover even half of the economic losses they suffered under Saddam Hussein, then they will be significantly better off in material terms as a consequence of forcible regime change."[31]

Outside of Kurdistan, economic reconstruction after March 2003 is universally acknowledged to have been fitful at best. Rebuilding amid an insurgency and a civil war, of course, is not easy. Insurgents attacked military and economic targets as well as civilians. There have been nearly 500 attacks counted on Iraqi oil and gas pipelines, installations, and personnel since June 2003—although they have numbered only one a month since the summer of 2007.[32] Normal investors do not take risks in a war zone. Electricity production has only consistently surpassed prewar levels since January 2008, and the average daily hours of supply across the country are still just less than twelve, causing deep difficulties for hospitals, sanitation, normal business operations, and household comfort (in either hot or cold weather).[33] Iraqi agriculture has been suffering from a severe drought since the summer of 2006. It received only a third of its normal rainfall in the winter of 2007–8, leaving families to abandon their farms, adding to the stocks of displaced people. Food can be imported with Iraq's improved oil revenues, but the drought leads to halts in the operation of hydroelectric plants and adds to sanitation and public health crises.[34] The U.S. model of replacing direct public administration with contractors was also highly problematic. The CPA's and subsequent U.S. expenditures on reconstruction went, following congressional law, largely to American contractors—high-priced compared with their Iraqi counterparts. These contractors often imported cheap non-Iraqi labor rather than face the security risks or the higher wage costs associated with hiring Iraqis.

American-directed reconstruction failures have been amplified by those of the transitional federal Iraqi governments under Iyad Allawi (late 2004), the elected federal governments since 2005, and of many provincial governments outside of the Kurdistan Region. The federal government has been extraordinarily weak in exercising its formal functions. Vulnerable to insurgents and penetration by militias, its officials have been scared, inept, and predatory. Iraq has the distinction of being ranked 178th out of 180 countries surveyed for their perceived reputation for corruption in 2007 by Transparency International, and its ranking has fallen each year since 2003.[35] Assassinations and kidnappings of the technical intelligentsia have only aggravated the difficulties in creating a new and effective government. As Iraqi oil revenues improved dramatically from early 2007, it became more apparent that the Baghdad ministries were often incapable of spending their allocated budgets—causing understandable impatience in the provinces, conditioned to being supplied from Baghdad but often better at administrative initiatives. These administrative failures extend to the federal oil ministry, which somehow manages to spend only a small proportion of its investment budget despite the proven necessity of infrastructure repair following poor and myopic extraction methods under Saddam and by the actions of insurgents since his removal from power. There are exceptions to this picture. The Federal Ministry of Water Resources, whose minister is Latif Rashid, has designed and implemented a strategic plan to restore and preserve the southern marshes. A regrowth of the Hammar and al-Hawizeh marshes has occurred, and the indigenous inhabitants have returned in large numbers.[36] But as Rashid told me in the summer of 2008, "The Garden of Eden will take longer to repair than Saddam took to destroy it."[37]

The successes of the Water Resources Ministry need to be matched elsewhere before one can speak confidently of Baghdad's new regime. But the hike in world oil prices, and in Iraqi oil production is expected to boost Iraq's total oil revenues to $80 billion in 2008. The Council of Representatives has just been able to grow Iraq's budget from $48 billion to $70 billion, but the immediate questions are, "will it be spent?" and "will it be well-spent?" Until Baghdad's governance improves it will not be easy to conclude—as I would like to—that Iraqis could hardly do worse than the Americans in managing their economy. But that cannot be a decisive consideration, either for Americans or Iraqis. Iraq is formally sovereign again, and principled American and Iraqi policy must endeavor to make that sovereignty meaningful. That means leaving Iraqis to manage their own economy, according to their own Constitution and political institutions. Freedom includes the right to make your own mistakes, and freedom to make them is what Iraqis seek.

Preferences

America is a democracy; Iraq is becoming one. Public opinion should therefore eventually have decisive weight in shaping important policies in both countries. The body count and economic damage of the intervention in Iraq have not, when compared with the past under Saddam, been apocalyptic. But perceptions do not always converge with admittedly contestable facts. It is not surprising given what has happened in Iraq since 2003 to find a strong convergence of opinion among Americans and Iraqis surveyed in the last two years. Majorities in both countries favor the immediate, or the phased, or the intended withdrawal of U.S. forces, though there are considerable nuances that need to be emphasized while respecting this broad convergence.

U.S. Opinion

The American public has made it clear that it wants the United States to withdraw from Iraq—subject to certain constraints.[38] In July 2008, 63 percent of Americans polled answered "not worth it" to the question, "all in all, considering the costs to the United States versus the benefits to the United States, do you think the war with Iraq was worth fighting or not?" In the same poll, 60 percent did not think the United States had to win the war in Iraq for the broader war on terrorism to be a success, while opinion was almost equally divided over whether the United States was making significant progress toward restoring civil order in Iraq.[39] The previous month a poll showed 68 percent opposing and 30 percent favoring "the U.S. war in Iraq."[40] In the same June 2008 poll, 64 percent favored the next president's removal of most U.S. troops within a few months of taking office.[41]

The desire to withdraw is matched by a negative reading of how the war is faring and the reasons for intervening. In a different June 2008 survey, 55 percent of Americans thought the United States had made the "wrong decision" in "using military force against Iraq," in contrast with 39 percent who thought it had made the "right decision"[42]; and while 44 percent thought the U.S. military effort in Iraq was going fairly or very well, 52 percent thought to the contrary. In the same survey, 52 percent were in favor of bringing home U.S. troops as soon as possible, while 43 percent favored keeping troops in Iraq "until the situation has stabilized." By contrast, and of note, 50 percent thought the United States would probably or definitely succeed in achieving its goals in Iraq, by comparison with 42 percent who thought it would probably or definitely fail.[43] Another poll in the same month asked: "Do you believe that the United States should bring most of the troops home from Iraq in the next year or two, or should the U.S. wait until Iraq is relatively stable, even if it takes four more years or more?" Those who thought they should be brought home within the next year comprised 56 percent of the sample, whereas 39 percent were prepared to delay four years or more to achieve stability.[44] The same respondents were asked whether the United States was right or wrong in going to war with Iraq: 57 percent thought it had been wrong, 35 percent that it had been right. In a *Los Angeles Times*/Bloomberg Poll, conducted during June 19–23, 2008, respondents were asked "should the United States withdraw troops right away, or should the U.S. begin to withdraw troops home within the next year, or should troops stay in Iraq as long as it takes to win the war?" A plurality, 43 percent, favored withdrawal within the next year, 26 percent favored staying as long as it takes to win the war, while 25 percent favored immediate withdrawal.

These views on the intervention have had repercussions for the public's view of the Bush administration. In one poll conducted in June 2008, disapproval of President Bush's "handling of the situation in Iraq" was at 64 percent, admittedly an improvement over his 72 percent disapproval rating nearly a year earlier in response to the same question. Those questioned were divided between 40 percent who thought the U.S. goal of "achieving victory in Iraq" was still possible and 54 percent who thought it was not. A more subtle question asked, "When it comes to the war in Iraq, which of the following statements comes closer to your point of view? The most responsible thing we can do is find a way to withdraw most of our troops from Iraq by the beginning of 2009. The most responsible thing we can do is to remain in Iraq until the situation in the country is stable." Those who favored staying until stability had been accomplished, 45 percent, were just outnumbered by those who favored a rapid withdrawal.[45] In late July 2008, a Gallup Poll found Americans almost evenly divided between those who favored planning a withdrawal without a timetable (50 percent) and those who favored a timetable (47 percent).[46]

As with all polls and surveys, respondents are affected by the way questions are phrased, but when we take the numerous snapshots of U.S. opinion in June and July 2008, and combine them with data since polling on the Iraq intervention began (which are far too numerous for me to report here), we can conclude that:

1. Americans disapprove of President Bush's handling of the situation in Iraq and think the decision to intervene was a mistake, or wrong, and they do so in proportions of roughly two to one, which almost reverses their attitudes in the late spring of 2003; see, for example, Table 4.1.
2. Americans in general now favor a timetable for withdrawal, especially when given an unqualified choice between a timetable or no timetable (perhaps because some think the "no timetable" option may permit an indefinite commitment), whereas in the immediate aftermath of the intervention they were likely to back "staying the course," or "as long as it takes."
3. When told that Iraqi leaders favor a withdrawal with a timetable, Americans are more likely to endorse both.
4. Americans are less likely to favor an immediate end to the U.S. military presence in Iraq, especially when reminded of its implications for instability, than they are to disapprove of the intervention in the first place or than they are to disapprove of President Bush's management of the intervention.

The intervention in Iraq is the third American military intervention since polling began to generate majority opposition in domestic public opinion.

TABLE 4.1 American Opinion on the Intervention in Iraq, 2003–8

Annual average percentages of Americans polled answering "Yes, a mistake," to the question: "In view of the developments since we first sent our troops to Iraq, do you think the United States made a mistake in sending troops to Iraq, or not?" (Percentages rounded to one decimal place.)						
	2003	*2004*	*2005*	*2006*	*2007*	*2008*
Average percentage saying that sending troops to Iraq was a mistake	32.3	45.9	50.8	54.1	57.5	59.8

Source: See http://www.gallup.com/poll/106783/Opposition-Iraq-War-Reaches-New-High. aspx.

The Korean War was the first. Opposition to the Iraq intervention is now nearly as high as those who in 1990 regarded the American war in Vietnam to have been a mistake.

American public opinion remains highly malleable. In late August 2008, nearly half of those polled were reported as applauding the surge, about which the public had been highly skeptical a year earlier; more Americans have come to think that the American intervention in Afghanistan is more important than that in Iraq; and Iraq's salience as a political issue likely to shape presidential voting decisions appears to be receding.[47] Nevertheless, the next American president can expect extensive popular backing if he organizes a substantive and effective withdrawal, especially if he manages to do so while minimizing further instability within Iraq. He will win even further approval from Americans if he can appear to do so while seeming to have fulfilled some of America's declared (or imputed) war aims.

Iraqi Opinion

Before summarizing the polling on Iraqi preferences, two important qualifications are in order. First, polls and surveys in Iraq are less reliable than those in the United States. This is not just because polling and surveying are new freedoms in Iraq. They are less reliable because the war-torn environment outside of the Kurdistan Region raises issues about the samples (given the absence of reliable census data and large-scale evidence of displacement), of the conduct of the polls and surveys (given that the staff employed may be fearful for their security),[48] and of the responses (given that pollsters and surveyors may be suspected of being spies or police).

Second, as the history of Iraq should by now have taught most Americans, "Iraqis" are not in the least socially or politically homogeneous. Iraq's three largest communities should be treated separately in any analysis. Unfortunately, many polls and surveys simply report Iraqi opinion as a whole—and their sample sizes by province or regions are sometimes not large enough to draw reliable conclusions about opinion within the big three communities. Iraq has two major languages and two major nationalities: Kurds, who speak Kurdish, which is related to Farsi, the language of Persians, and Arabs, who speak Arabic. That means there are issues in ensuring that everyone is being asked the same question. Then there are numbers: Kurds comprise about one-fifth of all Iraqis, and Arabs and Kurds together likely make up over 95 percent of Iraq's population. In instances in which Arabs have unified views, these are likely to dramatically outnumber those of Kurds if Kurds disagree. Most Iraqis are Muslims, over 95 percent or perhaps higher, but they are divided between Sunni and Shia Muslims (and within each of these major sects). Arab and Arabic-speaking Sunni Muslims perhaps constitute one-fifth of Iraqis. Arab and Arabic-speaking Shia Muslims constitute at least fifty and perhaps as much as sixty percent of Iraq's population. Where Shia Arabs are split, then aggregate Iraqi opinion will be skewed by whether Sunni Arabs or Kurds are the more unified or hold the more intense preferences on the relevant subject. Where I am able to report these three major communities' opinions from very recent polls and surveys I do so, but unfortunately, that is not possible on a significant scale.

In March 2008, the Oxford Research Bureau (ORB) polled Iraqis for the United Kingdom's Channel 4 television. Seventy percent said that they wanted Coalition forces to withdraw, with four-fifths of this group wanting them to leave within six months and a slightly higher number within a year.[49] A little earlier, in February 2008, a survey of Iraqi opinion carried out for the BBC, ABC News, ARD, and NHK asked the question, "What is the single biggest problem facing your life these days?" Just 5 percent of Iraqi respondents named the U.S. occupation or presence.[50] When we combine the responses that specified security concerns such as civil war, sectarian violence, and terrorist attacks with those that named political matters (instability, weak government, and bad leaders), as well as those supposing that the country was breaking apart, a full third of Iraqis cited security or political issues without directly blaming the U.S. presence. Moreover, the overwhelming majority of respondents named economic or social problems as their biggest personal concerns—including unemployment (10 percent), insufficient electricity supplies (11 percent), and other failures in public and social services. By comparison, in a survey with many of the same questions, published on March 19, 2007, 48 percent of respondents cited security considerations as the biggest single problem in their lives.[51] A lot of attitudinal change can occur in a year.

Open questions are important in assessing public opinion because they enable respondents to make their own selections rather than being cued by the surveying organization into fixed options. When asked another variation on this open question, "Not personally, but in terms of Iraq, what in your opinion is the single biggest problem facing Iraq as a whole?," a mere 6 percent named the U.S. occupation or presence—that is, half as many as named terrorist attacks (12 percent), and just 1 percent more than named the presence of al-Qaeda and foreign jihadists. In response to a far more strongly structured question, "From today's perspective and all things considered, was it absolutely right, somewhat right, somewhat wrong, or absolutely wrong that U.S.-led Coalition forces invaded Iraq in spring 2003?" Iraqi opinion was divided: 49 percent thought it had been somewhat or absolutely right, whereas 47 percent thought it had been either somewhat or absolutely wrong. Table 4.2 shows the responses to the same question over time. An important feature of these responses is their comparative stability, especially by comparison with U.S. opinion. Iraqi opinion in the spring of 2008 broke down more or less to where it was in 2004—though there are no more "don't knows" or "refuseds," and those believing the intervention to have been "somewhat wrong" have risen. Strong opinion in favor of the intervention dipped in August 2007, but it has since

TABLE 4.2   Iraqi Opinion (2004–8) on the U.S. Intervention in 2003

"From today's perspective and all things considered, was it absolutely right, somewhat right, somewhat wrong, or absolutely wrong that U.S.-led coalition forces invaded Iraq in spring 2003?" (Figures rounded to whole percentages.)

	2004	*2005*	*2007 (Feb.)*	*2007 (Aug.)*	*2008*
Absolutely right	20	19	22	12	21
Somewhat right	29	28	25	25	28
Somewhat wrong	13	17	19	28	23
Absolutely wrong	26	33	34	35	27
Refused/don't know	13	4	—	—	—

Source: D3 Systems (Vienna) and KA Research (Istanbul).

recovered. Strong hostility to the intervention has never had less than a quarter of the public's support and has risen to as high as a third before dipping.

By contrast, in the same survey Iraqi opinion was much less divided over the performance of U.S. and other Coalition forces and on the issue of their presence (see Table 4.3). In the spring of 2008, those who thought U.S. and Coalition troops were performing their responsibilities quite or very badly (70 percent) were over twice as numerous as those who thought otherwise (29 percent). And those who somewhat or strongly opposed their presence in Iraq (72 percent) outnumbered even more those who thought otherwise (26 percent). These assessments were made *after* the impact of the U.S.-led surge had made itself felt—and had moved opinion slightly back to more positive dispositions toward the foreign troops.

TABLE 4.3   Iraqi Public Opinion 2004–8 on U.S. and Coalition Troops: Performance and Presence

Performance: "Since the war, how do you feel about the way in which the United States and other Coalition forces have carried out their responsibilities in Iraq? Have they done a very good job, quite a good job, quite a bad job, or a very bad job?" (Figures rounded to whole percentages.)

	2005	2007 (Feb.)	2007 (Aug.)	2008
A very good job	10	6	3	6
Quite a good job	27	18	15	23
Quite a bad job	19	30	32	35
A very bad job	40	46	48	35
Refused/don't know	5	—	1	1

Presence: "Do you strongly support, somewhat support, somewhat oppose, or strongly oppose the presence of Coalition forces in Iraq?" (Figures rounded to whole percentages.)

	2004	2005	2007 (Feb.)	2007 (Aug.)	2008
Strongly support	13	13	6	5	7
Somewhat support	26	19	16	16	19
Somewhat oppose	20	21	32	26	31
Strongly oppose	31	44	46	53	41
Refused/don't know	10	3	—	—	1

Source: D3 Systems (Vienna) and KA Research (Istanbul).

Opinion on these questions has shifted significantly over time. Since 2004 those strongly supporting the U.S. and Coalition troop presence has halved to 7 percent, and those somewhat supporting their presence has fallen by a quarter, to 19 percent. The bare majority that opposed their presence in 2004 (51 percent) has now become a supermajority of 72 percent. This pattern has been strongly evident since 2006.[52]

Surveys have shown that half of all Iraqis supported the removal of Saddam's regime by foreigners, and another quarter have thought it somewhat wrong (presumably because of doubts about the motivations of the interventionists and the consequences) but not flat out wrong. But, by contrast, there has always been a majority opposed to the long-term presence of foreign troops, and that has increased over time. At the peak of intercommunal violence between 2005 and 2007, three-quarters to four-fifths of Iraqis in these surveys thought foreign troops were doing a bad or very bad job. While there was and remains strong and winnable support for the removal of Saddam's regime, there has always been at least as much skepticism and outright hostility toward the longer-term presence and performance of foreign troops. Such hostility appears to have peaked in the two surveys conducted in 2007 by the same teams. They found majorities (of 51 and 57 percent in February and August, respectively) who considered attacks on Coalition forces "acceptable" by comparison with the nearly four-fifths who considered them "not acceptable" in 2004.[53]

Like American opinion, Iraqi opinion is more nuanced on when, and according to what standards, there should be a withdrawal of U.S. troops (see Table 4.4), especially when provided with cues for their consideration. Those who favor an immediate withdrawal have increased since 2005, peaking at 47 percent in surveys taken in the summer of 2007 (see Tables 4.4 and 4.5). But those who want to place conditions on foreign troop withdrawal have so far always outnumbered them in these surveys. Most prefer a simple (but ambiguous) standard, namely, until the restoration of security, whereas others would prefer their withdrawal to be conditional on improvements in the capacities of the Iraqi government or Iraqi security forces. The same survey I have focused on here also asked a simpler question in 2008 focused just on American troops: "If the American forces left the country entirely, do you think the security situation in Iraq overall would become better, become worse, or remain the same?" A plurality of respondents, 46 percent, thought it would get better, 23 percent thought it would remain about the same, whereas 29 percent thought it would become worse. In August 2007, the same survey organizers put a hypothetical sce-

TABLE 4.4 Iraqi Public Opinion 2005–8 on U.S. and Coalition Troop Withdrawal (Percentages)

	2005	2007 (Feb.)	2007 (Aug.)	2008
Leave now	26	35	47	38
Remain until security is restored	31	38	34	35
Remain until Iraqi government is stronger	19	14	10	14
Remain until the Iraqi security forces can operate independently	16	11	7	10
Remain longer but leave eventually	3	2	2	3
Never leave	1	1	—	1
Refused/don't know	4	—	—	—

Figures rounded to whole percentages.
Source: D3 Systems (Vienna) and KA Research (Istanbul).

nario to Iraqi respondents, at a moment when there was a peak in support for the immediate withdrawal of U.S. and Coalition troops (as we can see from Tables 4.3 and 4.4). The question was, "Suppose the United States withdraws from Iraq before civil order is fully restored. Do you think U.S. withdrawal would make each item I read more likely, make it less likely, or U.S. withdrawal will not make much difference in whether that happens?" Respondents were presented with four possibilities—a full-scale civil war in Iraq, parts of Iraq becoming a base of operations for international terrorists, Iran taking control of parts of Iraq, and increased violence in the Kurdish areas. The responses are provided in Table 4.5. In no case did outright majorities of respondents affirm the worst-case scenarios predicted in

TABLE 4.5 Iraqi Public Opinion in August 2007 on a Hypothetical Withdrawal of U.S. Troops Before Restoration of Civil Order (Percentages)

	More Likely	Less Likely	Have No Effect	Don't Know
Full-scale civil war in Iraq	35	46	19	—
Parts of Iraq becoming base of operations for international terrorists	46	40	14	—
Iran taking control of parts of Iraq	46	29	24	—
Increased violence in Kurdish areas	9	45	44	—

Figures rounded to whole percentages.
Source: D3 Systems (Vienna) and KA Research (Istanbul).

much U.S. public commentary, although pluralities believed that the likelihood of increased international terrorist bases and Iranian control would rise after such a U.S. withdrawal.

These D3-KA polls are not always reported with community breakdowns, and that is true of the 2008 survey analyzed here. We can surmise that Sunni Arabs (on average) have been the most opposed to the initial U.S. intervention and the presence of U.S. and Coalition forces, the most hostile toward their performance, and, until recently, the most supportive of their immediate withdrawal. We can also surmise (on average) that Kurds have been the most supportive of the original U.S. intervention and the presence of U.S. and Coalition forces, and the least hostile toward their performance (partly because Coalition forces have scarcely been present in the Kurdistan Region). The average attitudes of Shia Arabs lie somewhere between those of Sunni Arabs and Kurds. Published data from the August 2007 D3 and KA surveys support these suppositions with regard to Sunni and Shia Arabs. For example, 93 percent of Sunni Arabs regarded attacks on Coalition forces as acceptable; 70 percent of Sunni Arabs thought the U.S. intervention absolutely wrong, and another 27 percent somewhat wrong; 73 percent of Sunni Arabs strongly opposed the continuing presence of Coalition forces, and another 25 percent were somewhat opposed; and 72 percent of Sunni Arabs favored the immediate withdrawal of Coalition forces (by comparison with 44 percent of Shia Arabs).

A March 2007 survey conducted for BBC's *Newsnight* and other news organizations, which sampled some 2,200 people, reported that more than eight in ten Shia (as well as 97 percent of Sunni Arabs) opposed the presence of U.S. and other forces in their country, while more than seven in ten Shia Arabs and nearly all Sunni Arabs thought the presence of U.S. forces in Iraq was making the security situation worse.[54] In contrast, three quarters of Kurdish respondents supported the U.S. presence, and in all surveys overwhelming numbers of Kurds have thought attacks on Coalition forces to be unacceptable.

Drawing on the survey data discussed here and on other polling data from 2003, we can draw four conclusions about Iraqi public opinion that will play a decisive role in the period ahead.[55]

1. Most Iraqis, especially Arab Iraqis, want to see an end to the presence of Coalition troops as soon as possible. This preference is much higher among Arabs than Kurds and has been consistently exceptionally high among Sunni Arabs.

2. Most Iraqis, but not Kurds, do not think the security situation will be worsened by a U.S. military withdrawal, and significant numbers of Iraqis (sometimes majorities) appear to believe that intergroup relations within Iraq will improve after a withdrawal of U.S. and Coalition troops. Kurds are more fearful of the negative consequences of a U.S. military disengagement.

3. Relatedly, and consistently, most Iraqis favor the visible affirmation of Iraqi sovereignty on the presence of foreign troops—their departure from Iraq should be subject to Iraqi preferences, and their presence in Iraq should be regulated under Iraqi policies and laws.

4. Polls and surveys, nevertheless, show some interesting nuances. High numbers of Iraqis appear to favor continued U.S. support (in training and materiel) to the Iraqi security forces. As many as eight in ten favor U.S. participation in operations against al-Qaeda and other foreign jihadists within Iraq (which is not consistent with a total U.S. troop withdrawal). Iraqis, including Arab Iraqis, realize that the security situation is still fragile, so despite recent improvements in public order, and despite their adverse judgments on the performance and presence of Coalition troops, they sometimes favor qualified or paced withdrawal—depending on where they live (or used to live), and their estimations of what may happen to their communities.

Iraqi public opinion as a whole is somewhat malleable, and there are palpable differences among its three major communities. They may change their judgments on a U.S. withdrawal depending on its nature and depending on how it is interpreted by their leaders—in political parties, mosques, militias, and immediate kinship groups. They may come to care less intensely about the presence of foreign troops if the security situation continues to improve dramatically and if the foreign troops are visibly returning to their bases—and largely deployed in a supportive or training role. But with provincial and federal Iraqi elections scheduled for 2009, it is sensible to expect majority opinion in Iraq to mobilize strongly behind a "U.S. troops out" platform. That has already started to happen—with politicians pushing in the Council of Representatives for their timetable of withdrawal.

The next American president can therefore expect extensive popular backing within Iraq as well as the United States if he sets forth to organize a substantive and effective withdrawal of American troops. Within Iraq he will need to assure Kurds that their recent political gains will not be lost, and assure Arabs that their recent security gains will be consolidated. He will need to perform a delicate balancing act to discourage Sunni and Shia Arab insurgents, militias, and parties from believing that they can win a decisive victory over their internal rivals after a substantive U.S. withdrawal. That will require credible American commitments to uphold a power-sharing equilibrium within Iraq, which we will explore later.

The Potential Benefits of a Successful Substantive Withdrawal

For Americans the potential benefits of a successful withdrawal from Iraq will include staunching the loss of the lives and limbs of American soldiers and will involve limited economic benefits from reduced military commitments to Iraq. These economic benefits cannot be exaggerated given that any president will be under strong pressure to "reset" the armaments of U.S. military forces and given that a substantive withdrawal may still include significant defense commitments to Iraq.

The benefits of a U.S. withdrawal will include following the current dispositions of American and Arab Iraqi public opinion and therefore will likely reap electoral rewards for politicians in both countries, provided, of course, the withdrawal is not a disaster. The benefits will include abandoning any direct or indirect U.S. governing of Iraq, which has opened the United States to accusations of neocolonialism. Abandoning efforts at state-building (or nation-building) in Iraq, at which successive American administrators and diplomats have proven inept (partly because of their instructions from the Bush administration), can only be of net value.[56] America has, unfortunately, proved better at state smashing than at state reconstruction. Many of the Americans who went into Iraq were blind to its realities. Indeed "blindness" is a favored metaphor in American commentary.[57] But many of the Americans who criticized the Bush administration have been equally blind to what Iraq was and is really like—under Saddam, and after—and especially oblivious to its binational and religious character and what that might require for political coexistence.[58] For these reasons, among others, American administrators, legal advisors, and diplomats have not been best suited to assist in the reconstruction of Iraq, and therefore it is difficult to argue against those Iraqis who want to manage their own affairs. They deserve the benefits (and costs) of self-government, as the polls and the Arab parties of Iraq tell us they want. Provided that those benefits do not include any loss to the rights of Kurdistan, such an outcome would reject both imperialism and clumsy paternalism.

All these potential benefits are contingent on two prerequisites being met: a workable Iraqi security settlement that will survive a substantive U.S. withdrawal, and a matching Iraqi political settlement within the framework of the 2005 Constitution (in which Kurds, Sunni Arabs, Shia Arabs, and others can play their role as equal citizens). The prospects for these two goals are assessed in the next two chapters.

Chapter 5
Securing the Iraqi Federation for All Its Peoples

American success or failure in Iraq may well depend on whether the Iraqis (as the people are called) like American soldiers or not. It may not be quite that simple, but then again it could.

—U.S. Army, *A Short Guide to Iraq*, 1943

You crushed the heads of Leviathan; you gave him as food for the creatures of the wilderness.

—Psalm 74:14

The Shia are afraid of what happened in the past; the Sunnis are afraid of what will happen in the future; the Kurds are preoccupied with the past, the future, and with what is happening right now.

—Nechirvan Barzani, Prime Minister of the Kurdistan Regional Government

Some people openly prefer despotism to anarchy. Throughout the ages numerous Christian and Muslim philosophers endorsed tyrannical kings and sultans or acquiesced in their excesses, believing the horrors of civil war to be the much worse alternative.[1] Many atheists have been similarly inclined, including disguised atheists like Thomas Hobbes, who told his readers to prefer the biblical sea monster Leviathan—the state—rather than what he saw as its sole alternative, the war of all against all.[2] And some contemporary political scientists have suggested that systems of control, where one group dominates another, however morally reprehensible, are preferable to intercommunal civil wars.[3]

The wisdom of the ages and of today's self-styled realists commend the peace of the cemetery. Such wisdom is not merely timid, but poor empirical counsel. Democratic conservatism, liberalism, and socialism are based on the assumption that we do not have to choose between absolutism and anarchy. We can design and enforce our political institutions to inhibit both despotism and anarchy. We can have law and freedom. Constitution-alized law and order remove the need to surrender to despots. Democratic freedoms, if appropriately organized, mean we do not have to take up arms in fear of our neighbors.

Even the most casual study of historical data shows that far more have died in our times from governmental terrorism than from nongovernmen-tal violence. State terrorism exterminated more people than unofficial ter-rorism in the twentieth century.[4] And so it has been throughout the history of governments. Saddam's Iraq and its aftermath are not exceptions to this generalization. This is not, however, to preach the merits of either anar-chy or civil war, and still less to plead that war should be given a chance, as Edward Luttwak suggested at the end of our bloodiest century.[5] Anarchy and civil war can be horrendous, as they have been in Arab Iraq since 2003. But only a fair fraction of the resulting deaths can be directly blamed on America. A significant quota of the violence in Arab Iraq was caused by the death throes of Baathism, whose followers held bloody hopes of a restora-tion. They sought to collapse the new Iraq and thereby compel an Amer-ican withdrawal. In appearing to succeed, they were not alone in getting more than they bargained for.

The Imprudence of the Ultrarealists

Some American commentators favor a dictatorship to resolve Iraq's cri-ses.[6] Significant numbers of Iraqis in some early opinion polls reacted the same way.[7] The suggestion that authoritarianism would be preferable to today's violent chaos has a long pedigree. But quite apart from its question-able ethics, this policy recommendation hardly seems practicable. A dicta-tor requires the support of a strong army, police, or party. Until recently, Iraqi security forces have been too weak and too divided to control most of the country's territory. Even if they are becoming stronger, why should we believe they would unite to support a powerful new central dictator? Which party could win a military contest for power? From which one of Iraq's communities would the dictator be drawn? A Kurd would be unac-ceptable to Arabs (and there are no sane Kurdish applicants for the job). Why would Shia Arabs accept a new Saddam? Or, why would Sunni Arabs accept the dictatorship of a Shia Arab when they are less than delighted with Shia dominance under democratic rule? So how would any strongman gain the allegiance of the existing Iraqi security forces?

Between 1958 and 1963, Brigadier Abdul Karim Qasim emerged as the sole leader of Iraq. He came from the Free Officers movement, which in a spectacularly violent coup overthrew the Hashemite monarchy (imposed by the British in 1920). The Brigadier became the commander-in chief, prime minister, minister of defense, and the official leader of the Free Officers. His precarious five-year claim on power was enhanced, it was widely agreed, because he could claim to be from each of Iraq's major communities. His father was a Sunni Arab, and his mother was a Shia Kurd.[8] Few of Iraq's present generals or officers can claim such a mixed heritage. And even if they could, it would offer no immunity or guarantee of widespread popularity: Qasim himself died in a hail of bullets.

The United States is in no position to pick and enforce a dictator, quite apart from the fact that such a policy would entirely undermine America's stated commitment to a democratic Iraq. Still, many have promoted as a possible Iraqi strongman Iyad Allawi, who in 2004–5 served as Iraq's (American-appointed) prime minister. He has some cross-sectarian appeal among Arabs, but his party was decisively defeated in the January and December 2005 parliamentary elections. Allawi appears to enjoy greater support among wistful Americans and in neighboring Sunni Arab majority states than he does in Iraq. Foreign Sunni Arabs like him because he is the least Shia of the Shia Arab leaders—and because he was a Baathist before he went into exile. That almost automatically disqualifies him from having significant electoral support from his community of origin. There are absolutely no grounds for supposing that Allawi would be able to win the loyalty of the Iraqi security forces, and even less to imagine that be might be able to impose his writ more effectively than he did before. His only prospects of returning to power lie in his party's winning a pivotal position in the next federal elections. Even if it did that, however, the other parties would likely prefer someone else from Allawi's party to be the prime minister because they have not forgotten his utterly uncollegial style of rule.[9]

Leave and Pick a Winner?

Some have put forward even more cold-blooded recommendations. They have suggested that nothing will prevent a deeper civil war after most American troops have left Iraq—that America is already "baby-sitting a civil war." They reason that instead of trying to limit the flow of blood itself, the United States should pick a side, and presumably supply it with arms, in the hope that it will prevail.[10] This policy may be feasible. But it would be morally and politically incredible *unless* the proposed policy backs the existing elected federal Iraqi government and the elected Kurdistan Regional Government.

There is no plausible way in which the United States can now switch sides and back Sunni Arab militias in assaults on the new government in Baghdad. Equally, there is no way that the United States can plausibly support an all-out sectarian onslaught by a coalition of formal and informal Shia Arab forces, in which the Mahdi Army and the Badr Organization drive the remaining Sunni Arabs out of Baghdad and its satellite towns. If the Shia Arabs were to win decisively through the use of their militias, the outcome would probably help the Sadrists, and the least progressive factions in Iraq and Iran. Iraq's democratic prospects would therefore be terminated. But the Shia Arabs are not likely to win such a conflict decisively, or, differently put, they are only likely to be decisively victorious in southern Iraq and the Baghdad metropolis. They are split among multiple factions and may not cohesively cooperate to conquer all of Arab Iraq. The Sunni Arabs have demonstrated significant prowess in guerrilla and terrorist warfare against the United States since 2003, so they would not be pushovers. They would also continue to have some support from Sunni Arab majority states, at least in arms purchases.

Quite apart from its moral repugnance, any switching would neither make good public relations nor good strategic sense. Such scenarios also usually fail to consider Kurdish responses. Would the Kurds secede from Iraq in such circumstances, with or without the disputed territories, and would Kurdish secession prompt Turkish and Iranian interventions? Or, would the Kurds back one side—and if so, which one? Or would they, as seems more likely, stand aside and offer to mediate?

We can, therefore, draw one reasonable conclusion from this inspection of the unthinkable. The United States is rightly constrained politically and morally to support the democratic governments in Baghdad and Erbil. Therein lies the sole option. Making them into "winners," as we have seen, is not going to be easy, especially since they often disagree.

There Will Not Be a Baathist Restoration

Even if there were to be a precipitously, disorderly, and recklessly irresponsible American military withdrawal from Iraq in 2009, we now know there will be no Baathist restoration. The Shia Arabs in the Iraqi army and police, and their militias, as well as Kurdistan's Peshmerga, will prevent any attempt by the Baathists to regain power. No legions will march from Damascus, Riyadh, Amman, or Cairo to return the Baath to power. The key killer and his psychotic sons are dead. The Hussein Tikriti clan will never rule again. In the end they helped destroy themselves, partly because they had killed and pushed aside too many able Baathists who were not of their immediate kin. The surviving Baathists have no aircraft, helicopters, tanks, or chemical weapons. Their party's organizational structure is wrecked beyond repair. Most Sunni Arabs do not want a restoration of the Baath party, as opposed to a restoration of some of their prestige as a people. The neo-Baathists who have gone into the new Iraqi politics and competed in elections—those in the Iraqi National Dialogue, for example—lament an Iraq of their imaginings, but do not seriously contemplate an armed return to power.

The Baathist cadres who fought the United States and the other members of the multinational Coalition and the new Iraqi government often ended up fighting under nominally Islamic banners. True, their driving motivation was a Sunni version of Iraqi nationalism derived from Baathist doctrine, as is evident from reading their proclamations, and from their conduct. The claim that the new Iraqi government is Persian figures prominently in their rhetoric. But the Baathist cadres are now divided and scattered. Some have been incorporated into the new Iraqi security forces, where they are watched to prevent any conspiracies within the army. Some, under new guises, tribal, neotribal, or religious, have made peace or ceasefire agreements with the U.S.-led Coalition forces, or with the Iraqi government. They have done so because they foresaw the complete destruction of their people, especially if more of them had followed the tactics and governance favored by the foreign jihadists. "Better to negotiate with the Americans than to die with jihadists or to lose to the Shia" is a rough approximation of their sentiments.

Barry Posen of the Massachusetts Institute of Technology suggested in 2006 that four sources of energy motivated the Sunni Arab insurgents: "the anger of a group that once stood at the pinnacle of power and privilege in Iraq and now has been thrust to the bottom; tight kinship ties among this group caused by high birth rates, large families and first-cousin marriage...that draw new family members into the insurgency as others are killed, captured, or roughed up; nationalism, both Iraqi and pan-Arab; and the recent flowering of religious fundamentalism in the Islamic world."[11]

This fluent assessment needs qualifications. As we shall see, Sunni Arabs were not "thrust to the bottom" in the new Constitution of Iraq, but it is fair to acknowledge that they thought otherwise. This formerly dominant religious and ethnic minority displays political traits found among similarly situated groups elsewhere in the world—a strong fear of, or contempt for, democratization. That is because meaningful democracy underlines its status as a minority.

It is important to be frank about the political psychology and emotions of the Sunni Arabs. Many still openly express contempt toward their presumed racial inferiors (the Kurds) and their presumed religious inferiors (the Shia).[12] They are not just motivated by resentment and fear, as Posen suggests, but also by supremacist hatred and contempt. Posen is perhaps too quick to suggest that the Sunni Arab insurgents could indefinitely tap vast reserves of manpower. He sensibly claims, however, that "they will not reconcile themselves to a diminished position in Iraq until they discover that they cannot beat the Shia and the Kurds in a fair fight." Most of them now appear to recognize that they cannot beat "the Shia and the Kurds" in either a fair or a foul fight. That is why it may be possible for them to be incorporated into the new Iraq, although not on their most preferred terms. Given that they can occasion tremendous insecurity to others it is clear, however, that a sufficient number have to be part of any sustainable security settlement.

The mere possibility of a significant withdrawal of American military forces—and their move away from direct counterinsurgency, pacification, and policing duties throughout Arab Iraq—is already creating a major dilemma for Sunni Arab leaders, whether they are urban or rural, tribal or party, Islamist or nationalist. The insurgents will be tempted to claim credit for the American departure. But that departure will leave Sunni Arabs far more exposed to the long-run consequences of their displacement from domination. Some of them, I suspect, think like the playwright George Bernard Shaw, who hailed from the soon to be formerly dominant minority of Irish Protestants. In 1912, amid heated controversies over whether England should concede home rule to Ireland, Shaw claimed that he "would rather be burned at the stake by Irish Catholics than protected by Englishmen."[13] Analogously, some Sunni Arabs may claim to prefer to have their eyes blindfolded and the back of their heads drilled by Shia Arab militiamen than to be protected by Americans. But such bravado, I suspect, is a diminishing taste among a minority that must staunch its losses and assess what it can recover.

Sunni Arabs are reconsidering their need for alliances within Iraq. Many of them have rationally concluded that they cannot return to dominance throughout Iraq, at least not through force. Most have now acknowledged that the Shia Arabs outnumber them and that the Kurds may be their demographic equals. Resentment at loss of power may be giving way to a more rational sense of fear. They are tentatively exploring new vistas. Sunni tribal leaders in the northwest have made some practical alliances with Sunni Kurds close to the Kurdistan Democratic Party. In the Council of Representatives in Baghdad, some Sunni Arab nationalists are seeking alliances with those among the Shia Arabs and the Turkomen who favor a unitary and centralized Iraq. Generations of Arab nationalists, not just Baathists, have sought a unitary and centralized Iraq, and some Sunni Arabs believe it is not too late to repair bridges with some of their Shia co-nationals.

It is, however, utterly unrealistic to expect, in the short or medium term, that the remaining or the former Sunni Arab insurgents would voluntarily engage in comprehensive disarmament or decommission their weapons. Most Sunni Arabs distrust the new army, which they see as an instrument of a new Shia or Kurdish ascendancy. Even the Iraqi Islamic Party, the sole major Sunni party to endorse the Constitution in 2005, maintains its own militia. The Sunni Arabs often distrust the new police even more than the army, seeing them as controlled by the Badr Organization. These perceptions, of course, are reciprocated. Kurds and Shia Arabs have not forgotten how Sunni Arabs conducted themselves when they had their hands on the whips. They fear Sunni Arabs have not lost their urge to dominate Iraq, especially through the army, so they want to ensure that the new army is incapable of being the vehicle for a Sunni Arab general to seize power through a coup d'état—one reason why they are most reluctant to incorporate the Sunni Awakening Councils into the Iraqi army.

All this might suggest a security impasse, in which it is impossible to see how anyone's security can be improved except at the expense of others. That's what leads many American and Iraqi analysts to anticipate further and more extensive bloodshed after a substantive American withdrawal. They think America's substantive withdrawal or full exit will pave the way toward a fight to the finish. That is a possibility, but no longer the most likely one. Most Sunni Arabs have now imbibed a more realistic assessment of their long-run prospects. It is, however, obvious that any worthwhile security settlement must allow some Sunni Arabs to be armed, and that other Sunni Arabs must have some reasonable confidence in the security institutions in their neighborhoods. Granted the necessity of these premises, only two plausible policy courses within Iraq satisfy these conditions (though they can be combined).

Legalizing, Provincializing, and Regionalizing Sunni Arab Militias

The most plausible way to begin the incorporation of armed Sunni Arabs into the new Iraq must lie in their significant enrollment into provincial police forces, especially in Anbar, Salahaddin, and Ninevah. There cannot, of course, be a wholesale enrollment, and there will have to be appropriate screening and training before many of them are considered fit for their new roles (including, one hopes, more than nominal human rights and minority rights training). More ambitiously, Sunni Arabs might eventually be enrolled into the regional guard of any Sunni Arab-dominated region, which their elected provincial leaders will be able to establish under Iraq's new Constitution and under a new law that came into force in the summer of 2008. They could form a region either by upgrading the status of any of their existing provinces or by joining together two or more provinces (the available procedures by which this can take place are discussed in Chapter 6).

The legalization, provincialization, and regionalization of Sunni Arab militias, including former insurgents who are prepared to work within the new Iraq, offers the most obvious and one of the best ways to consolidate the federalization of Iraq. This policy, however, cannot be significantly advanced before there are fresh provincial elections. Sunni Arabs boycotted the first set of such elections, in January 2005, and therefore do not have provincial governments with which they can identify. When there are such elections, their former strategic error can be reversed. If the new provincial leaders opt to take substantial security powers into their own hands, then the lawful "provincialization" of security can begin in earnest. Sunni Arabs can then enjoy some lawful self-government. But before there are such provincial elections it would be better if there could be agreements on their boundaries, especially where the northern borders of Salahaddin, Ninevah, and Diyala are demarcated from the southern border of the Kurdistan Regional Government. (A decision to exclude Kirkuk from provincial elections seems highly likely.)

The more ambitious "regionalization" strategy, by contrast, cannot be developed before there are significant reversals of preferences among Sunni Arab politicians and their public. At present most of them reject regionalization, which they see as a mechanism for the destruction of Iraq. They think regionalization is the Trojan horse of Kurds and Iranians (and their Shia Arab proxies) bent on the breakup of Iraq. It is just possible that a period of significant provincial self-government may eventually alter their opinions, especially since provincial governments, unlike regional governments, will be subject to greater executive and legislative regulation from Baghdad. Since under any democratic arrangements the federal government in Baghdad will be dominated by Shia Arabs, it follows that Sunni Arabs will have to reflect in the future whether they want to grant Baghdad significant authority over their security. Provincialization offers them a way out.

The other strategy to incorporate Sunni Arabs into the security arrangements of the new Iraq, which would also involve legalization, is integration (a course currently preferred by American diplomats and commanders). Under integration, former Sunni Arab insurgents and existing Sunni Arab forces that currently cooperate with Coalition forces would join the Iraqi army and the Iraqi police in significant numbers—again after screening and training. They could then operate within centralized security forces throughout Iraq. The logic here is to create a common army and police, without quotas, that all Iraqis know to be integrated, and that they might therefore be more likely to respect and trust. The objective sounds fine, in principle, but in practice it is fraught with difficulties, and almost certain to fail if tried on a large scale.

An integrationist security personnel policy cannot apply to Kurds, who speak Kurdish and want to continue doing so. Kurds do not want to be policed by Arabs, or defended by them—in the recent past Arab soldiers killed their relatives in very large numbers. Only high-ranking Kurdish commanders tend to be bilingual, and extraordinarily few Arabs speak Kurdish. For the Kurdistan Region, therefore, the logic of Iraq's new Constitution should prevail for domestic security. The Peshmerga forces will operate as the Kurdistan regional guard, under Kurdish-speaking officers, responsible to the Kurdistan Regional Government and the Kurdistan National Assembly. Minorities within the Kurdistan Region may be integrated into these regional security arrangements. But they may also have their own policing units in their own languages, where their numbers warrant such a policy. The Kurdistan Regional Government has shown itself willing to operate such arrangements for Turkomen—including in the disputed city of Kirkuk.

Reciprocally, only very limited integration can apply to Kurdish participation in the federal Iraqi military. Kurdish-speaking soldiers can be organized in divisions, regiments, brigades, or battalions and they can serve under Kurdish officers working within the Iraqi federal forces. Such units can be deployed, as they are now, in the external defense of Iraq's borders or in aiding the federal government of Iraq.[14] But they will not become Arabic-speaking units, and their officers will need to be fluent in both of Iraq's official languages. They can be integrated—in a limited sense—as Iraqi federalists, but they will refuse to be Arabized. Their first loyalty is and will remain to the Kurdistan Region, and in many cases to its principal political parties, the KDP and the PUK.

Critics of this argument typically agree that an exception must be made for the linguistically different and largely territorially concentrated Kurds. But, they then say, Arabs share a common language, and they are still mixed, especially in a range of central Iraqi cities, so surely integrating the security forces must be the right policy goal in Arab Iraq. The argument has some merit, and it wins significant nominal support among Arab Iraqis. But it is nevertheless ethically abstract and tries to paper over the recent history of sectarian conflict among Arabs.

There is a profoundly naïve view, which can nevertheless be articulated with great sophistication in American social science, which holds that if there are better opportunities to have multiple voices of reason and moderation heard, and if there are more, diverse and better sources of information, then beliefs different from those of ethnic or sectarian hard-liners would form and expand among mass publics.[15] I am all for the Enlightenment but not for naïveté in explanations of people's conduct. The integrationist viewpoint usually suggests that it is the control of information, education, and history by manipulative elites that generates ethnic and sectarian conflict. Sometimes that is so. But at least as often sectarian and ethnic leaders are leaders precisely because they express, in a representative fashion, the beliefs of their peoples. These beliefs resonate, moreover, not just because of manipulation, which is an ineradicable feature of human conduct, but because of the actual histories and considered experiences of such groups, rather than their imaginations—manipulated or otherwise. Mass publics may rationally fear that integration will be at the expense of their identity and interests. When they favor integration, they do so on their own cultural and political terms. That is one reason why, amid sectarian or ethnic conflict, that what people say they would like (integration) is often not what they are willing to do (integrate).

The old, largely Sunni Arab-officered Iraqi army repressed Shia Arabs as well as Kurds. The Shia have not forgotten. The Shia Arab-dominated government has moved very slowly, awkwardly, and with palpable reluctance to regularize or integrate some members of the Sunni Awakening Councils and the Sons of Iraq.[16] They have done what little they have about integration only under intense American military and diplomatic pressure. Many of the Shia Arabs in Iraq's Council of Representatives agree with one of their members, Sheikh Jalaladeen al-Sagheer, who maintained in August 2008 that "the state cannot accept the Awakening. Their days are numbered."[17] These forces, at present largely financed by the Pentagon at a rate of approximately $300 per member per month, operate outside the formal law and Constitution of Iraq. They violate both Iraq's Constitution and laws and the status of forces agreement between the U.S. and Iraqi governments. They are America's own private Iraqi militia—hired to protect buildings, installations, and U.S. troops.

Until recently the bulk of the Awakening members were engaged in ferocious attacks on the Americans, the security forces of the Iraqi federal government, and often against Shia Arab civilians. Shia Arabs do not find it easy to accept that those who yesterday called them Persians, apostates, and traitors sincerely want to cooperate with them in an integrated military and police. They did not notice a chorus of Sunni Arab condemnation of the grotesque excesses of the foreign jihadists when Shia Muslims were being murdered on pilgrimages, outside and inside mosques, or in marketplaces.

In the late summer of 2008, Iraqi security forces, in a direct chain of command to Iraq's prime minister, were pursuing orders to arrest hundreds of members of the Awakening movement who used to serve as leading members of organizations such as the 1920s Revolutionary Brigade and the Islamic Army of Iraq. From the perspective of the law of Iraq, they are criminals. Amnesties and vetted incorporation of some of these forces are therefore not likely to be speedy, despite current American pressure on the Baghdad government.

Peter Galbraith has observed that "much of the discourse about Iraq in the United States, even among critics of the war, seems to assume that the composition of the security forces somehow is not Shiite or Sunni or Kurdish, but Iraqi. In fact, the security forces are *more* sectarian than the population. . . . While the U.S. military can train them to be more effective fighters, it cannot train them to be Iraqis—that is, loyal to an inclusive Iraq."[18] He therefore expects that "once U.S. forces withdraw, the civil war will escalate." He may be right. There is, however, a way to halt that prediction from materializing, that is, in the interim a decisive shift toward the regionalization and provincialization of security, consistent with the federation sketched in Iraq's 2005 Constitution, should be advocated. That strategy offers the best hope of addressing each group's fears, and putting checks on their ambitions that provoke fear among the others.

One of the arguments for federalism is that it provides a mansion with many rooms. If you cannot have the whole mansion, you can at least have a suite of your own. This recipe is not, however, a panacea for Iraq's security problems, although it can address many of them. In still mixed areas where there are histories of recent conflict, the two major internal security options cannot work on their own—that is, provincialization (or regionalization) or integration for Iraq as a whole. Instead, these policies have to be combined in such places. The minorities in the relevant province or region are not likely to be happy with being policed by gendarmes from the local majority group. They may prefer their own police. That, in turn, suggests the necessity of mixed and cooperative patrols of differently composed police and gendarmerie in such places. Alternatively, at the district or subdistrict level, one can try to obtain integrated policing units that represent the local mixture of peoples. These approaches will not be easy, but neither are they fantastic visions. Such exceptional arrangements in mixed places can work alongside a general pattern of provincialization (or regionalization).

There is a further practical difficulty with integrationist security policy. The facts on the ground have been changed. The mass expulsions and mass flights, especially those that occurred during the peak of sectarian cleansing in 2006–7, have radically reduced the degree of mixed living within Iraq. Homogenization because of flight has not, however, neatly separated Iraqis into three clearly regionally demarcated bundles of Kurds, Sunni, and Shia Arabs. In fact, even the Kurdistan Region has become more heterogeneous. It houses the largest numbers of internally displaced people who have fled there because its security situation is more stable. No one doubts that there is greater territorial segregation of Arabs by religion. Therefore, at district and subdistrict levels in Baghdad and the mixed cities of central Iraq, it will become necessary to recruit community police, who will be overwhelmingly either Sunni or Shia in particular areas, and to establish provincial policing boards in which elected representatives can hold the police accountable for impartial enforcement of the law. Iraq is some distance from this goal, but it is no longer ludicrously optimistic or impossible.

The Jihadists Are Being Defeated

The Sunni Arab insurgency was predominantly indigenous to Iraq. Foreign Salafi jihadists were always a minority among those attacking Coalition and Iraqi governmental security forces, though they were a persistent majority among suicide bombers and possibly among the killers of Shia civilians. The agenda of the foreign Salafi jihadists was theocratic and cosmopolitan—the restoration of the caliphate in the lands of Islam. That objective contrasts strongly with the agenda of Iraqi Sunni Arabs, who were and are overwhelmingly concerned with removing non-Arab foreigners from Iraq and reestablishing their former status. They had a local nationalist and sectarian agenda. The two groupings were therefore in an alliance of convenience. It did not hold.

The strategy of the Salafi jihadists, especially their deliberate attacks on Shia civilians, produced its own form of "blowback": mass-supported defensive and offensive Shia actions against Sunni Arabs, which almost drove them out of the Baghdad metropolis. The governance of the Salafis, where they tried to build pockets of Islamist governance in Anbar and Diyala, in "liberated territories," alienated them from local Iraqis, especially tribal Sunni Iraqis. The Sunni Arabs rejected another form of alien, puritanical, and arbitrary rule, which most of them judged to be worse than that of the Americans. That is ultimately why the foreign Salafi jihadists will be defeated. Not because of the superb leadership of Coalition forces, or the political efficacy of American diplomacy, or the deft use of large stacks of dollar bills, but because they have been rejected by Sunni Arabs. Speeding the establishment of lawful self-government among Sunni Arabs in the provinces where they are a majority will consolidate this process.

The Awakening Councils emerged semi-spontaneously from clashes between Sunni Arab insurgents and al-Qaeda operatives who were trying to build an Islamic Salafi state, especially in Anbar. After one such set of clashes, in which al-Qaeda killed relatives of Abdul Sattar Buzaigh al Rishawi (Abu Risha), the American military and Sunni tribal leaders converted Abu Risha into the head of the Anbar Salvation Council, later renamed the Anbar Awakening Council. In September 2007, shortly after meeting with President Bush, Abu Risha and two of his bodyguards were killed in an explosion.[19] But the movement did not die, and now has upwards of 100,000 people being paid monthly allowances by the Pentagon.

Contracting out the repression of al-Qaeda to Sunni Muslims is the best global policy the United States can promote—both in Iraq and elsewhere. But it should not be directed by the United States at the expense of Iraq's Constitution or law. If the Iraqi federal government reaches an accommodation with the Awakening Councils and the Sons of Iraq, that is well and good. If it chooses to rehabilitate some and not others among their members, that, too, is an Iraqi governmental prerogative. And if the Iraqi government chooses not to accommodate them, that does not mean that all or most of the relevant Sunni Arabs will go back to being insurgents or will realign with al-Qaeda, as some American generals fear.[20] In cooperating with the Americans, the Awakening and Sons of Iraq personnel have provided their biometric identities and registered their weapons. They have taken pay from the allies of the Iraqi government. It will therefore be easier to monitor, arrest, and kill them should they return to insurgent activity. They are aware of this reversal of their power. They know that now there are and that there will be more numerous informants within the insurgent movements, and among any foolish enough to realign with al-Qaeda in Iraq. In short, while making peace with the Americans, the former Sunni Arab insurgents in the Awakening Councils and the Sons of Iraq have not yet made peace with the Iraqi federal government. However, their blackmail potential over the Baghdad government has significantly receded. They cannot dictate their terms, even with American pressure. Other Sunni Arabs, who were not involved as insurgents, are more likely to be recruited and rewarded for being loyal to the federal government.

By early fall 2008, al-Qaeda in Iraq appeared to be cornered in Mosul city in the northwest and Diyala in eastern-central Iraq; it was also believed to persist in small pockets of Baghdad's satellite towns. Sunni Arab insurgents appear to be in retreat, judging by the radically reduced killings of American and Coalition troops. Although both groups are much weakened, they are still deadly. One of their current most preferred tactics is to assassinate key leaders of the Sunni Awakening Councils and the Sons of Iraq. On August 17, 2008, in a crowded street in front of the famous Abu Hanifa mosque in the Adhamiya district of Baghdad, a Sunni Arab stronghold, a male suicide bomber, who some eyewitnesses claim was dressed in an *abaya*, the robe worn by many Arab women, exploded a bomb he was carrying. He killed fifteen people, including his likely principal target, Faruq Abdul Sattar, a deputy commander of the local Sunni Awakening Council.[21] This episode is typical of current conflicts between those Sunni Arabs fighting Americans and those who are collaborating with them. Many more turncoat collaborators like the murdered Abu Risha, who founded the Anbar Salvation Council, are likely to die at the hands of their former comrades.

That there will be setbacks suffered among the Sunni Arabs who have decided to align with the Americans rather than the Salafists or the insurgents is therefore not in doubt. But neither is the overall pattern. The jihadists are on course for a comprehensive defeat. The Sunni Arab insurgents are looking for a settlement they can live with rather than the one of their dreams. The pressure of a substantive American withdrawal, for which they originally fought with such vigor, is now turning on them. They know the emerging strength of the Shia-dominated Iraqi forces could soon be exercised against them with much less restraint than Americans have recently displayed.

What is the right way for Americans to respond to these emergent trends? They must take advantage of them, but not by pandering to the most unreasonable of the Sunni Arabs' demands, such as abandoning federalism, granting one of them a powerful executive role as president, centralizing oil management and allocation, or a total end to de-Baathification, which will only put American policy at loggerheads with America's allies, the Kurds and the Shia Arab factions supporting the Iraqi federal government of Prime Minister Nuri al-Maliki. Instead, it should be to encourage Sunni Arab party and tribal leaders and their followers to make their peace with federalism. That will give them, minimally, provincial self-government, control over their own security, and their lawful entitlement to a proportional share of Iraqi oil revenues. To achieve these goals, available to them under the Constitution, Sunni Arab leaders will also have to recognize that the Constitution mandates territorial adjustments in the disputed territories, and that its democratic provisions mean that as a group they will never dominate the Baghdad government.

Building Wisely on "The Surge"

"The surge"—the deployment of an additional 30,000 U.S. troops into Iraq in the first half of 2007—and its effects have both been controversial in United States domestic policy. The improvements in Iraqi security that followed have been hotly debated. One camp boasts it is proof of the merits of President Bush's commitment to stay the course. Alternatively, it has been argued that the benefits that have flowed since the surge owe nothing to the surge itself but rather stem entirely from the switch in conduct by some Sunni Arabs and their abandonment of alliances with the jihadists and former Baathists. That in turn encouraged the Mahdi Army to enact a cease-fire. Iraqis are resolving matters themselves. In short, on this view, the surge was an epiphenomenon: the United States got lucky.[22]

Neither of these orthodox Republican or Democratic activist responses is appropriate or convincing. We should neither lionize the surge and its practitioners in the manner of the *Weekly Standard*[23] nor conclude that everything positive since the surge has flowed from an independent switch in strategy by Sunni Arabs, in Anbar and elsewhere, or maintain that all is down to luck or prior sectarian cleansing. Let us acknowledge, first, that without additional troops to stabilize Baghdad, the sectarian cleansing of the city might not have been halted. What the surge did, in short, was to prevent the Mahdi Army from winning the sectarian war of militias over Baghdad. Let us also acknowledge that the switch in strategy, argued for and implemented by Generals David Petraeus and Raymond Odierno, toward a complete focus on counterinsurgency, was sensible, important, and long overdue. U.S. military strategy in Iraq between the fall of 2003 and 2006 had been coercive and brutal, sowing dragons' teeth.[24] It also did not always conform to the standards required to fight a just war, *ius in bello*, also known as "international humanitarian law," in which torture, punishment of civilians, and mass detention of civilians are outlawed.

These standards were, of course, entirely and more egregiously violated by the Baathists and jihadists, who directly targeted civilians in indiscriminate attacks that had no obvious military purpose. But U.S. military conduct between 2003 and 2006 was often reckless when it came to civilians. Its greater concern for "force protection" than for Iraqi lives lost it public support among Arab Iraqis—as seen in the polls discussed in the previous chapter. Indiscriminate mass internment added fuel to the fire. A policy of immediately conducting humanitarian assistance—social as well as police work—in the aftermath of clearing out pockets of insurgents was therefore the right one, especially when it was carried out with Iraqi authorities.

If fortune did play a role, it was in the conjunction of the switch in U.S. counterinsurgency strategy and the political realization among Sunni Arabs that they were doomed to lose any continuing Iraqi civil war. The latter realization helped prompt the Anbar Awakening Movement. Had there not been a significant U.S. military presence, the Sunni Arabs would have been driven out of all of the mixed cities where they confronted Shia Arab militias and the Iraqi security forces (not always distinguishable). But well-managed counterinsurgency cannot work without a political strategy and without opponents who realize they cannot win all they want. When General Petraeus began his duties in Iraq he put the Baathists back in control of Mosul, which is why in that city, as KRG Prime Minister Nechirvan Barzani used to regularly say to me in the summer of 2005, "three Kurds are killed every night."[25] From 2003 until 2006, Sunni Arabs fought, by and large, for a restoration. Even if U.S. military policy had been better conceived earlier, much of the Sunni Arab constituency would not have been politically pliable. What has made more of them flexible now is that as a community they are staring comprehensive defeat in the face. American policy should encourage that clarity of recognition and not further any illusions.

Some critics have concluded that if Prime Minister Maliki's government does not immediately incorporate the Sunni Arabs from the Awakening and Sons of Iraq movements into the Iraqi security forces, then there will be a reignition of the insurgency, and a return to sympathy for the jihadists among Sunni Arab civilians. But we already know that any such responses will be much less unified and less threatening now because the authorities have the intelligence required for deep and sustained disorganizing penetration. American policymakers continue to insist that concessions be made to the Sunni Arabs on the Constitution, especially regarding their preferences for a more centralized Iraq, but these calls now lack strategic efficacy, even if one believed them to be politically astute. The Iraqi federal government does not have to make major concessions to the former Sunni Arab insurgents. If it is skilled, as I have suggested, it will encourage their provincialization (after vetting and training), but it is unlikely to bring them into the new army and police in large numbers.

Iraqi Security Solutions for Iraqi Security Questions

A future is opening in Iraq in which Iraqis will finally gain control of their own security decisions. In 2008 Iraqi security forces, with American support, removed al-Qaeda from Ramadi and have since operated an appropriate humanitarian relief policy, calming that much troubled city. On his own initiative Prime Minister Maliki then launched an all-out assault against the Sadrists in Basra deep in the south of Shia-dominated Iraq. Initially ridiculed, especially because of a media focus on the poor performance of one military unit just out of training, Maliki and the Iraqi forces prevailed—with American and eventually British back-up (when the battle was won). Since then, Basra has been recovering from the rule of criminal gangs and its own ruthless Shia puritans.

Historians may subsequently treat these twin events as decisive turning points. They showed that the federal Iraqi government could enforce its writ in a Sunni majority and then in a Shia majority city. They compelled the flight of al-Qaeda operatives and a cease-fire from the Mahdi Army. They won the federal government much needed credibility and legitimacy among a public keen on order but not on militia or freelance clerical order. Equally important, the federal government is not merely focused on establishing its security prerogatives for their own sake. Its key parties are also interested in future votes. The Shia religious parties, Da'wa and the ISCI, are keen to defeat the Sadrists in competition for votes among the Shia. They have calculated that their electoral strategy requires firmness before the provincial and federal elections, exposing the Sadrists as sources of disorder and criminality and opening the opportunity to break their independent militia. They have also calculated that their election strategy must include the substantial withdrawal of America from Iraq, and in fairly short order.

Grand Ayatollah Sistani, the father of Iraqi democracy, issued an opinion in 2008 that any political understanding to keep the U.S. "guests," as he has always called them, on Iraqi land (however limited the duration) must have broad political support throughout the country. The Washington and the Baghdad governments have been in negotiations since March 2008 to specify the terms of U.S. military responsibilities and rights within Iraq. The agreement, a memorandum of understanding, rather than a treaty, is needed to replace the UN mandate authorizing the presence of U.S. and multinational forces in Iraq. There have been disagreements on several matters, but there is now a draft text. It awaits approval by the U.S. and Iraqi executives and the Iraqi parliament.

The Iraqi foreign minister, Hoshyar Zebari, a Kurd, and the Shia Arab prime minister, Nuri al-Maliki, have insisted that there should be a withdrawal timeline. Media reports in the summer of 2008 confirmed that the Iraqi Council of Ministers is insisting on the end of 2011 for a complete withdrawal of U.S. combat troops. In the interim, the Baghdad government wants the withdrawal of all U.S. troops from Iraq's cities and villages by the end of June 2009. U.S. combat troops would be withdrawn to their bases in Iraq, where they would be available to assist the Iraqi forces if called upon to do so. American military forces would therefore be visible primarily in training and support roles between 2009 and 2011.

Debate between the two governments is over whether these dates are "aspirational" or firm "deadlines." The Iraqi federal government is equally keen to establish its sovereignty by ensuring that U.S. soldiers and officials do not have legal immunity for any crimes they commit under Iraqi law. The possible compromises on this matter may confine their immunity to when U.S. personnel are carrying out their official duties and on base. The formation of joint Iraqi and American committees to address such questions may also ease matters. The United States, throughout its history, has insisted that it retain exclusive legal jurisdiction over its troops, including when they are abroad working with allies, on the grounds that it is a U.S. constitutional imperative. Such insistence, of course, is seen as treating the sovereign rights of U.S. allies with disdain.[26]

Whether the draft memorandum of understanding will be ratified remains to be seen. In a sense it does not fundamentally matter whether it is negotiated with the Bush administration or with its successor. The content of the draft agreement confirms, consistent with the argument of this book, that elected Iraqis, Kurds, and Arabs want and are negotiating for a substantial withdrawal of U.S. forces from Iraq, although not an immediate pullout—indeed some Kurds would prefer a relocation of U.S. forces to Kurdistan rather than a full withdrawal from Iraq. They are doing so on the basis of a broad-based political consensus. These developments prove both that the federal government is not a puppet government and that the Iraqi military, at senior levels, is confident that it can soon take control of the defense of the provinces of Arab Iraq. Many provinces in Arab Iraq already no longer have a U.S. military presence. The Iraqi military is no longer as it was shortly after the CPA's efforts to reconstruct it. Then its soldiers often fled or were disorganized when first confronted with serious combat.[27] It has been bloodied. Its ability in 2008 to take Ramadi from al-Qaeda in Iraq and Basra from the Sadrists, albeit with Coalition support, has had a transformative impact on its morale.

The Kurdistan Region's security has already been extensively accomplished. At present the security of the KRG is maintained without a single U.S. soldier on its soil—and without any Iraqi federal forces recruited from outside Kurdistan. Erbil and Sulaimania have experienced fewer suicide bombings than London in recent years. The success of Kurdistan's security is not because it has had no threats since 2003. On the contrary. Ansar al-Islam (the Sunni jihadist allies of al-Qaeda), al-Qaeda in Iraq, and Sunni Arab and Turkomen militants in the disputed territories have tried to attack the region, its population and its institutions, with occasional success—including the Erbil bombings of February 2004, which killed deputy Prime Minister Sami Abdul Rahman and large numbers of the KDP and PUK leadership in the city. In the remote and inaccessible mountains of the KRG are guerrilla bases of the Kurdistan Workers' Party, or PKK, the party of Turkish Kurds, formerly organized as Marxist-Leninists and nominally led by Abdullah Ocalan, who lives under 24-hour surveillance in a Turkish prison.[28] They are said to use their bases in the Kandil Mountains to attack positions in Turkey before retreating. The Turkish military has launched both air and land attacks on these areas—on the grounds that the KRG has not done enough to prevent the PKK's activities. The PKK has also spawned PJAK (the Party of Free Life for Kurdistan), which is a subunit of its organization, made up of Iranian Kurds.[29] The KRG's Minister of Peshmerga, Jafar Barzinji, has accused the Iranians of supporting Ansar al-Islam in order to pressure the KRG to attack PJAK.[30] Both of the KRG's large neighbors, Turkey and Iran, accuse the KRG of being soft on Kurdish guerrillas, and have bombed its territory.

The KRG has largely been free of violence because its government is legitimate and has won the cooperation of the vast bulk of its public. The number of Kurdish Islamists is electorally small: they have about one in twenty votes. The cadres of Islamist parties are isolated, watched, and reported on by a vigilant public, which does not wish to repeat the experiences of Arab Iraq. The Islamist parties are subjected to extensive surveillance, and their fund-raising is limited since they are required to rely on government funding. The KRG's officials follow Turkish practices in appointing all the imams in mosques—a supervisory role made easier after an infamous scandal in which a sheikh used mosque-based resources and sexual blackmail to organize a jihadist network.

The KRG's security policy operates under Article 117 of the Constitution of Iraq, which makes regions responsible for their own police, security forces, and guards. The Kurdistan National Assembly has passed a counterterrorism law, which guides the police and puts them under judicial regulation—in contrast to what often happens in Arab Iraq. Firearms regulation and control are far more vigorous than in the rest of Iraq, where weapons are ubiquitous. Each of the two major Kurdish parties has covert intelligence branches, the Parastin in the case of the KDP and the Zanyari in the case of the PUK. The Asayesh, which is not party-based, is the KRG's equivalent to the FBI. It engages in both counterintelligence and counterterrorism and enjoys widespread public support.

The KRG's Minister of State for the Interior Karim Sinjari, who showed me around Kurdistan's police training colleges in 2004 and 2005, sits at the center of an effective network of now well-trained although underresourced police and gendarmes. The Peshmerga regional army units are spread out to defend the major urban centers of Dohuk, Erbil, and Sulaimania from potential attacks along the major roads from Mosul, Kirkuk (especially Hawija), and Khaniqin. Multiple vehicle checkpoints and intense surveillance of Arab visitors and residents combine to create an effective external security perimeter. Kurdish forces also successfully protect the infrastructure within the existing KRG and within the disputed territories, including oil extraction and pipelines. The KRG offers a positive model of what may be possible in the rest of Iraq if the local politicians pursue either regionalization or provincialization.

The major security problems for the KRG are threefold. They arise, first, from a lack of diplomatic and political engagement with Turkey and Iran to address the PKK-PJAK questions to all parties' mutual satisfaction. Second, there are patterns of distrust between the federal government and the KRG that create mutual anxiety. Federal officials suspect the Kurds of planning independence and land and oil grabs. Kurds suspect federal officials of seeking to prevent the resolution of the status of Kirkuk and the disputed territories and of blocking their economic development (on oil exploration and development).

This distrust flows over into budgetary relations. The federal government and the KRG have not agreed to the funding of pensions for the Peshmerga, which has been lawfully recognized as the official army of the KRG as far back as 1992, or the salary and benefit payments for Peshmerga units operating inside and outside the KRG. Arab politicians and public opinion tend to think the Kurds have done well since 2003 and can afford to pay more; the Kurds think that Arabs are breaking their promises again and free-riding on Peshmerga support for the new Iraq. Third, the disputed territories are a cause for concern. Here Kurds, Turkomen, and Arabs contest the appropriate location of districts, subdistricts, and (in the case of Kirkuk) a governorate and their boundaries. Jihadists have sought to exploit Arab and Turkomen fears and so have Turkish special forces.

On these matters, sensible American policy should shift decisively toward better diplomacy with Turkey and Iran and supporting Iraq's Constitution, which obligates (in Article 140) the resolution of the disputed territories (which is discussed more fully in Chapter 7). Kurdish negotiators will likely tie the holding of the next set of provincial elections to boundary settlements of the disputed territories—especially over Kirkuk, which may be excluded from the elections until there is a resolution. These in turn will need to be accompanied by agreed-upon policing arrangements, which will enable each linguistic community to police itself. Otherwise the probability of interethnic violence will increase. Constructive U.S. diplomacy can help here. The American government should also seek to help deliver a long-term settlement of federal-regional financing arrangements, one that is fair to its most loyal ally since 2003, namely, the KRG. It should realize that a security policy that only oils the squeaky wheels is a mistake. The KRG will benefit immensely from technical, training, and equipment assistance to improve its intelligence and policing operations.

Obliging the Sadrists to Choose

We have examined the prospects of self-management of security policy among Sunni Arabs and Kurds, but what about Iraq's largest community? Here the biggest threat to the new constitutional order is currently posed by the Sadrists, including the Mahdi Army, who have thrived on the insecurity in Arab Iraq since 2003. Their anti-Americanism, their links to the poor Shia through urban religious charities, and their informal links to criminals and to Shia who were Baathists have made them formidable communal contenders. They have invested in politics—receiving a disproportionate share of the United Iraqi Alliance list in December 2005—and in violence, both as defenders of Shia communal interests and as aggressors against the Coalition and Iraqi security forces. The other religious party leaders hoped to co-opt Sadr through generous placement of Sadrists on the list of the United Iraqi Alliance. They failed in this endeavor. However occasionally astute their nominal leader was, the Sadrists were never coherent or disciplined—it is a movement with a high number of poorly educated people. They were powerful and cohesive enough to ride the enraged Shia mass anger after the holy Samarra mosque was bombed in February 2006. To lead spontaneous rage is their forte, but policy with gravitas seems beyond them.

In Jordan at the end of 2006, journalist Patrick Cockburn interviewed Abu Kamael, a lawyer, a Mahdi Army member and self-described death-squad leader, about his actions: "It was very simple, we were ethnically cleansing. Anyone Sunni was guilty. If you were called Omar, Uthman, Zayed, Sufian, or something like that, then you would be killed. These are Sunni names.... [The Mahdi Army] is supposed to kill only Baathists, Takfiris [Sunni fanatics who do not regard the Shia as Muslims], those who cooperate with the occupation, and the occupation troops....It does not always happen like that though, and it can turn into a mafia gang."[31]

The platform for which Sadrists formally stood—Shia and Sunni unity against U.S. forces and al-Qaeda in Iraq—had a decent chance of being a political and electoral winner. The platform embodies pan-Muslim, Arab, and Iraqi colors. But his supporters and his militia now seem irredeemably stamped as Shia sectarians and criminals. Far from being free from foreign control, the Sadrists were used and abused by Iranian intelligence and security forces. The Sadrists' protection rackets and the petty criminality of their members eventually rendered them often less popular in key Iraqi cities than the Iraqi federal government, which from 2005 had been widely condemned for failing to provide basic services.

The high political point for the Sadrists was their critical role in ensuring that al-Ja'afari and then al-Maliki of Da'wa would become the federal prime minister instead of al-Mahdi of ISCI (who now serves as one of Iraq's two vice presidents). The Sadrists hoped to delay ISCI's plans to oversee region formation in the south of Iraq, and they did. Sadr then threw his weight around, trying to force the Maliki government to call for an immediate withdrawal of American forces. He regularly withdrew his ministers and parliamentarians from supporting the federal government, and just as often put them back in. In the end these maneuvers lacked credibility. Sadr also failed to build strategic or long-lasting alliances either with Shia religious leaders or with Sunni Arab nationalist political forces. The bloodletting and expulsions of 2006 have probably made the prospect of a sustained alliance between Sadrists and Sunni Arabs unrealizable.

Sadr not only rejected the idea of a southern super-region or regions, as articulated by Hakim's ISCI, but he and his immediate entourage have harbored the ambition to control all of Iraq from the central government. Their conduct, however, has made the Kurds and the Sunni Arabs reluctant to have anything to do with them. Occasional alliances of convenience with Sunni Arab centralists are not out of the question, but there appears to be no prospect of a lasting strategic alliance. One reason to expect that situation to continue is that the Sunni Arabs who will be returned at the next federal elections may be even more divided than they are now, especially as the Awakening Councils seem likely to form political fronts. No Sunni Arab politician seems likely to win votes on a platform of cooperation with Sadr. By contrast, there is reason to believe that the alliance of the Kurdish parties, the KDP and the PUK, and the Shia religious parties prepared to work with the Americans—Da'wa and ISCI—has prevailed in the war of succession to Saddam.

The Sadrists and their supporters are being forced to choose between operating within or outside the law that will now have some effective Iraqi force behind it. Their leader is seeking to reestablish his credibility as a religious and charitable organizer, critical of violence. He has formally asked his supporters not to join the extant militia. He has said that he sees the future of his movement in welfare rather than war. His opponents are gearing up to ensure that neither his militia nor his movement will be successful in future provincial or federal elections. Breaking the Sadr militia is part of their plans for electoral success. If they succeed, then the man who begins his sermons with his father's chant, "No to Satan!, No, no to America! No, no to the occupation! No, no to Israel" will receive the "No!" that matters— a "No!" from the majority of the Shia Arab electorate. If the Americans leave Iraq on the terms of the alliance in the federal Iraqi government, then neither Sadr nor the Sadrists will receive the plaudits they might once have expected. It has, of course, been foolish to discount Sadr and the Sadrists in the past, and they may yet experience a revival. But if they do, then the federal coalition government will only have itself to blame.

Achieving sustained security success in neutralizing the now fragmented and discredited Mahdi Army (like the Sunni Arab insurgents) is essentially a matter of managing to organize effective policing, delivering basic governmental services (health, education, and rations, where needed), and relying on intelligence from cooperative populations that do not want a return to chaos. Strange as it may seem to some ears, it may be easier for the Iraqi government to be more effective in all these respects when it no longer has the American military to rely upon if need be. That is because it will have to be effective if it wishes to survive.

If the preceding analysis is broadly right, then the succession to Saddam may have been won institutionally and militarily and may also be won electorally in the future. The dominant players in the Iraqi federal government want to demonstrate that they have reestablished Iraq's sovereignty. That, of course, will facilitate a substantive American withdrawal from Iraq. Civil wars either end in victories or with negotiated settlements. In this case the evidence points toward a victory for the federal government of Iraq and its allies in the Kurdistan Regional Government. That will be confirmed if they are the major winners, along with Sunni Arab parties willing to operate in the new order, of the future provincial and federal elections. Electoral successes by the Sadrists, if they have wholly switched to democratic politics, will certainly cloud that assessment. They need not necessarily fundamentally damage it.

The question will then become whether Iraq will experience a long period of sustained but lower-intensity violence—from continuing Sunni Arab insurgents, Sadrists, and criminals—or, alternatively, enter a more comprehensive peace process. The latter would obviously be the most desirable outcome. It would require sustained cease-fires and active intra-Iraqi negotiations with the leaders who made and maintained such cease-fires; the tacit support of former insurgents and Sadrists in dealing with "spoilers"; the former insurgents and Sadrists to take sufficient numbers of their followers into constitutional politics; and mechanisms to integrate some former insurgents into provincial or federal security institutions or into civilian employment. Amnesties, already offered, might have to be extended, while assurances, recognition, and compensation need to be organized for the victims of violence. Merely to list these desiderata, the features of successful peace processes the world over, is to signal how far Iraq is from achieving them. So what must now be asked is whether Iraq's Constitution, and its new institutions, are sufficiently flexible to allow this currently low probability outcome to emerge and to explore how U.S. and multinational foreign policy might facilitate that outcome.

Part III
Leaving with Integrity

Iraq has been killed, never to rise again. The American occupation has been more disastrous than that of the Mongols, who sacked Baghdad in the thirteenth century.... Only fools talk of "solutions" now. There is no solution. The only hope is that perhaps the damage can be contained.

—Nir Rosen, *Current History*, December 2007

What you are reading is the work of a fool, according to Nir Rosen (see the epigraph on the facing page). This book does not accept that Iraq is dead. It assumes that its extinction is exaggerated. Though Iraq's days may conceivably be numbered, a death certificate is premature. This book also maintains that there remain ways to address Iraq's deep conflicts that have the potential to do more than staunch the flow of blood. Rosen offers no proposal to contain the damage. His counsel, as well as his analysis, is hopeless—in all senses.

The claims made here suggest that more than the triage gestured at by Rosen is possible. His posture, however, amply conveys the received wisdom of the English-speaking intelligentsia. Readers may have noted some restraint being exercised by this author. The argument has been unfolded as calmly as possible in a deliberate effort to avoid the enraged tone that accompanies this subject in the Middle East, North America, Europe, and in Iraq. Perhaps I may therefore be excused from briefly abandoning this tenor to reject Rosen's portrait of the American occupation of Iraq as more disastrous than that of the bloodthirsty grandson of Genghis Khan.

Rosen's judgment displays both ignorance and arrogance. The Mongols executed urbicide in Baghdad, not a mere sacking. In 1258, after a siege led by the Mongol prince Hulagu, the city was ravaged and plundered, and most of its inhabitants slaughtered. "So powerful was the stench of the unburied corpses that Hulagu was forced to withdraw temporarily from the city for fear of a plague."[1] This event terminated the Abassid Caliphate, which had lasted five centuries.[2] The last holder of the post was wrapped in a carpet and trampled to death by horses (because the Mongols never shed royal blood). The figures for the numbers killed "vary widely and increase the further away the writer is in time and place."[3] "The caliphate had long ceased to exist as an effective institution, and the Mongols did little more than lay the ghost of something that was already dead." "Baghdad and Iraq [then defined without Kurdistan] never again recovered their central position in the Islamic world. The immediate effects of the invasion were the breakdown of civil government and the consequent collapse of the elaborate irrigation works on which the country depended for its prosperity.... Iraq now became an outlying frontier province, abandoned to the destructive inroads of the Bedouin..., leaving...the fallen city of the caliphs to centuries of stagnation and neglect."[4]

One can and should be critical of the American occupation. But that does not mean we have to accept the premise that American leaders, generals, soldiers, and officials have been worse than the Khans and their hordes. In 2003 American soldiers should have stopped the looting of "the city of peace." But Baghdadis carried out the looting, not foreign invaders. The mass killings and expulsions in Baghdad should also have been stopped by better American policies. But they were carried out mainly by the city's inhabitants, by men from its satellite towns, and by foreign jihadists, not by American troops. The reconstruction of Iraq should also have been better managed. But sincere efforts were made in this direction, some of which have borne fruit, and some American tax dollars and expertise have been allocated to revive the infrastructure of Iraq. Americans took no authorized spoils from Iraq, unlike the hordes of Hulagu. After May 2003 it was mostly Arab Iraqis who destroyed the infrastructure of their country. They did so for political reasons, not because they were mad. Had the Americans been like Hulagu, there would be few Iraqis left to regret their political choices.[5]

Samantha Power is a thoughtful scholar who avoids the ahistorical hyperbole of Nir Rosen. She is the author of a superb study of genocide and the failures of successive American governments to prevent it.[6] But she opposed the U.S. intervention in Iraq because she did not like the fact that it was not motivated by concern for Iraqi humanitarian needs. Unlike the Kurds, Shia Arabs, and me, she was not persuaded that the effect of the intervention—the removal of the genocidal dictator and his regime— would make the intervention worthwhile, even if genocide-prevention or genocide-punishment were not the prime goal of the interventionists. If quoted correctly, Power believes that in 2003 that Iraq "was, in a sense, a postgenocidal state."[7] That suggestion has several problems. How does any one know when a state has become postgenocidal, or, differently put, why should any one expect a genocidal regime not to be a serial offender? Why give a genocidal regime the benefit of the doubt? Were the assaults on the Shia Marsh Arabs and the southern governorates in the late 1990s neither genocidal nor recent? As important, Power's argument might suggest that a postgenocidal regime should be immune to any intervention to punish the perpetrators. Last, the behavior of Baathists and other Iraqis after 2003 showed that significant numbers of Arab Iraqis were very far from a postgenocidal mentality. Had Saddam's regime not been removed in 2003, it is entirely rational to think its genocidal character would have resurfaced.

Refloated on enhanced oil revenues (after the decay of the UN embargo), the regime would have been in a position to resume its customary repression and aggression. And Saddam's sons, by all accounts, would have been worse rulers than their father.[8]

But whatever the debates about the past, the point now must be to ensure that any withdrawal from Iraq renders none of its three major communities (or any of its smaller minorities) more vulnerable to further efforts at extermination. That is the acid test by which any withdrawal should be evaluated. None of us will have the luxury of looking back 800 years after the March 2003 intervention to assess its long-run impact. It has been a terrible five years, but not entirely so, and all is not yet lost. It remains possible that a withdrawal with integrity will enable a federal Iraq to be stabilized. It may also be possible to ameliorate some of the worst consequences of recent irresponsible and misguided polices. The following pages are offered in that spirit.

Chapter 6
Respecting Iraq's Constitutional Integrity

> The illegal we do immediately. The unconstitutional takes a little longer.
>
> —Attributed to Henry Kissinger, *Washington Post*, January 20, 1977

Iraq has a Constitution, but it is not properly respected by the U.S. government. That makes it more difficult for the Constitution to command the respect of others, but we can still hope that under the next administration the United States will respect Iraq's Constitution—even if it will have taken longer than it should have. The Constitution is worth defending precisely because it is a power-sharing settlement for a pluralist federation. It is a settlement that partly works in practice, although more because of the internal balance of forces in Iraq's domestic politics than because of a deep respect for constitutional legality. The Constitution newly defined the state as a "free union" and "a country of many nationalities, religions and sects."[1] It made Iraq officially both bilingual and a plurinational federation. The federation comprises multiple nationalities—including Arabs, Kurds, and Turkomen. Although Islam is named as the official religion of the state, the Constitution recognizes Iraq as a land of multiple religions— including Muslims, Christians, and Yezidis.[2] It recognizes the religious sects (or "components," the more delicate and diplomatic Arabic expression) within these religions, including, most importantly, the Sunni and Shia variants of Islam. Shamefully, only Jews conspicuously fail to have their religion formally recognized, although there are very few Jews left in Iraq after a century of exchanges, expulsions, persecution, and exodus.[3]

Iraq's federal chamber, the Council of Representatives, is elected by proportional representation. That makes it unlikely that any list or party will obtain a governing majority in the Council and makes it highly likely that the federal executive, the prime minister, and the Council of Ministers must be built anew after each election as a multiparty or multilist coalition government. This formula therefore promotes power sharing in Baghdad. When combined with the extensive regional and provincial autonomy envisaged in its Constitution, Iraq therefore has some of the traits necessary to establish both a pluralist federation and a working "consociational democracy," namely, a democracy with the following four traits: (1) a federal executive with cross-community support; (2) proportional representation of key parties, groups and communities in core institutions; (3) territorial and cultural autonomy for key nationalities, linguistic groups and religious groups; and (4) formal and informal veto powers that prevent a simple majority in the Council of Representatives from imposing its will on others. Iraq also has the potential to be a "liberal consociation"[4] because its Constitution does not have any overt quotas. It does not, as in a corporate consociation such as Lebanon's, mandate that particular political posts have to be allocated to representatives of particular ethnic communities or religious sects but instead allows people's votes to determine who shall hold office in a structure that nevertheless obligates power sharing and respect for pluralism.[5]

Pluralist federations and consociational arrangements require suitable internal and external support structures. Internally, the fact that Iraq lacks a community with a preponderant and cohesive majority that will rally behind just one list or party makes coalitional politics possible—and necessary. The internal balance among the three major communities may also assist coalitional politics. As long as Shia and Sunni Arabs deeply distrust one another, they are less likely regularly to join together to oppress Kurds—although some have tried to block the constitutionally authorized referendum to determine whether Kirkuk province may join the KRG. As long as Kurds cannot win independence because of implacable opposition from Turkey and Iran, they have a strategic interest in alliances with Arab parties and politicians who are willing to respect Kurdistan's autonomy.

They also have an interest in preventing either Arab sect from totally dominating Iraq, because if they did they would likely impair Kurdistan's autonomy. Most Kurds share the same branch of Islam with Sunni Arabs, although they support a different school of law in the Sunni tradition[6] and are much less religiously zealous. And most Kurds share with some leading

Shia Arabs an interest in building an Iraq of its regions rather than a recentralized Iraq. Here their joint history as victims of Baathism makes them partial allies. The Sunni Arabs, displaced from power, have mostly learned that they are unlikely to win back power through guerrilla struggle or terrorist methods. They are in search of new political strategies. Some have considered experimenting with alliances with the Sadrist Shia in the interest of promoting a recentralized Iraqi nation-state, and others, who are less religious, have looked toward secular Kurds and secular Shia. Altogether these internal conditions make federal coalitional and consociational politics possible.

Externally, consociations require regional powers or great powers either to balance against each other or to make explicit agreements in such a way that they do not disturb the internal equilibrium that makes coalitional and consociational politics possible. The regional powers must practice self-restraint, avoiding interventions on behalf of their co-ethnics or co-religionists. They are more likely to keep out if the relevant internal group with which they feel most affinity is reasonably well treated and satisfied with the status quo. Otherwise the regional powers must be kept out by the threat-capacities of great powers. The critical question for Iraq's future, addressed in the next two chapters, is whether the United States has the capacity and the interest to support the external conditions necessary to give coalitional or consociational politics within Iraq a chance to stabilize.

Iraq's Constitution provides the right mix of institutional incentives to make a durable power-sharing settlement possible, consistent with the security needs of its people. That does not mean the Constitution cannot be modified, but it is best not modified in the directions preferred by U.S. policymakers. Leaving Iraq with integrity requires the United States to support Iraq's constitutional integrity.

Working for, Not Against, Iraq's Constitution

World opinion is deeply skeptical that Iraq's parties can develop the parliamentary democratic federation proclaimed in the first article of its new Constitution or the pluralist provisions evident in its new definition of the state as a "free union" and of "a country of many nationalities, religions and sects."[7] This skepticism has some basis. The Constitution's birth took place in the midst of a long bloodbath and was preceded by a sandstorm. Its birth was rushed, and its lack of polish shows in places. But for at least one of Iraq's three major peoples, it was a triumph. Kurdish film-maker

Hineer Saleem's recollection of his grandfather's words seemed like an epitaph for his people in the 1990s, "Our past is sad. Our present is a catastrophe. Fortunately, we don't have a future."[8] These words no longer apply. The Kurds of Iraq, at least, have reasons to hope.[9]

The Constitution also met the aspirations of Shia Arabs. For the first time in the history of modern Iraq, the Constitution enables their demographic majority to count democratically. And indeed for the first time since the party of Ali was defeated on the plains of Karbala in the seventh century, the long institutional ascendancy of Sunni over Shia is over. Sunni Arabs do not regard the Constitution as a victory, but it offers them securities as individuals and as a minority that will ease their loss of dominance.

The arguments in favor of Iraq's Constitution are profoundly neglected. The new Constitution deserves the conditional support of other democratic federations and other democratic and Western governments, and analysts should cease their futile and unhelpful efforts to persuade the Shia-dominated parties and their allies from Kurdistan to make dramatic changes to its text. Foremost among the arguments in the Constitution's favor is its legitimacy: it was endorsed by four out of five of Iraq's voters in 2005. It also reflected the most feasible bargain that could have been made by Iraq's major parties in the summer of 2005. It is the sole obvious framework through which Iraq may stabilize as an entity that resembles a democratic state. The Constitution underpins the federalization of Iraq with sensible proposals to federalize Iraq's natural resources. That does not mean the Constitution cannot be improved or modified to assuage the sentiments of Sunni Arabs, but there are limits to what can feasibly be amended. If Iraq breaks up—as many confidently or pessimistically assume—that eventuality should not be blamed on its new and only partly tested Constitution. The Constitution, moreover, provides the best mechanism through which that break-up can be managed if that proves to be the final outcome—although I neither favor nor expect that.[10] Let me elaborate this case.

A Legitimate and Feasible Constitution

The new permanent Constitution was ratified in the referendum held on October 15, 2005. It was validated by the United Nations Election Assistance Unit. The process by which it was made was not ideal. The text was drafted in Baghdad amid extraordinarily high security, with the U.S. ambassador, Zalmay Khalilzad, playing a key mediating role, although not a dictatorial one.[11] The United States noted; it proposed from time to time, but did not dispose, except when asked to arbitrate (as it was on the question of the participation of Shia clergy on the federal supreme court). Kurdish and SCIRI leaders, aided by their respective advisors, did the real bargaining over the content of the text. The party leaders took over the process precisely because the parliamentary process was not working.[12] Though Khalilzad hailed the Constitution, it was not what the United States had sought—on regions, on natural resources, on security, and on centralization. It was not a Constitution made in Washington D.C.; if it were, it would be difficult to explain why Washington has sought so often to have it changed.

The campaign that preceded the Constitution's popular ratification scarcely met the best standards of democratic transparency, but the public security provided on referendum day was effective. UN advisers rightly blocked a Machiavellian effort by some in the proconstitution parties to construe in two separate and self-serving ways an ambiguity about the meaning of "voters" in the Transitional Administrative Law's rule of ratification.[13] The UN ruling ensured that the ratification process was proper. But the Constitution, as the world knows, was opposed, with both bombs and ballots, by most of Iraq's formerly dominant minority of Sunni Arabs.

The Constitution, however, offers means through which Iraq may hold together without dictatorship or permanent civil war. It does not guarantee that outcome but is rightly regarded as a work in progress. This argument rejects two standard skepticisms, which conveniently have been represented in cartoons. The vulgar view is typified by America's satirical magazine, *The Onion* (see Figure 1).[14]

Merciless satire is often instructive. *The Onion's* cartoon was not wholly racist because it laughed at the United States' own Constitution, which specifies a right to bear arms and under which Native Americans now operate gambling casinos under treaty rights. But it also laughed at intergroup hatred in Iraq and at the Iraqis presumed shared hatred of Americans, suggesting nothing lasting could come from this constitutional enterprise. Here the cartoon is an utter distortion. Intergroup hatred is not pervasive in Iraq. Saddam's major victims, the Kurds and Shia Arabs, may not love one another but they have pragmatic affinities. Their leaders became opposition allies under Saddam. They made and are now the de jure champions of the new Constitution. The also got their respective communities to vote for it—admittedly in a rush and without ideal public debate. Americophilia, genuine and strategic, is widespread among Kurds. Americophobia is also intense among Sunni Arabs, but now some of their politicians seek

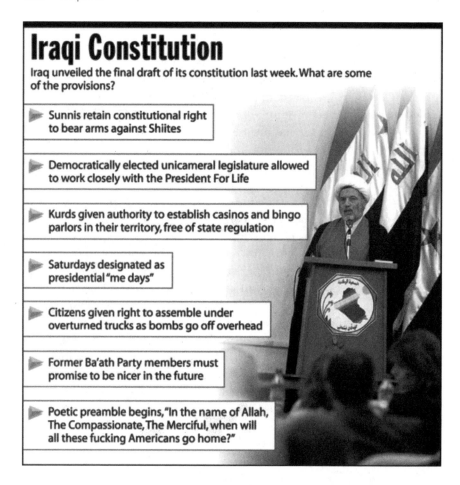

Figure 1. The vulgar view of Iraq's Constitution. *The Onion*, September 7, 2005. Reprinted with permission of *The Onion*. Copyright © 2008 *The Onion*.

the withdrawal of American troops from central Iraqi cities *rather than their total withdrawal.* Shia Arabs are ambiguous and divided about America. The Sadrists campaign for an American withdrawal, but the more prudent leaders of Da'wa and ISCI, the Iraqi Supreme Council of Islam, do not want that exit to reverse the political gains of their people. They favor a controlled departure.

Another and more elegant cartoon represents the "impossibilist thesis" about Iraq's Constitution (see Figure 2).[15] It shows a parchment, morphing into a cloth with its threads unraveled at the end, connected to a signature

Figure 2. A knitter's nightmare: the sophisticated impossibilist view of Iraq's Constitution. Illustration by Phil Foster. Reproduced with permission.

pen that awaits use. Copper-toned stereotypes of a Kurdish Peshmerga, a Sunni Arab with a typical *kafiyya* (cloth headdress), and, in front, a turbaned Shia Arab, flank the unraveling cloth. The Arabs have beards. The Kurd does not. They have their backs to one another pointing perhaps toward the "three state solution." The cartoon conveys the impossibility thesis, namely, that Iraq is unworkable because of its ethnic (Arabs versus Kurds) and sectarian (Sunni versus Shia Islam) conflicts. But Kurdish and Shia Arab politicians intensively negotiated face to face—in the Baghdad compound of Mas'ud Barzani, the president of the Kurdistan Democratic Party and now the president of the Kurdistan Region. An accurate cartoon would have shown some Sunni Arab negotiators threatening chaos while being targeted for assassination by insurgents from their own community and while claiming, with some cause, that the Shia Badr Organization and the Mahdi Army had them in their sights.

The truth is that no successful negotiations could have materialized in 2005 from the inclusion of representative Sunni Arab politicians. The

Sunni Arabs present in the Iraqi Assembly had demands that were unacceptable to their Constitution-making partners: the elected representatives of roughly four-fifths of Iraq's population.[16] Many Sunni Arab political leaders had boycotted the elections to the constitutional convention, or they were supporting armed violence against the transitional government and its civilian supporters. Others among them were intimidated from indicating what willingness to compromise they then possessed. The Sunni Arab boycott of the January 2005 elections backfired spectacularly against their interests, and some of their leaders compounded this strategic error with poor negotiating tactics, because they still had demographic fantasies about their people's numbers. The Sunni Arab leaders "negotiating" in Baghdad, notably Salih al-Mutlak, were determined to block the formation of an Iraqi federation because they saw that, as they said endlessly, to be "the end of the country." They thought their best hope was to prevent a settlement, precipitate fresh elections under the provisions of the Transitional Administrative Law,[17] and return with new strength to a new set of negotiations. They did their best to become procedural obstructionists. That strategy strongly reduced the likelihood that other Iraqi politicians would treat their concerns seriously.[18] The Sunni negotiators' second best hope, they thought, was to campaign for a "no" vote, which most of them tried—apart from the Iraqi Islamic Party. Though they mobilized their voters, they failed to achieve the requisite blocking supermajority of two-thirds in three governorates.

Throughout 2005 many Sunni Arab leaders, the elite of a formerly dominant minority, remained strongly inclined to see Shia Arabs and Kurds, approximately eight in ten of Iraqis, as "special interest groups."[19] The Sunni Arab elite acted like a deposed *Staatsvolk*—the people who own the state. In 2005 there were just not enough key Sunni Arab elites, or voters, who were democratic, let alone federalist or pluralist, who were capable of being viable negotiating partners. There was therefore no workable political inclusion strategy for the other groupings in Iraq, short of outright surrender of their vital interests to the traditionally dominant ethnoreligious community. These facts of political life in 2005 rendered impossible the hope of combining successful constitution-making with a comprehensive and inclusive peace and security settlement.

The facts on the ground since then may have changed matters. Sunni Arab leaders recognize they erred in boycotting the January 2005 elections and hope to win sufficient allies to modify parts of the Constitution. Most now know they cannot overthrow it by force, as many have sought to do for nearly three years. A successful political settlement, defined as the end of most of the Sunni Arab insurgencies and the stable withdrawal of multinational forces from Iraq, necessarily requires significant Sunni Arab compliance with the new constitutional dispensation. But that compliance cannot be wished into existence. When significant numbers of Sunni Arabs accept federalism and negotiate under its terms, only then will the intra-Arab civil war terminate. That vista is now within sight. Its realization is made more difficult when American and British policymakers continue to insist that it is necessary for the Constitution to be dramatically modified to appease Sunni Arab demands and interests. Sunni Arabs should not now be able to succeed in overthrowing its key provisions on the back of massively violent blackmail, which has failed in the field. Their legitimate concerns can and should be addressed, but within the framework of a decentralized federation and through any necessary modifications of the existing Constitution.

A Framework for Better Possibilities

The 2005 Constitution remains the sole obvious framework through which Iraq may stabilize as an entity that resembles a democratic state. While Sunni Arab insurgents fight or reconsider their options, we should recognize that Kurdistan and most of southern Iraq could flourish and function, respectively, with or without widespread Sunni Arab compliance with the new Constitution and with or without the presence of the Coalition's multinational troops. That was so even before the Constitution was made; it is now even more evident with the consolidation of the Kurdistan Region into one governing unit in 2006 and with the recent establishment of federal Iraqi control over Basra and other cities in the south. The democratic leaders of the Shia Arabs and the Kurds have the ability, if they wish, to insulate themselves from what they regard as Sunni Arab aggression.

Kurdistan is institutionalized; its civil war is long healed; and relations between the KDP and PUK are much improved, as their joint negotiating team proved in Baghdad in 2005. Since 2006 the two parties have created and have continued to support a unified power-sharing coalition government in Erbil. Kurdistan's public often favors independence as an abstract ideal, but its leaders are prudent. I often tested the abstractness of the ideal by asking my Kurdish friends in Erbil and Sulaimania the following questions: "Would you favor an independent Kurdistan, even if it meant a Turkish invasion and occupation would follow? Even if it meant that an Iranian invasion and occupation would follow?" They would either answer "no," or they would deny that either Turkey or Iran would do as my questions suggested. I would also ask them to make a choice between just two options. I would ask if they favored independence without unification with Kirkuk, or, instead, autonomy in Iraq with Kirkuk's becoming part of the Kurdistan Region. Without exception, they preferred the latter option. Integrating Kirkuk and other "disputed territories" into the Kurdistan Region through peaceful and democratic means is therefore best construed as Kurdistan's price for committing to the federation of Iraq.

The Shia Arabs' institutions, religious and political, are slowly taking on a resilient shape in the south. There has been far more chaos, warlordism, criminality, and general disorder in the south than in the Kurdistan Region, but that is partly because its liberation from Baathism is much more recent. The southern provinces are not unified—different Shia parties and factions vie for influence, sometimes violently. Military action in 2008 by the federal government, with the support of Coalition forces, has led to the consolidation of its grip on the south. Significant defeats for the Mahdi Army and criminal networks in Basra and other cities have been registered.

Since the summer of 2008, under an Iraqi law that implements key provisions in the Constitution, Iraqis outside of Baghdad and Kirkuk are free to form regions through combining governorates. They can upgrade any existing governorate to the status of a region (including Baghdad). They can also make their governorates have most of the powers already exemplified in the Kurdistan Region, if they wish, without even forming regions. The Shia Arabs have the votes and numbers, lawfully under the Constitution and under the new statute to follow these courses of action.

The map of Iraq may shortly be transformed in ways that match the existing emergent regionalization of security. For that to happen, the Shia Arabs will have to follow the advice of the dying leader of ISCI, Abdul Aziz al-Hakim, and develop their own region or regions in the south. That is not a settled course of action because other Shia parties, especially the Sadrists, but also some within the prime minister's Da'wa party, prefer for now not to follow in the path of Kurdistan. But even if the centralists defeat the regionalists among the Shia Arabs, they are not going to be able to impose their version of centralism upon the Kurds, and they are unlikely to make workable coalition deals with centralist Sunni Arabs. Noticing that Shia sectarians are the most enthusiastic of the potentially successful centralists in Iraq should concentrate the minds of Sunni Arabs, if not in the very near future then at least eventually.

Major armed conflict in Iraq may shortly, with luck and skilled politics, be confined to Baghdad and its environs, including parts of Diyala, and the two Sunni Arab majority governorates of Salahaddin and Nineva, that is, the previously "ungoverned territories"; Anbar is calm for now. Differently put, the remaining territorial concentrations of disorder will be in two places. The first lies amid the northern disputed territories. Here local Kurdish majorities live below the borders Saddam drew for Ninevah, Salahaddin, Kirkuk, and Diyala and below the boundary of the KRG he created through his withdrawal from Kurdistan. Here there are border and local power-sharing issues to be resolved, largely between Kurds and Sunni Arabs but also with Turkomen, especially in Kirkuk. For now these districts and subdistricts are not especially disordered because Kurdistan's Peshmerga supply most of the local security. But they are suffering because their territorial status is not resolved—the KRG has no official jurisdiction over them and the Baghdad ministries neglect them. The second significant areas of disorder lie in the mixed districts of Arab cities and in Sunni Arab majority provinces. Therefore Sunni Arabs have territorial and power-sharing disputes to resolve with both Kurds (in the north) and with Shia Arabs (largely in the center), but they are not in a position to dictate terms in either set of places. The political question therefore will become what Kurds and Shia Arabs can offer Sunni Arabs to reassure them.

There will, of course, be persistent conflict elsewhere in Iraq, but much less than at the edges of the Sunni Arab heartlands, provided that further international interventions can be inhibited. Some Shia Arab leaders have expressed interest in imitating Kurdistan's security perimeter, lawful under its constitutional right to organize internal security. All this thinking foreshadows an important opportunity. The regionalization program of the Constitution, which recognizes and makes possible a bigger and more powerful Kurdistan and which allows the emergence of a big and powerful south or multiple souths, or powerful governorates, also enables the internal regionalization of security—and its legalization. In the worst-case scenario, this shift has the possibility, eventually, to confine Sunni Arab violence to Sunni Arab-dominated territories and areas at the edges of their heartlands where they are or have become local minorities. In the best-case scenario, in which Sunni Arabs take charge of their own security, within functioning provinces (or in a region or regions), the majority within each of the three major communities will be able to breathe easier and be less of an intrusive threat to the others. The push toward regionalization has regrettably not simply been the result of logic, persuasion, reasoned discourse, and information about pluralist federations, but owes much to the territorial homogenization flowing from sectarian and ethnic expulsions.

Against Significant Recentralization

The Constitution of Iraq allows and encourages a highly decentralized federation. The *exclusive* powers of the federal government are as follows:

Article 110:

1. Formulating foreign policy and diplomatic representation; negotiating, signing, and ratifying international agreements and treaties; negotiating signing, and ratifying debt policies and formulating foreign sovereign economic and trade policy.
2. Formulating and executing national security policy, including establishing and managing armed forces to secure the protection and guarantee the security of Iraq's borders and to defend Iraq.
3. Formulating fiscal and customs policy; issuing currency; regulating commercial policy across regional and governorate boundaries in Iraq; drawing up the national budget of the State; formulating monetary policy; and establishing and administering a central bank.
4. Regulating standards, weights and measures.
5. Regulating issues of citizenship, naturalization, residency, and the right to apply for political asylum.
6. Regulating the policies of broadcasting frequencies and mail.
7. Drawing up the general and investment budget bill.
8. Planning policies relating to water sources from outside Iraq and guaranteeing the rate of water flow to Iraq and its just distribution inside Iraq in accordance with international law and conventions.
9. General population statistics and census.

And that is it. Where a regional government exists, its writ is supreme in every other domain of politics. This text specifies a truly decentralized constitution because even provinces that choose not to be regions may choose (outside the powers listed in Article 110) whatever role(s) for the federal government that they wish. Aside from Article 110(2), which mandates a national security *policy* and Iraqi armed forces that are necessary for the federation to qualify as a state rather than as a confederation, the Constitution envisages an exceptionally limited federal government, especially where regions (and provinces) opt for that preference. Amendments to the Constitution that would weaken regional powers are blocked unless the relevant region's parliament and people consent to them (Article 126(4)). Even in foreign affairs, an exclusive federal competence, regions "shall" have offices within embassies and diplomatic missions to pursue the broadranging matters within their powers, a right that the Kurdistan Region already exercises (Article 121(4)). Exclusive federal military authority is confined to the external borders and defense of Iraq because internal security (policing and regional guards) is a defined power of the regions (Article 212(5)).

But U.S. policy under the second President Bush has favored a recentralized Iraq. The Bush administration, contrary to some of its critics, did not go to Iraq to carve it up. It was both insistent on preserving Iraq's territorial integrity and on creating a strongly centralized federation—as was evident in the negotiations over the Transitional Administrative Law and the making of Iraq's Constitution. Washington's encouragement of this centralist disposition has been pursued under both Secretaries of State Colin Powell and Condoleezza Rice and a succession of diplomats. It is relatively unchallenged by most U.S. think-tank commentary, in which there is a presumption that a centralized federation (read "like the United States") is a good thing, whereas a pluralist, decentralized federation is a bad thing (read "like Bosnia Herzegovina," rather than the European Union). What explains this deep policy bias, which both disrespects and disregards the merits of Iraq's Constitution?

The Bush administration's preferences have been partly driven by geopolitical considerations. It wanted to appease Turkey's fears of an independent Kurdistan, even though Turkey's Parliament, fortunately, voted in 2003 not to join the American intervention in Iraq—an outcome that was perhaps the single most important piece of luck (at least for the Kurds and other Iraqis) and sound judgment (by the Turks) in recent Middle East international politics. Washington, equally, has a long and sometimes shameful record of favoring a strong Iraq to counterbalance Shia Islamist Iran. Three predominantly Sunni Arab populated states and one future state are on Iraq's western flank, namely, Jordan, Saudi Arabia, and Syria,[20] all of which will be joined in some future form by Palestine. The Gulf ministates are ruled by Sunni Arabs. These external considerations have led U.S. policymakers, since the fall of the Shah, to favor a strong centralized Iraq under Saddam and his successors.

The Bush administration's preferences were also driven by its political estimations of what is required to stabilize Iraq. The squeakiest wheel always gets the grease. Sunni Arabs have been the angriest respondents to the American-led intervention in Iraq. That has led the administration to appease what it regards as reasonable Sunni Arab interests in Iraq. Since Sunni Arabs and Americans both favor a centralized Iraq, their preferences converge. This convergence is consolidated by the false belief that a regionalized Iraq would deprive Sunni Arabs of access to Iraq's natural resources and that it would increase the prospects of Iraq's breaking up through secessions. Fresh U.S. military thinking, to the extent that it occurred under General David Petraeus, inclines nevertheless in the same political direction. Since the insurgents deemed to matter most have been Sunni Arab centralists, it is widely believed among Petraeus's advisors (who have not included Kurdophiles) that the best policy is not to antagonize this constituency.

This mind-set, which favors a strongly centralized Iraq, needs to be broken if America is successfully to disengage from Iraq. Americans should remind themselves that a centralized oil-rich Iraq was not a force for stability. It started two wars with its neighbors, Iran and Kuwait. It paid the families of Palestinian suicide bombers. It committed genocide against Kurds and Shia Arabs. These facts alone should give pause to those who wish to restore a centralized Iraq. In fact, those who most favor a centralized Iraq, sectarian Sunni Arabs and sectarian Shia Arabs, are those most likely to seek to oppress one another. A fully centralized Iraq has in any case become unattainable because of the unintended consequences of democracy promotion. Kurds will resist any involuntary recentralization, and the intellectual policy elite among Shia Arabs is also committed to avoiding a recentralized Iraq, especially one that looks like a Sunni Arab Phoenix.

Mowaffak al-Rubaie exemplifies that Shia Arab policy elite. Al-Rubaie is an important man in Iraq. He was elected to the Council of Representatives in December 2005, on the list of the United Iraqi Alliance. He was born in Kadhimiya and left Iraq in the early 1980s to study in Britain. He is neurologist and a member of the British Royal College of Physicians. He is a Shia Muslim, and in London he was a spokesman for the Da'wa party. He was appointed a member of the Iraqi Governing Council by the CPA, and in April 2004 was made Iraq's National Security Advisor by Paul Bremer. He held this post until September 2004, when the transitional Prime Minister Iyad Allawi sacked him in a controversy over how to deal with Muqtada al-Sadr and the Mahdi Army. In 2006, al-Rubaie was reappointed National Security Advisor under the new government, led by Nouri al-Maliki. I have detailed his credentials to underline the importance of an article he chose to publish in the *Washington Post* on February 18, 2008. Under the heading "Federalism, Not Partition. A System Devolving Power to the Regions Is the Route to a Viable Iraq," Mowaffak al-Rubaie briskly made all the arguments advanced in this chapter.[21]

Writing in a personal capacity, he maintained that "the political objectives of Iraq's three main communities are unrealizable within the framework of a unitary, centralized state.... The absence of any truly national parties and leadership that reach the Iraqi people exacerbates the problem.... Resolution can be achieved only through a system that incorporates regional federalism, with clear, mutually acceptable distributions of powers between the regions and the central government.... A key condition for success is that the balance of power should tip decisively to the regions on all matters that do not compromise the integrity of the state.... Iraq needs a period of time during which the Shiites and Kurds achieve political control over their destinies while the Sunni Arab community is secure from the feared tyranny of the majority."

While expressing flexibility on the exact territorial configuration of a federalized Iraq, al-Rubaie insists "it should permit the assignment of nearly all domestic powers to the regions, to be funded out of a percentage of oil revenue distributed on the basis of population. The federal government should be responsible only for essential central functions such as foreign policy (including interregional affairs), defense, fiscal and monetary policy, and banking." In this crisply articulated vision he suggests that a regional and decentralized federation will better match religious, educational, and cultural policy preferences than could a central government and that "a regional framework for economic policy would also fit better with traditional trade patterns and markets."

Mowaffak al-Rubaie also foresees the exact territorial configuration of regions: "Iraq's political geography suggests five likely federal units: A 'Kurdistan province,' including the current Kurdistan and surrounding areas; a 'Western province,' including Mosul and the upper Tigris and Euphrates valleys; a 'Kufa province,' built around the Middle Euphrates governorates; a 'Basra province,' including the lower Tigris and Euphrates valleys; and a 'Baghdad province,' built around Greater Baghdad, which may include parts of Diyala and Salahadin Governorates. The Kurdish region would be given special constitutional status as a recognized society and culture with a unique identity (similar to the Canadian province of Quebec)."[22]

Map 3 sketches what al-Rubaie's propositions would look like if implemented. These proposals are not only remarkable for their clarity; they

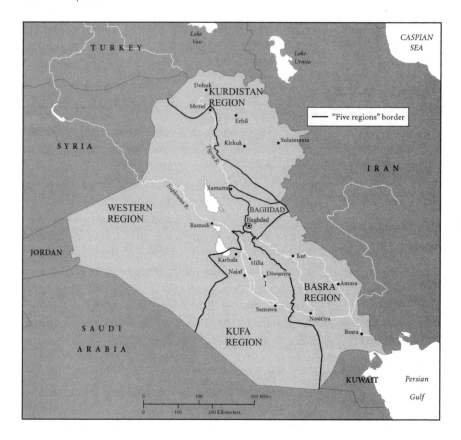

Map 3. The five-region proposal of Mowaffak al-Rubaie.

show the considered depths of reappraisal of Iraq by a leading Shia intellectual and policymaker, whose chief responsibility, we should recall, is
security for the whole of Iraq. He will happily cede "surrounding areas" to
Kurdistan (i.e., Kirkuk and the disputed territories) and grant it special status as a nation, as he thinks Quebec is now recognized in Canada. He wants
to see his own community divided among three large regions (running
from Baghdad and parts of Diyala downward). He contemplates a mixed
central region in Greater Baghdad. He packages his proposal with a caution: "Iraq's constitution was ratified before its communities reached agreement on many vital issues, such as provincial powers." He therefore favors
a referendum on a reformed constitution, but reformed around a regional
federal consensus. That regionalism, he thinks, should be funded though

a per head allocation of oil revenues. Al-Rubaie's lucid federal vision provides an appropriate junction to consider the federalization of Iraq's natural resources.

Federalizing Natural Resources

A central corollary of the centralist wisdom that drives America's policymakers is the conviction that Iraq's central authorities should be firmly in control of ownership of its natural resources and of the revenues from these resources. The International Crisis Group, which vehemently articulates this perspective, has intemperately called for a "total revision of key articles concerning the nature of federalism and the distribution of proceeds from oil sales" and argues that revenues from natural resources be "centrally controlled." It warned that if Shia Arabs construct a nine-province Shia region, as permitted by the Constitution, it would "leave the Sunni Arab community landlocked and without oil."[23] This perspective usually judges the Constitution as a partisan document with provisions on natural resources that privilege Kurdish and Shia Arab regions while collectively punishing Sunni Arabs for the sins of the Baathists. Kanan Makiya, the author of perhaps the best book on Saddam's Iraq, has described the Constitution as a "punitive" document that penalizes Sunnis "for living in regions without oil." The Constitution suggests, allegedly, that the "state owes the Sunnis of the resource-poor western provinces less than it does the Shiites and Kurds."[24] Yahia Said, another centralist and the son of an Iraqi Communist leader, has argued that the Constitution means that "Baghdad and the non-oil-producing regions will be at the mercy of the oil-producing ones."[25] American political scientist Donald Horowitz, explaining Sunni Arab alarm at the Constitution, traces that fear to a provision that "seems to tie the distribution of future oil revenues to the location of the resource in one region or another. Iraq's oil is in the Kurdish north and Shiite south."[26] Many who believe this conventional wisdom also see natural resource fights as at the heart of the struggle for Kirkuk. Why else, the argument goes, does Kurdistan want to incorporate Kirkuk, if not for the fact that it sits on top of some of the world's largest oil fields?

Some supporters of a centralized Iraq argued with breathtaking early revisionism that the Constitution actually mandates their preferred world. This appears to be the curious position of the federal oil minister, Hussain al-Shahristani, appointed in 2006, who claimed on assuming office that the federal government's (alleged) control over exploration extended to all oil fields in the country, including those that are not yet in production. The Turkish government took a similar line, seeking through its official spokesmen to play down the extent to which Iraq's Constitution gives any control over oil to Iraq's regions.[27]

By contrast, I maintain that the Constitution's provisions on natural resources are appropriate for a pluralist federation. They are coherent and politically and morally defensible. A centralized Iraq, with Baghdad in charge of its oil and gas, would repeat the institutional arrangements that made Iraq a prison for a significant share of its population and a threat in the region and maximize the prospects for corruption. The decentralized 2005 Constitution precludes no community from equitable treatment, differing markedly in this respect from the status quo ante, in which the Baathists pocketed oil money and which disproportionately benefited Arabs, especially Sunni Arabs. The new Constitution provides for an adequately resourced federal government in Baghdad but not one that owns and controls oil and gas. It does not link Kirkuk's future territorial status to that of oil and gas, a major accomplishment of the negotiations. Contrary to the policies of the Iraqi federal oil minister, who was not involved in the key negotiations, the Constitution does not hand control over exploration in new fields to Baghdad. Nor does it leave Sunni Arab-dominated regions without their own future oil. The Constitution also provides for an important federal role in perhaps the most important long-run natural resource of all: water.

Let us look at these claims more carefully. In doing so we need to keep an important political point in mind: The Constitution's federalizing provisions, especially as regards natural resources, cannot be substantively renegotiated. That is because the Kurdistan Region enjoys a veto over any such proposed amendments and, if necessary, will use this blocking capacity.

The Waters of Babylon and Kurdistan

Let us start with water, the natural resource that will be of greatest importance in the long run for the peoples of Iraq, the land of the two rivers, which is heavily dependent upon the mountains, streams, and rivers of Kurdistan.[28] The Euphrates flows from Kurdistan in Turkey and through Kurdistan in Syria, and major tributaries in the Kurdistan region of Iraq mightily amplify the Tigris. The interdependence is obvious. There were no fundamental difficulties in negotiating the relevant clauses for water, and the consensus that they express may suggest that a loose pluralist federation may be able to work. Article 50, the constitutional oath of the members of the Iraqi Council of Representatives, places an obligation on the members to "ensure the safety of [Iraq's] land, sky, *water*, wealth, and federal democratic system" (my emphasis). Water, however, is federalized differently from oil and natural gas.

Article 110, which specifies the "exclusive" powers of the federal government, grants the federal government exclusive responsibility for policy related to water flowing from outside Iraq into it and provides for a federal role in ensuring both the rate of flow within Iraq and in internally just distributions. This may fairly be interpreted as giving the predominantly Arab parts of Iraq a federal stake in the rivers that begin in Kurdistan and as warranting the federation an international lead role in negotiating water responsibilities with Iraq's neighboring states.

Article 114 of the Constitution, which specifies powers shared by the federal government where both the federal government and the regional governments may legislate, declares at clause 7 "to formulate and regulate the internal water resources policy in a way that guarantees their just distribution, and this shall be regulated by a law." This article must be read in conjunction with article 115, which grants supremacy to regional law, and with article 121(2), which grants regions the power of nullification over federal laws outside of the exclusive competencies of the federal government. Article 115 does not require extensive commentary:

> All powers not stipulated in the exclusive powers of the federal government belong to the authorities of the regions and governorates that are not organized in a region. With regard to other powers shared between the federal government and the regional government, priority shall be given to the law of the regions and governorates not organized in a region in case of dispute.

Nor does article 121, which is a provision under the constitutional chapter dealing with "Powers of the Regions" with which article 115 should be read, require the services of a constitutional lawyer:

> (1) The regional powers shall have the right to exercise executive, legislative, and judicial powers in accordance with this constitution, except for those authorities stipulated in the exclusive authorities of the federal government.

> (2) In case of a contradiction between regional and national [read "federal government"] legislation in respect to a matter outside the exclusive authorities of the federal government, the regional power shall have the right to amend the application of the national [read "federal government"] legislation within that region.

These two articles, 115 and 121, powerfully express regional legal supremacy in domains outside of the exclusive powers of the federal government. How then should we reconcile the apparent clash between the "exclusive" power of the federal government to plan for "just distribution" of water inside Iraq (Article 110(8)), with the "shared competence" of the federal government and the regional governments for "just distribution" for "internal water resources policy" (Article 114(7))? As follows: The federal government has exclusive powers for planning the external dimensions of water policy. It is obliged to plan a just distribution within Iraq. But any regional government is entitled to nullify (or modify) any application of the law as regards "just distribution," since the determination of "just distribution" is specified as a shared competence. The relevant articles acknowledge Iraq's interdependence as regards water and grant the federal government the minimum necessary planning authority, but they also express the historical distrust of Baghdad governments by Kurdistan. They ensure that the KRG can veto any law that in its judgment does not match international law and conventions on "just distribution."

The Bremer dinars, the currency that may be L. Paul Bremer III's most lasting contribution to the new Iraq, include a graphic that represents a beautiful waterfall at Gali Ali Beg in Kurdistan. The waterfall is not named on the currency and is not named as being in Kurdistan.[29] But the waterfall on Bremer's currency may be taken as a metaphor for the treatment of water in the Constitution. The relevant clauses recognize interdependence and the hidden power of Kurdistan. They balance federal and regional interests but prevent the former from usurping the latter. They obligate the federal government to follow international law and conventions in planning distribution, or else it will face the nullification of the relevant statute by the KRG. Given the importance of water resources for Iraq's urban populations and for agriculture, the interdependence between water policy and hydroelectric power, and Saddam's past abuse of central authority to build huge dams without local consultation or planning, these articles and subsections express a principled bargain.

The law that must be made, according to the Constitution, must be a federal law, but nothing in the Constitution prevents regions from modifying or nullifying the law's provisions as regards "just distribution," provided they do so within the conventions of international law. Regional and federal courts will have to develop the requisite expertise in these domains. In the broad-based coalition government formed in Baghdad in May 2006, a Kurd, Abdul Latif Rashid, was given responsibility for the federal ministry of water and is widely acknowledged to have done a good job.

Iraq's Oil and Gas in the Constitution of 2005

The deeply controversial subject of oil and gas must begin through an examination of Article 111: "oil and gas are owned by all the people of Iraq in all the regions and provinces." This article is not straightforward. Its construction is best understood as follows. There is no explicit indication how this provision is to be regulated, or by whom. It is, however, *not* a subclause of Article 110, which specifies the exclusive powers of the federal government. That was deliberate, as a comparison with the relevant article in the Transitional Administrative Law (TAL) makes clear.[30] It follows that oil and gas ownership are *not* within the exclusive powers of the federal government. Article 111 must be read in conjunction with Articles 115 and 121(2), discussed above, which establish regional legal supremacy on matters outside the exclusive powers of the federal government. Article 111 is also *not* specifically listed among the shared powers of the federal government and regional governments (specified in Article 114). Therefore, there can be no presumption that Article 111—or Article 112, which I shall examine presently—must be treated as a wholly shared power, that is, one for which both the federal and regional governments are permitted to legislate. By implication, the federal government can automatically legislate only for governorates that are not regions.

This construction establishes that Article 111 is subject to the supremacy of the law of any established region, which for the present simply means Kurdistan but would include any future regions, as the negotiators intended. Does it have any other constitutionally constraining meanings? Yes, in my view. There cannot be any exclusively non-Iraqi ownership of oil and gas. There is, however, no statement saying that ownership has to be *exclusive* to Iraqis; the article just requires that all Iraqis must be owners of all the oil and gas, although presumably not that in all cars or trucks on roads between Basra, Baghdad, and Erbil. A reading of Article 111 as a requirement that oil and gas be exclusively owned by Iraqis or exclusively governed through a single public corporation may be read by a court to contradict Article 112, which commends the "most advanced techniques of market principles and encouraging investment." Any reasonable court may presume Article 111 prohibits non-Iraqis from having more than 49 percent of equity in any oil and gas enterprise, but it need not presume that

Article 111 prohibits foreign direct investment, or equity sharing, in which Iraqi governments (note the plural) would have a golden share. Last, Article 111 does not mandate the continuation of a centralized, vertically integrated industry.

The other critical article, 112, has two parts:

(1) The federal government, with the producing governorates and regional governments, shall undertake the management of oil and gas extracted *from present fields*, provided that it distributes its revenues in a fair manner in proportion to the population distribution in all parts of the country, specifying an allotment for a specified period for the damaged regions which were unjustly deprived of them by the former regime, and the regions that were damaged afterwards in a way that ensures balanced development in different areas of the country, and this shall be regulated by a law.

(2) The federal government, with the producing regional and governorate governments, shall *together* formulate the *necessary* strategic policies to develop the oil and gas wealth in a way that achieves the highest benefit to the Iraqi people using the most advanced techniques of market principles and encouraging investment [my emphases].

These provisions are also subject to regional legal supremacy. Article 112(1) makes it clear that the federal government's prescribed role is managerial. It does not require that the federal role take the form of managing a single public corporation. Moreover, the federal managerial role is confined to currently exploited fields. Equally vital, the federal managerial role is shared with the respective regions and governorates where production takes place. The Arabic version subtly implies a lead role for federal management as regards Article 112(1). This interpretation is not contested by Kurdistan, provided, of course, it is not abused.

Article 112(1) makes it mandatory that the federal government and the regional governments plan a per capita formula for the distribution of revenues from oil and gas production from currently exploited fields. So, Sunni Arabs and Sunni Arab-dominated regions or governorates are not cut out of revenues from currently exploited fields. Far from it; no Iraqi is. At present, nearly all of Iraq's oil and gas revenues flow from fields that were being exploited in 2005. However, the per capita formula, may, by statute, be modified by time-limited support for regions deprived under Saddam and "damaged after." An "allotment," which dictionaries treat as a synonym for quotas, shares, rations, grants, allocations, allowances, slices, and (informal) "cuts,"[31] will be specified by law to go to the regions unjustly underdeveloped under Saddam (read: Kurdistan and Kirkuk governorate, and the nine southern governorates), as well as regions "that were damaged afterwards." Any allotment has to be time-limited, and it has to be consistent with a "balanced" development strategy. Therefore it would be unconstitutional for the Iraqi authorities wholly to dwarf the per capita allocations by the allotment reparations. Sensible advice to the Sunni Arab community should focus on developing a statute that places a premium on the per capita revenue allocations and that limits (or removes) the period of reparations. That offers much better prospects for collective reassurance than non-negotiable demands to restructure the Constitution.

Which are the regions that "were damaged afterwards"? Knowing the negotiators' intentions, this phrasing does not mean the Sunni Arab-dominated provinces damaged by the actions of insurgents and counterinsurgency operations. But it would be open to the Kurdistan Region and the federal government to interpret the clause in that generous spirit. The clause was intended to cover southern governorates damaged under Saddam (during the Iran-Iraq War and after the Shia uprising) and Kurdistan (which did not gets its fair share of Iraq's revenues during the period between 1992 and 2003 and which was outside the grip of the regime from 1992).

Article 112 is equally important because of what it does not say. Its complete silence on future (or unexploited in 2005) oil and gas fields removes any role for the federal government in their management as well as over legislation. The injunction on future policy planning specified in Article 112(2) has an important "together"—and the Arabic version is equally clear on this. The "together" implies a full regional veto as regards the content of Article 112(2).

How then should the substance of Article 112(2) be constructed? It obligates regional and provincial governments to formulate necessary strategic policies together with the federal government. The necessary policies flow from Iraq's membership in the Organization of Petroleum Exporting Countries (OPEC). It would be odd if Iraq's regions were to develop completely different exploitation and pricing policies. Iraq's OPEC membership may reasonably be held to necessitate regional (and producing provincial) agreements on production quotas. But necessity does not dictate a single vertically integrated oil or gas industry; and necessity does not require regions to link their new (or old) fields to existing Iraq-wide pipelines.

Regions are constitutionally free to have their own investment strategies, oil and gas industry infrastructures, and exploration strategies. They are also free to deem "necessary" whatever they wish to the federal government and to revise such judgments. Unquestionably, it was the intention of the negotiators to grant future supremacy in ownership and management to the regions (and governorates) over unexploited fields of oil and gas. Article 112(1) and (2) must be read together: the obligation to achieve the "highest benefit to the Iraqi people" is confined to policy as regards "present fields." Regions are not, by implication, required to make any federal-wide distribution of benefits from new fields of oil and gas. Nothing stops them from agreeing to that, but they are not obligated to do so. President Barzani of the Kurdistan Regional Government has, however, indicated his government's willingness to commit to such distributive arrangements, provided others (especially in the south and Baghdad) do likewise.[32]

In Defense of These Arrangements

The constitutional provisions governing three key natural resources—water, oil, and gas—are consistent with the vision of a pluralist federation. In addition, they permit the federal government to work. There will be a sufficient revenue base, from present oil and gas fields, for a workable federal government, including enough for it to meet its significant security obligations. Iraq's present fields have long lives ahead of them. As and when regions other than Kurdistan develop, there will be a corresponding reduction in the necessary revenues for the federal government to execute its functions, especially if the regions exercise their constitutional right to monopolize internal security. In the long run, the federal government, which lacks the independent power to tax, will have to develop revenues from other sources, which will require the consent of the regions if duties other than those on imports and exports are to be levied. That is as it should be. The Constitution spells the death warrant of a highly centralized Iraq, but it delays the execution—to enable the regions and provinces to grow.

These arrangements are both just and gradualist. There is a constitutional obligation to have per capita allocation of revenues from existing fields to all regions and governorates, and there is a constitutional obligation to redress past misallocations. The gradualism of the arrangements is less well known. In 2008, fully 100 percent of Iraq's oil revenues will flow from current fields; it is reasonable to project that 90 percent will do so in 2018 and that 80 percent will do so in 2028. There will therefore be a slow adjustment from a time when all oil revenues from currently exploited fields fund all of Iraq's governments to a time in which there will be an Iraq of its regions, with greater revenues from the yet-to-be-exploited fields. This gradual shift will enable appropriate development strategies. Well-run governorates and regions will plan according to their respective futures and tailor their cloths appropriately. Economic diversification planning should start now.

The Constitution and likely future revenue shifts permit Iraqis to share all future revenues from regions. Given that they do not know, contrary to rumor, who stands to gain most from future regional revenues from currently unexploited or undiscovered fields, they may sensibly bind themselves to a distribution rule that benefits them all, whatever the geological and financial facts turn out to be. That is precisely what Kurdistan has proposed.

If one relied on the bulk of English-language press reporting, one would believe that the Iraqi Constitution licenses the Shia Arabs and the Kurds to deprive the Sunni Arabs of any access to Iraq's oil and natural gas. This may be called the myth that the Constitution leaves Sunni Arabs to diet on sand and the Quran, and, sadly, often-sensible commentators, such as Kanan Makiya and the International Crisis Group, have propagated it. It is a myth for three reasons. First, the Constitution guarantees that revenues from currently exploited fields, which will supply the overwhelming bulk of Iraq's oil exports for decades to come, must be allocated across Iraq as a whole on a per capita basis (see Map 4 in Chapter 7 for their locations). The draft federal oil law negotiated by the federal government and the KRG in 2006 but not yet agreed to by Baghdad respects this obligation. Second, the Constitution does not prevent regions, which now control revenues from future fields, from agreeing to share revenues with the rest of Iraq on a per capita basis. This is not merely a hypothetical defense of the Constitution. Such provisions are part of the draft federal oil law accepted by Kurdistan, which has agreed, in advance, that 83 percent of the revenues to be extracted from new fields in its region will go to the rest of Iraq. What is not agreed is the attempt of the Baghdad Oil Ministry to monopolize the granting of licenses for exploration, nor is there any agreement on the precise mechanism through which the revenues should be allocated. Third, it is not true that Sunni Arab majority areas have no future prospects of oil and gas development. The current geological wisdom says the opposite: Allah in his infinite generosity has blessed Anbar as well as Basra and Kirkuk.[33] There are extensive opportunities for exploration throughout Iraq. All three major communities predominate in some territory where there are good prospects of new fields. Baghdad, which should become a region itself, also straddles good prospects.

What matters politically is that the historically underdeveloped regions must have constitutional assurances that Iraq's future will not be like its past. The political development of oil-rich states that were not democ-racies before they discovered and exploited their oil fields has generally been dreadful. Oil wealth weakens the prospect of a chain of accountabil-ity between governments and taxpayers, encourages corruption and clien-telism, and heightens dependency on government.[34] The "curse of oil" is indeed one of the major potential threats to the prospects of Iraq's suc-cessful democratization. For that very reason democrats should welcome the fact that the Constitution recognizes decentralization provisions over control and ownership of oil and natural gas and the fact that Kurdistan's oil law and the draft federal oil law have state-of-the-art transparency pro-visions. These arrangements can prevent the type of overcentralized, rent-ier state that led Iraq to disaster. Kurdistan's proposal, so far resisted by the Baghdad Oil Ministry, to process all revenue allocation through an interna-tionally supervised trust remains on the table.

The constitutional arrangements on natural resources may also facilitate the settlement of the status of Kirkuk. The 2005 settlement creatively and deliberately separated deciding the final territorial status of Kirkuk prov-ince from the question of the ownership, management, and revenues of the Kirkuk oil field. Under Article 112(1), the long-exploited Kirkuk oil field must be federally managed, in conjunction with *either* the Kurdistan Regional Government *or* Kirkuk province (*or* both), and the revenues dis-tributed according to the per capita formula and a balanced development requirement. Therefore, it is not true but false that if the Kurdistan Region unifies with Kirkuk governorate, the rest of Iraq loses its entire stakes in Kirkuk's oil field. The better this constitutional fact is appreciated, the greater the likelihood that the heat can be taken out of the referendum on Kirkuk's territorial status or any other agreed-upon way of resolving the sta-tus of Kirkuk. Recognition of this fact by responsible international organi-zations and commentators is overdue.

The presence of the entirety of the Kirkuk oil field within the Kurdistan Region would, of course, have one important bearing on power relations within Iraq. Before Kurdistan's other oil and gas fields come on stream the federal government and legislature would not be able to blackmail the KRG by depriving it of its rightful share of Iraq's oil revenues or by blocking its right to develop its own region in accordance with its consti-tutional rights. Anxieties on these matters have been at the heart of dis-putes between the KRG and federal oil minister Hussain al-Shahristani since 2006. Kurdistan has had nearly eighty years of experience of finan-cial dependence on Baghdad, during which Baghdad governments took the oil revenues from Kirkuk but forbade the development of other fields within Kurdistan. That is why the Kurdistan Region insists on its autonomous right of development and has proposed that all of Iraq's oil revenues should go into an internationally supervised trust fund, which would make allocations to the federal, regional and provincial governments based on agreed per capita allocations. This proposal is not motivated by a plot to secede but by decades of experience of underprovision from Baghdad, or, in other words, fear of theft.

The bargain of 2005 on natural resources was part of a coherent remaking of Iraq as a pluralist federation and it deserves a chance to work. The differences between the KRG and Baghdad, although not yet resolved, are not huge and may yet be bridged. It would be helpful if American policy toward Iraq incorporated recognition of Iraq's Constitution rather than remained tilted against it. There are practical as well as principled reasons to favor the Constitution. As a matter of practical fact, Article 126(4) of the Constitution empowers Kurdistan's voters and the Kurdistan region to block any amendments to the Constitution. No one should expect Kurdistan to accept amendments detrimental to its interests, especially those dealing with natural resources. The principled reason is to look carefully at who supports a centralized Iraq within Iraq, namely neo-Baathist Sunni-Arab elites, jihadist religious fanatics, and the followers of Muqtada al-Sadr among the Shia. Why should the international democratic community, with or without the United States, sympathize with these reactionary and unnatural bedfellows? Why should it not instead favor the modernized Kurds and Shia who have committed to a pluralist federation? International opinion may be as it is because it believes, unfortunately and inaccurately, that the Constitution, and it provisions on natural resources, materially disadvantages Sunni Arabs.

Winning Over Sunni Arabs to Make a Federal Iraq Work

The Constitution normatively establishes a pluralist, democratic framework acceptable to Kurdistan and the majority of Shia Arabs. It also does not harm any others' rights, including those of Sunni Arabs, in a democratic political order. The provisions against Baathism have, it is true, been primarily borne by Sunni Arabs, but steps have been and will continue to be taken to alleviate some of their repercussions. But otherwise the Constitution provides incentives for Sunni Arabs to accept new democratic realities. In those parts of Iraq in which they constitute majorities within provinces, Sunni Arabs are free to decide exactly what levels of self-government they wish to exercise and which powers they wish to leave to the federal government or to share with it. They have the right, under the law, to manage security within provinces or a region where they constitute a majority, although they have no automatic right to provide amnesties. The Constitution, as I shall show, does not establish Shia Islam at the expense of Sunni Islam. If Sunni Arabs wish to weaken the influence of Shia versions of law and morality, they are free at the federal level to build alliances with secular Arabs and Kurds and Sunni Kurds, or, if they prefer, they can ensure in their own provinces—or their own region—that Sunni Islam will set the tone of public law and morality. The existing Constitution, through enabling regional legislative supremacy, grants regions sovereignty over the regulation of rights, including religious rights.

Conceding all the nostalgic demands of Sunni Arab leaders for a unitary and strongly recentralized Iraq is both unacceptable and impossible for the overwhelming majority of Iraqis—Kurds and Shia Arabs. Kurds will only accept that level of centralization required to build security forces sufficient to defeat the Sunni Arab insurgents and the Sadrists. They do not want another Arab conquest of Kurdistan. A federal Iraq is not, contrary to what Sunni Arabs are inclined to say, a recipe for breaking up the country; it is the only way that Iraq can survive without permanent civil war. Blocking Kurdistan's interest in secession requires accepting its autonomy and respecting it. Blocking the possibility that Shia Arabs may prefer to downsize Iraq in the future requires Sunni Arabs to become partners with their fellow Arabs rather than act as their implacable enemies.

There are three positive ways to win enough Sunni Arabs into accepting the new order. First, they should be encouraged to take advantage of its provisions on provincial and regional autonomy to build their own forms of self-government. They are entitled to and will have a common interest with the KRG in ensuring that they receive their proportionate shares of oil revenues. Second, they should work with Kurds to ensure that the federal executive, especially the Council of Ministers, is more collegial. Kurds and Sunni Arabs have a shared interest in preventing too much Shia Arab power within the federal government. They might also consider maintaining the three-person Presidency Council, which has served to protect minority rights, or consider how to raise the powers of the deputy prime ministers. These are positive ways in which Sunni Arabs may achieve both self-government and shared government. Third, they should work, again with possible allies among the Kurds, to build a second chamber for the federal union and a federal legal system that will protect them against any new tyranny of the majority. But all these positive possibilities come with a price. Sunni Arab politicians will need to work within the new order and accept a range of other changes, including internal provincial border changes and changes in control over oil revenues. They can have all the rights of a well-treated minority. They cannot have the rights of a *Staatsvolk*—the people who control the state.

There are negative ways in which many Sunni Arabs already feel obliged to accept the new order. Some acknowledge they have been defeated and misplayed their hands. Some of them prefer the new Iraq to the prospects of Salafist government. Others know they cannot win—either through violence or through the ballot box. They have been unable to defeat the Americans. The coming departure of the Americans will in fact weaken their leverage, leaving them vulnerable to the ascendancy of the new Shia majority. Their security position—after the collapse of Baathism and after the failed insurgencies against the new order—is weaker, not stronger, because of their resort to violence. The violence they have supported has made them lasting enemies among some other Iraqis. They know they could be quarantined from the rest of Iraq. Their economic position is terrible—and can only start to recover if they work within the new institutions. If they appraise their future realistically they have to decide, as my friend Khaled Salih has put it, whether they wish to emulate the fate of the Palestinians—who have found each succeeding political settlement offered them by their principal protagonist since 1947 to be less appealing than the one before.

Protecting the Federacy of Kurdistan

Kurdistan's strikingly asymmetrical status in the Transitional Administrative Law of 2004 made it likely that it would evolve into a "federacy."[35] A federacy is an asymmetrical unit of government with different powers and status than that of other entities in a common state. It is semisovereign, different in its institutions and constitutional powers, and is not a mere local government. Federacy is not devolution; it is not a revocable gift from the federal government.[36] A federacy can veto any changes in its status or powers, and, ideally, its status and powers are internationally protected in a treaty. In a federation, a federacy is normally culturally different from the other units (states or provinces) in the federation and may enjoy different powers to those units or choose to exercise the same powers strikingly differently. The division of powers between a federacy and the federal government is entrenched and cannot be unilaterally altered by either side and, for it to work, normally must have established arbitration mechanisms, domestic or international, to deal with difficulties that might arise between the federacy and the federal government.

Under the Transitional Administrative Law, Kurdistan was the sole recognized region. All the other federative entities were governorates. It was recognized as it was before 2003, as were its laws since 1992; that is, the legality of its revolution against Baathist Iraq was recognized. Its National Assembly was recognized. Of the federative entities, the Kurdistan Region alone was entitled to amend federal legislation. It was the largest federative entity in territory and the second largest in population (after Baghdad). It was the sole federative entity dominated by another nationality, and speakers of the other official language, Kurdish. It was the sole entity granted exclusive jurisdiction in policing and internal security. Kurdistan was different, QED.

In negotiating the Constitution of Iraq, Kurdistan's politicians did not seek to stop Arab Iraq from adopting a more centralized U.S.-style federation, if that was what Arabs and other Iraqis wanted, within Arab Iraq. What they did not want was to be ruled from Baghdad except in those limited domains they were prepared to grant to the federal government. As it happened, SCIRI's negotiators also wanted to create a highly decentralized Iraq. That is why the powers and status accorded to the Kurdistan Region became the standard to which all future regions in Iraq are now entitled to conform.

The result is that on constitutional paper Iraq looks like a program for a symmetrical federation, in which other regions may form with powers identical to those of Kurdistan. That may not happen, however; we shall see. It may be that Shia Arabs, who can easily identify with the new federal government, will be less keen to establish regions (or keep provinces) with the same degree of autonomy as Kurdistan; and Sunni Arabs, for now, have mostly not warmed to federalism at all.

The most striking evidence of Kurdistan's status as a federacy may be found in Article 141 of the Iraqi Constitution. It provides for laws and contracts made by the KRG after 1992 to "remain in effect," unless they violate the Constitution, and, by implication, ratifies the legal status of the Peshmerga, who are not a militia. Kurdistan also has the capacity to veto any unilateral change to its definition and powers by the federal government. So, it is, for now, a federacy.[37]

Kurdistan has sought autonomy since the formation of Iraq. It now has that autonomy recognized, in a form with which it is content, provided that the federal government fulfills its obligations to resolve the status of the disputed territories, provided that the federal and regional governments can resolve their differences on the allocation of oil revenues (and the related question of budgetary support for security force personnel, past and present), and provided that the laws establishing the federal supreme court and creating a second federal chamber protect Kurdistan's rights. That is a significant number of "provided thats."

Kurds worry that after the withdrawal of the U.S. forces, the Arab parties in the federal government will renege on their constitutional obligations. Kurds will find themselves vulnerable once again to betrayals of their promises by Arab politicians in Baghdad and elsewhere, as well as being threatened by Turkey and Iran. They will have their secessionist option blocked by Turkey and Iran and be vulnerable to Baghdad governments, which might refuse to pay Kurdistan's share of all-Iraqi revenues, or seek to recentralize outside the text and spirit of the Constitution.

The United States has a debt of honor to the Kurds, who fought in Operation Iraqi Freedom and who subsequently supplied the most reliable troops for the alliance with the multinational Coalition and the defense of Iraq. How might a substantive U.S. withdrawal be compatible with discharging some of that debt of honor in a lawful way? One way is through support for the KRG's constitutional security powers—including its right to arm and protect its rights. Another may be through the negotiation of a treaty with Turkey, Iran, Syria, and the Federal Government of Iraq. That treaty would have to respect each country's borders and each country's sovereignty—and Iraq's specific constitutional provisions for Kurdistan. Such a treaty would place an obligation on all parties to protect the rights of the Kurdistan Region within Iraq's borders and establish arbitration mechanisms for resolving difficulties that might arise. Later I will spell out other elements of what is required in that treaty, or its equivalent, to protect the most important positive outcome of the U.S. intervention in Iraq, the federacy of Kurdistan.

Completing the Constitution

Iraq's Constitution remains unfinished business. Its transitional provisions allow for amendments to be proposed by a committee of the Council of Representatives, voted on by the whole house, and then put to a referendum with the same ratification rules as were used to make the Constitution. The date for these has expired but, by consensus, these procedures may yet be followed. They were intended to help Sunni Arabs participate in modifications of the Constitution. Once these measures are declared expired or inoperative, however, it will be more difficult to amend the Constitution—as most provisions would then require the support of two-thirds of the members of the Council of Representatives and (where regional powers are affected) the support of regional assemblies and their peoples.

The Constitution requires a law to be passed, with the support of two-thirds of the members of the Council of Representatives, to establish the nomination, rules, and powers of a federal second chamber (the "Federation Council" [or Council of the Union] in Articles 65 and 137). That is anticipated, according to the text, during the second electoral term of the Council of Representatives. A federal supreme court is also required to be established through a law that has the support of two-thirds of the members of the Council of Representatives (Article 92). That has not yet been passed. These unfinished institutions cannot come into being unless the Shia Arab parties can win enough votes from either Kurdish or Sunni Arab legislators. The high threshold requirement makes it likely that both institutions will only come into being with a broad-based consensus and if they are seen as likely to protect all of Iraq's major communities. These are subjects to which Iraqis are best left to themselves—although they may profit from such international advice as they seek fit to take.

Federalism and Religion

The prospects for making Iraq's Constitution work are enhanced by the fact that it manages the severe tensions that religious controversies may occasion with skill. Contrary to foreign expectations, the Iraqi negotiators had little difficulty in recognizing Islam as the official religion in Iraq. That had already been accepted in the TAL.[38] In the final constitutional provisions, Iraq, like a range of European countries, and in the Middle East, has an official religion:

> Islam is the official religion of the State and is a foundation source of legislation:
>
> A. No law may be enacted that contradicts the established provisions of Islam.
>
> B. No law may be enacted that contradicts the principles of democracy.
>
> C. No law may be enacted that contradicts the rights and basic freedoms stipulated in this Constitution. (Article 2(1))

But, unlike many European states, Iraq neither establishes nor endows a sect and its clergy. The permanent Constitution treats Islam as *a* foundation source rather than *the* source of legislation. That no law may be passed that contradicts the "established provisions" of Islam is an assurance for Sunni Muslims because, in principle, it prevents sectarian legislation by Shia federal representatives. Muslim jurists, both Sunni and Shia, would have to agree on what are the "established provisions," though there are not many (depending on how one reads "established"). Laws that meet this standard cannot, however, violate the "principles of democracy" (undefined) or "the rights and freedom" protected in the Constitution. That means that both legislators and courts have to take democracy and rights into consideration when framing legislation approved by Muslim jurists. The Constitution goes further:

> This Constitution guarantees the Islamic identity of the majority of the Iraqi people and guarantees the full religious rights to freedom of religious belief and practice of all individuals such as Christians, Yezidis, and Mandean Sabeans. (Article 2(2))

The phrasing does not confine such rights to these three named groups (two of which, Christians and Mandean Sabeans, have Quranic protection), although it may be debated whether full freedom includes atheism (which it should).

Iraq has had deep sectarian conflicts despite these reasonable and fair-minded provisions, proof if it were needed that constitutional texts without enforcement are worthless. But at least reasonable provisions are there. It will be Iraq's parliament and courts that will decide in the future how important a role Islamic jurisprudence will play.[39]

The Shia Marja'iyya wanted constitutional protection for their shrines—understandable given their treatment under Saddam and since—and for Shia Husseini rituals, which Saddam had banned. These were granted without controversy, and all places of worship are to be protected. The Shia negotiators also wanted their own status recognized, in particular the right to serve as judges on the federal supreme court. That was far more controversial. That demand was mediated by Ambassador Zalmay Khalilzad, the Sunni Muslim ambassador of the secular United States, whose priority was meeting the U.S. timetables for constitutional completion.[40] He argued that it would be reasonable to have Muslim jurists on the Supreme Court because they have the requisite expertise in Islamic law. Iraq's secular parties, including those from Kurdistan, met that counsel with intense disappointment.

How did they respond? In effect, Kurdistan's parties succeeded in stripping the supreme court of its right to review regional laws, implementing the "federalization of God." Religion, human rights, and all the rights enumerated in Chapter 2 of the Constitution are not listed as among the exclusive competences of the federal government. Therefore, at least in the view of Kurdistan's negotiators, these provisions are subject to the supremacy of regional law.[41] Kurdistan will be able to maintain its secular laws, while the rest of Iraq, through the federal government, through any new regional governments, or through provinces, may, if these areas wish, apply versions of Islamic law—though federal legislation would still have to abide by "democracy" and the "rights provisions."[42]

This constitutional bargain among Iraqis reflects local political choices. Sometimes democracy and liberalism diverge. The United States and outsiders have no right to impose particular provisions on rights and their regulation on Iraqis—although they are entitled to remind them to uphold those international human rights treaties to which they are parties. That is obviously easier to do when one's government respects these provisions.

The issue of how the supreme court will work is postponed. Shia jurists will not be able to dictate either the selection of judges or the powers of the court because one can expect the Kurds, Sunni and secular, Sunni Arabs, secular and religious, and secular Shia to prevent that possibility. Any supreme federal court that emerges will be weak; will be likely to have no preenactment role; and will likely have to be regionally representative and required to operate with a high threshold of consensus rather than majority rule.

Iraq not only has a federal, pluralist, and democratic constitution on paper, with de facto recognition of Kurdistan as a nationally distinctive federacy, it also has a constitution which its makers think is worth fighting to preserve: against foreign jihadists, Sunni Arabs bent on an undemocratic restoration, and Sadrist populist theocrats who would impose their version of Shia preferences on others. A well-organized American withdrawal from Iraq should support this Constitution rather than seeking its radical modification. That will ease the withdrawal, since it will not be encumbered by impossible benchmarks. America will be able to claim that it aided Iraqi regime change on Iraqi terms. And its diplomatic mission and its soft and hard powers can then be oriented toward the protection of Iraq and its Constitution.

Chapter 7
Respecting Iraq's Territorial Integrity

This era does not reward people who struggle in vain to redraw borders with blood.

—President William Jefferson Clinton, speaking in Pakistan, March 2000

Leaving Iraq with integrity requires support for Iraq's territorial integrity. That obligation is not owed because Iraq's territory is somehow sacrosanct or because all of its current boundaries are long-rooted in history.[1] Nor is it owed because the United States should always favor the territorial integrity of states at the expense of the self-determination of imprisoned peoples. The obligation arises for two core reasons. First, the promise to respect Iraq's territorial integrity was given at the outset of the intervention, not just to Iraqis but to the world; and second, the Iraqi Constitution establishes a federation endorsed by its citizens, including the Kurds, who rejoined Iraq in a "free union" in the words of the closing sentence of the preface to the Constitution. Iraq is in very important respects not like post-Communist Yugoslavia. The KRG has rejoined Iraq, not left it. Iraq has no "first-mover" secessionists—no political leaders and peoples determined to break free and establish wholly independent states. The Kurds would have had justice on their side if they had sought this path, but they have chosen to try to make the new Iraq work for them. Sunni and Shia Arabs have been in vicious contention over the nature of power in Iraq—but neither community articulates secessionist platforms.

The U.S. withdrawal from Iraq therefore, should not be accompanied by any plan to partition Iraq—which would be against international law for those who care to respect that law, which often protects regimes rather than peoples, and would be against the overt wishes of the democratically elected leaders of Iraq (and of its undemocratic leaders). Any division of Iraq should be left to Iraqis themselves to negotiate if they ever decide to make such a terminal agreement. Withdrawal with integrity will, however, be better if it is accompanied by diplomatic and technical support for key internal territorial adjustments within Iraq that are mandated by its Constitution.

Against Partition

A frequent American judgment is that Iraq should no longer be conceived of as a single country but instead partitioned into three entities reflecting Iraq's ethnic and sectarian divisions. There should be a Kurdistan, a "Shiastan," and a "Sunnistan," loosely modeled on the three Ottoman provinces from which modern Iraq was built by the British, namely Mosul, Baghdad, and Basra.[2] Plans along these lines had been intermittently promoted by Joseph Biden of Delaware, when he was chair of the Senate Foreign Relations Committee, and by Leslie Gelb, president emeritus of the U.S. Council on Foreign Relations.[3] Partition has been endorsed with qualifications by Senators Sam Brownback, Barbara Boxer, and Kay Bailey Hutchison as well as by American intellectuals and policy analysts, notably Peter Galbraith, Michael O'Hanlon, and David Brooks.[4] Some Kurds speak positively of the idea, as do a few Shia, but I have never heard a Sunni Arab inside or outside of Iraq speak in defense of this logic. We may distinguish two versions of this proposal: a plan to create three independent sovereign states, and a plan to create three entities that would remain linked in a formal Iraqi confederation (with Baghdad functioning as an ATM to allocate oil revenues, as Thomas Friedman, the commentator of the *New York Times*, has put it).[5] These partitionist proposals merit serious consideration, partly because they have been advanced by some very intelligent people and partly because, in extremis, if a substantive U.S. withdrawal from Iraq goes very badly, we can expect these arguments to resurface with vigor and to have more Iraqi proponents than they do now.

A partition is a fresh border cut through at least one community's national homeland.[6] In this case, it would be intended to create three separate political units under different sovereigns or authorities (in a confederation the member states retain their sovereignty and that includes the right to secede). Between them advocates of partition in Iraq make the standard arguments that were used to justify the major partitions of the twentieth century. We can summarize these claims without personalizing them or without attributing one shared view to all the proponents of partition.[7] They provide "historicist" arguments in which partition is deemed inevitable or is already happening; therefore the process should be speeded up or better organized to ease the pain. As David Brooks put it, "America's best course is...simply to inhibit the violence as Iraqis feel their own way to partition."[8] They make the "last resort" argument. All else has failed, so let us apply this form of triage. They make the cost-benefit case: partition, on balance, is a better proposal than any other for Iraq's peoples. They advance the "better tomorrow" claim: after partition there will be an end to or radical reduction in violence. Some even advance pursuing partition to the finish, with "population transfers" to remove enclaves. Realist rigor, it is suggested, requires thoroughgoing homogenization of the postpartition entities.[9]

The arguments against partitioning Iraq are more compelling. They also, I think, explain why Senator Biden adjusted his proposals in the Senate and sensibly crafted them to conform with Iraq's Constitution.[10] He did so by encouraging the regionalization process laid out in Iraq's Constitution. The arguments against the partition of Iraq also conform to the standard repertoire of arguments used against major partitions in the twentieth century.[11] Partition is not wanted by a majority of Iraqis, including majorities of Sunni and Shia Arabs. Kurds would, in general, prefer independence, if they could be sure that it would not lead to their destruction. But no Kurds favor partition if that would mean they had no control over the drawing of the boundaries of Kurdistan—their fate throughout the twentieth century. Partition would rupture the hard-won national unity of Iraq, according to most Arab Iraqis, both Sunni and Shia.[12] This conviction is not shared by Kurds, who regard themselves as a separate nation, but their leaders accept that partition would suggest that Iraq cannot function as a binational or pluralist federation. However, many of them say it has not yet been given a sufficient chance to do so properly. Why move toward something no community has endorsed (in elections or a referendum) and away from a political formula that four out of five voters endorsed less than three years ago?

A just partition, critics observe, is unrealizable. Would the partition be made by agreement? But that, as Samuel Goldwyn said, is two words: impossible. What ratification procedure would be used? All major partitions have been accompanied by major and long-running demarcation disputes. Would the partition be imposed? If so, by whom? The United States? The United Nations? Why should anyone think partition could be justly or impartially organized by either the United States or the United Nations and subsequently regarded as legitimate? The United States is, wrongly, deemed biased toward the Kurds. The United Nations is more accurately (with 22 Arab League member states) deemed biased toward the Arabs, especially Sunni Arabs. How would mixed territories and enclaves be allocated? Critics observe that all planned partitions generate more disorder and intense violence than the status quo because militias and governments try to establish facts on the ground and carry out expulsions. Critics also observe that partitions almost never accomplish homogenization, except through extraordinary violence, which historically has always proved worse than the prepartition scale of violence.

The Iraq Study Group, which produced what is known as the Baker-Hamilton Report, argued against partition in 2006 in the following fashion:

> Because Iraq's population is not neatly separated, regional boundaries cannot be easily drawn. All eighteen Iraqi provinces have mixed populations, as do Baghdad and most other major cities in Iraq. A rapid devolution could result in mass population movements, collapse of the Iraqi security forces, strengthening of militias, ethnic cleansing, destabilization of neighboring states, or attempts by neighboring states to dominate Iraqi regions.[13]

These counterclaims are too much. They ignore the fact that parts of Iraq are very homogeneous. Even the most cursory inspection of the votes on Iraq's Constitution (which took place before the most intense periods of expulsion and flight) entitles us to conclude that large parts of Iraq are very politically homogeneous, much more than the Baker-Hamilton gloss would suggest. Table 7.1 shows that nine out of ten Shia majority governorates endorsed the Constitution with "yes" votes of 94.5 percent of the vote or more. Three out of the four Kurdish majority governorates endorsed the Constitution with "yes" votes of 98.9 percent or more. Two of the three Sunni Arab majority governorates voted "no" at levels of 82 and 97 percent.

The genuinely mixed parts of Iraq (where local minorities number more than ten percent of the population) are all at the edges of the Sunni Arab heartlands and in the central Baghdad belt. It is therefore more accurate to say that Iraq has fourteen very homogeneous and four significantly mixed provinces:

- *Baghdad*, divided mostly between Shia Arabs (a clear majority) and Sunni Arabs, but with small numbers of Kurdish, Christian, and other minorities;

Table 7.1   Turnout and Votes in the October 15, 2005, Referendum to Approve the Constitution of Iraq (Percentages)

	Turnout	No	Yes
Shia Arab Majority Governorates			
Muthana	58	1.4	98.6
Misan	57	2.2	97.8
Thiqar	54	2.8	97.2
Qadissiya	56	3.3	96.7
Karbala	73	3.4	96.6
Basra	63	4.0	96.0
Najaf	56	4.2	95.8
Wasit	54	4.3	95.7
Babal	72	5.4	94.5
Baghdad	56	22.3	77.7
Kurdish Majority Governorates			
Erbil	90	0.6	99.4
Dohuk	85	0.9	99.1
Sulaimania	75	1.0	98.9
Kirkuk	79	37.1	62.9
Sunni Arab Majority Governorates			
Anbar	32	96.9	3.0
Salahaddin	88	81.7	18.3
Ninevah	58	55.1	44.9
Governorate Without a Majority Community			
Diyala	66	48.7	51.3

Figures rounded to one decimal point.
Source: Electoral Commission of Iraq.

- *Diyala*, also known as the "little Iraq," because it is the only province where all three major communities number more than fifteen percent, and none commands a majority;
- *Ninevah*, where Kurds form a significant minority in Mosul on the left or east bank of the Tigris and in other disputed areas, notably Sinjar; and
- *Kirkuk*, where Kurds are in a majority and Arabs and Turkomen form significant minorities.

These facts suggest that if the boundaries of Kirkuk, Ninevah, and Diyala can be successfully adjusted, then only Baghdad governorate will have a large minority. Strong demographic, ethnic, or sectarian bases are therefore present for a pluralist federation that recognizes these realities.

The Iraq Study Group's arguments, while important in rejecting any externally imposed partition, should not be abused, as they were, to argue against the federal Constitution of 2005, which recognizes one region and permits the formation of others through lawful and consensual processes. In the United States, unfortunately, some people have muddied the waters by using the language of "soft partition" to describe the federalization process available in the Iraq Constitution. This language confuses matters—and encourages Sunni Arabs, wrongly, to believe that partition and federalization are synonymous. The federalization process provides constitutionally authorized mechanisms to form regions out of existing provinces and mechanisms to resolve disputed territories through intra-Iraqi negotiations.

There are three telling objections to any proposals to partition Iraq, leaving aside the question of who would do it and by what means. The first is that no major elected representatives from any of its three major blocs have called for it to happen. Second, the formation of three smaller independent and homogenous states would require the international partition of the cities of Mosul and Baghdad—Mosul would have to be partitioned between Kurdistan and "Sunnistan," whereas Baghdad would have to be partitioned between "Sunnistan" and "Shiastan." Otherwise, the new states would not be strongly homogeneous and therefore would be no more likely to be peaceful or stable than today's Iraq. Third, each of the three new independent states would be much weaker in foreign and defense policy than they can be together. Turkey would dominate a 4–5 million person Kurdistan even if it did not invade it. So would Iran. A 4–5 million person Sunnistan would have less weight demographically than Jordan and would be dominated by Saudi Arabia or Syria. The Shia Republic of Iraq, with a population of 16–18 million, would be more substantial than the other two entities, but it would be overshadowed by its weighty Iranian neighbor. In short, the Kurds and Arabs of Iraq have some joint defense and foreign policy interests. Together they can be more influential in foreign policy and less dependent on or penetrated by their neighbors. Such "togetherness" requires neither love nor abiding affection among Kurds, Sunni Arabs, and Shia Arabs. Their respective leaders know that avoiding dependency on Turkey, Iran, or others is one of the strongest cases for an Iraqi federation (in the case of Kurds and some Shia Arabs) and an Iraqi state (in the case of Sunni Arabs and some Shia Arabs). As long as these three reasons remain jointly operative, a formal partition of Iraq is not likely. The key to making Iraq work is not any externally imposed partition but rather a combination of federalization and the successful negotiation of internal provincial boundary adjustments—as provided for in its Constitution. These internal boundary adjustments are required in the "disputed territories," including the famous cases of Kirkuk city and province.

Kirkuk Governorate and City

It is vital to ensure that the intra-Arab civil war, which may well be coming to an end, is not succeeded by Kurdish-Arab conflict. Kurds did not take advantage of the Arab civil war to annex the disputed territories that concern them. They will not, however, react well if they are rewarded for their constitutionalism and patience by failures to deliver on the part of the Iraqi federal executive powers. Since most Americans are not well briefed on these matters, it may be helpful to provide some background to what is at stake.

The key disputed territories at issue on the borders of the KRG are known to all Iraqis, which is why it was redundant to name them in the Constitution. They have been at issue since the March Proclamation of 1970, which brought a temporary respite to conflict between the Baathists and the Kurdistan Democratic Party of Mulla Mustafa Barzani. The most famous and important of these, in population and resources, are Kirkuk governorate and city.[14]

Iraq became resource-rich on October 15, 1927, when oil was struck at Baba Gurgur, very close to Kirkuk, and not far from the site of the "fiery furnace" described in the Hebrew Bible's Book of Daniel. Kirkuk province has since become truly "oil rich," although its inhabitants have not. The city sits atop 6 percent of the world's and 40 percent of Iraq's proven oil reserves (see Map 4). The oil field, however, is long and extends into Erbil governorate. These facts lead many to reason that all the controversy over Kirkuk's territorial status is about oil. Turkish commentators suggest that Kurds are planning an oil grab in Kirkuk to finance an independent sovereign state, and some have developed fearful fantasies of a well-funded Kurdistan air force that will subsequently contribute to the building of a Greater Kurdistan.

The mostly ignored fact is that any potential controversies over the distribution of Kirkuk's oil revenues are already resolved in the Constitution. Kurds agreed to play fair, unlike Saddam or his predecessors. They have made fairness a matter of Iraq's constitutional law. The revenues from Kirkuk's oil field, because they were already being exploited on October 15, 2005, when the Constitution was validated, must be shared across Iraq as a whole.[15] Any change in Kirkuk's territorial status will not mean that the

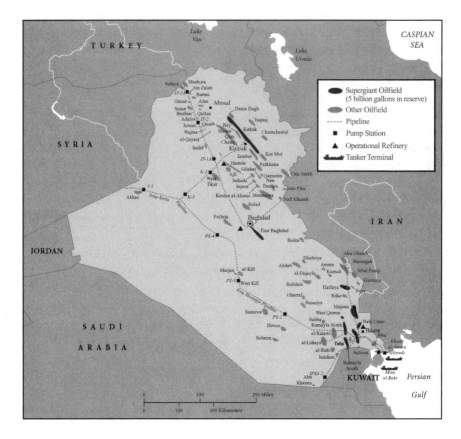

Map 4. Iraq: oil infrastructure.

Kurdistan Region obtains all of Kirkuk's oil revenues, as is often wrongly suggested. Instead, the KRG will obtain something on the order of 17 to 22 percent of these revenues, depending on the total population of the KRG after its boundary is definitively demarcated. If Kirkuk governorate joins the Kurdistan Region, then the revenue from its oil fields must accrue to the whole of Iraq, including, of course, Kirkuk itself; the same formula applies if Kirkuk does not join the Kurdistan Region. This is a remarkable constitutional compromise.

But what if the Kurds did secede? The same formula would apply in any negotiated secession because it would have to respect the 2005 constitutional deal on oil and gas revenues. A contested secession, by contrast, would be a recipe for suicide because Arab Iraq and the neighboring states could block the export of Kirkuk's oil. In short, provided the Constitution is implemented, all Iraqis stand to benefit from Kirkuk's currently exploited oil and gas fields, and the KRG has a strong interest in remaining in a federal Iraq to ensure the legality of its title to revenues from Kirkuk's oil field—apart from the necessity to ensure an export route.

The leaders of the Kurds of Iraq, whom I have advised, are not intent on winning independence. Their public may want it and may dream of it. They also deserve it because of maltreatment at the hands of successive Baghdad governments. But Kurdistan's public has so far followed their leaders, who have argued that the new federal Iraq gives them the substance of full domestic independence and protects them from Turkey and Iran. Grabbing Kirkuk's oil revenues and seceding would weaken Kurdistan's present standing as the most lawfully governed part of Iraq and jeopardize its legal entitlements under Iraq's Constitution. Neighboring states that refused recognition would block the export of Kurdistan's oil and gas, a fact of which Kurds are fully aware.[16] Sadly, some of these neighboring states and commentators nevertheless persist in believing that Kurdistan's leaders are embarked upon an organized plan to achieve both expansion and independence, abusing their allegedly naïve U.S. ally, even though the Kurdistan Region's interests point otherwise.

While Presidents Barzani and Talabani and their colleagues have skillfully managed the end of Saddam's dictatorship and peacefully navigated the bloody waters of Arab Iraq's civil war, they are not planning Kurdistan's independence. They do not wish to precipitate either a Turkish or an Iranian invasion. They need their political alliance with the major Shia parties of the south to make Iraq work, if only to be certain they can export oil and import Kurdistan's trade. They are willing to consider an accommodation with reasonable Sunni Arabs to balance against Shia Arab dominance. They do not benefit from a bloody Iraq and will not benefit from an unrecognized Kurdistan that would deter investors and economic development. They have in Iraq's Constitution what they and their relatives have fought for over several generations. Why would they risk so much, achieved against such odds, for a bloody romantic gesture? A Kurdish strategy to achieve independence does not exist. That does not mean, however, that Kurds will not fight to protect their homeland or their constitutional rights.

Kirkuk, of course, has been the site of oil grabs. The first came in the British decision to occupy the Mosul *vilayat* (province) of the Ottoman Empire and to incorporate it within Iraq. During World War I British strategists were well aware of the future importance of oil and that it might be plentifully available in Mosul *vilayat*.[17] They were followed by successive Arab-dominated governments in Baghdad, which confined the revenues to

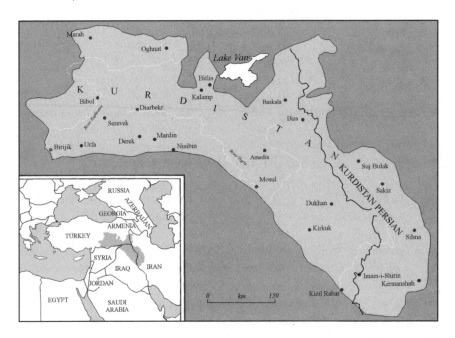

Map 5. Kurdistan in the Middle East, as presented on behalf of Kurdistan at
Versailles by Sharif Pasha.

the discretion of the central government and did not spend significantly
on Kirkuk city or governorate, or allow the development of other significant oil prospects in Kurdistan.

Kurds are fully aware that having Kirkuk within the KRG will mean that
they will be able to control, count, and cut revenue checks along with other
Iraqis. That will reduce their economic dependence on Baghdad and prevent political exploitation as the federal government strengthens. But
ultimately what drives Kurds is not oil but the defense of their national
territory, and justice. Their leaders sought a Kurdistan with Kirkuk at the
Versailles Peace Treaty before the wealth of the oil field of Kirkuk was
widely known. Map 5 shows that Kirkuk and all the relevant disputed territories were included in the presentation made by the Kurdish representative, Sharif Pasha, to the Paris Peace Conference in 1919. Kirkuk was a
Kurdish-majority locale, which is why Kurdish nationalists wanted it within
Kurdistan.

Kurdish nationalist territorial feelings magnified enormously after the
gross injustices perpetrated by the Baathists. Saddam betrayed his com-

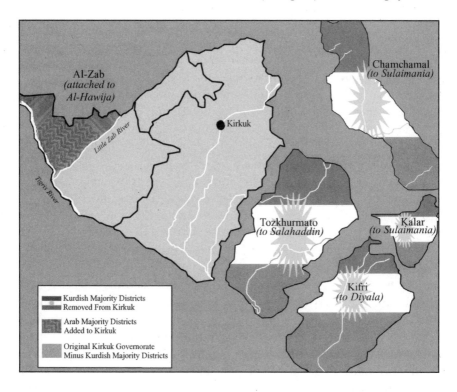

Map 6. The Saddam-ander of Kirkuk.

mitments to Mustafa Barzani after he realized that the Kurds would win any referendum held within Kirkuk in the early 1970s. He then went on to manipulate its administrative boundaries, organize ethnic expulsion, encourage coercive Arabization, and promote the infusion of settlers. These deeds, however, are not well known.

Saddam manipulated boundaries, transferring Kurdish-majority districts out of the province and adding Arab-majority districts. This "Saddam-ander," sketched in Map 6, was intended to make Kurdish-majority Kirkuk into an Arab province. The reduced province was renamed "Tamim," which in Arabic roughly means "nationalized."

The Saddam-ander explains why Kurds profoundly care about Kirkuk. They feel it is part of their homeland, taken from them by force. The surrounding region, if not all of the city, has been part of the Kurdish-speaking civilization for centuries. Although the governorate has numerous significant minorities, that should not affect its right to be part of Kurdistan.

The last relatively reliable census in Iraq was held in 1957. I have had the original census returns translated and inspected in the University of Pennsylvania Library. In 1957, of the three largest communities in Kirkuk governorate—Arabs, Kurds, and Turkomen—the Kurds constituted the plurality, approximately 48 percent of the governorate as a whole (49 percent if unknowns and foreign citizens are excluded) and a majority if Kurds are allocated an appropriately high share of those classified as "unknowns." Outside of Kirkuk city, Kurds were indisputably the majority community. In the city—then home to less than a third of the governorate's population—Turkomen (37.6 percent) were the largest group, just outnumbering Kurds (33.3 percent), who in turn outnumbered Arabs (22.5 percent). The objective summary is that in 1957 Kirkuk was a multiethnic city within a larger and heavily Kurdish population in the rest of the governorate.

Since Kurds were the poorest of the major groups in 1957, their higher population growth would have made them unambiguously the largest community by the mid-1960s. That is exactly why the Baathists subjected both the city and the governorate to brutal demographic engineering. Saddam reduced the size of Kirkuk governorate and its population (compared to what it would otherwise have been) to dilute its Kurdish majority status and added Arab majority districts, notably Al Hawija and Al Zab, to drive home the transformation. Mostly poor Shia Arab settlers from the south were encouraged by handsome bonuses to make their lives in Kirkuk. The Baathists are reported to have expelled between 100,000 and 250,000 Kurds and thousands of Turkomen.

Two sets of elections and one referendum took place in Kirkuk governorate in 2005. The pro-Kurdistan lists, which included some Turkomen and Assyrians, won a decisive majority in each election, including that in December 2005, when there was a high turnout and no Sunni Arab boycott. In the October 2005 referendum, the governorate's electorate endorsed Iraq's Constitution by a clear majority, with 63 percent voting "yes" and 37 percent voting "no" on a 79 percent turnout. The Independent Electoral Commission and the United Nations Electoral Assistance Unit validated the results. In voting "yes," voters were endorsing a mandatory referendum under Article 140 in the new Constitution that would enable the governorate to join Kurdistan after "normalization." These three separate votes in 2005 confirm that pro-Kurdistan voters are the majority group in the governorate, even that redesigned by Saddam—and that they are the largest group in the city, which now has more people than the surrounding rural areas. The return of a significant number although not all of expelled

Kurds in 2003 and the flight of some Arab settlers after the U.S.-led military victory have partially overturned Saddam's work, especially because the electoral commission rightly gave expelled persons from Kirkuk the right to vote in their governorate of origin.

Kurdish parties have sought to reverse Saddam's ethnic engineering through "normalization." The expression means restoring the pre-1968 boundaries of Kirkuk province, facilitating the return of expelled people and their descendants (mostly Kurds and Turkomen), and encouraging Saddam's settlers to leave with financial compensation. "Normalization," in short, means that Saddam does not dictate the electoral register or Kirkuk's boundaries from his grave.

Western media almost invariably call the city of Kirkuk a "powder-keg," a "tinderbox," or a "flash-point." (Put these phrases together with "Kirkuk" into Google if you wish to check this claim.) They speculate that local Sunni Arabs, Shia Arabs, local Turkomen, and the Turkish Army will forcibly seek to prevent Kirkuk's unification with the Kurdistan Region, or they anticipate a four-way fight between Kurds, Sunni Arabs, Shia, Arabs, and Turkomen. (Usually the Assyrian Christians are ignored as potential militants—and rightly so, for their numbers are small.)[18] Journalists also often portray the politics of the city as simply Kurds versus the rest (Kurds for unification with the Kurdistan Region; the rest for the territorial status quo or for some special status for Kirkuk governorate).

There is certainly contention. The Kurds and Turkomen have valid historical claims to the peopling of Kirkuk city and governorate. They correctly claim they were oppressed in the recent past (although, under Saddam, Turkey did nothing for the Turkomen, who are ethnically distinct from the Turks of Turkey).[19] Article 5 of the 1992 (draft) Kurdistan Region's Constitution named Kirkuk as its capital, and Kurdish leaders have referred to the city as their "Jerusalem." Sadettin Ergeç, the leader of the Iraqi Turkomen Front, wants to make Kirkuk the Turkomen's capital and earn it special status. Many local Arabs have a strong long-running desire to keep Kirkuk outside the KRG.

The powder-keg metaphor suggests that ethnic, national, and religious antagonisms in Kirkuk are so high that the slightest move to resolve the territorial status of the governorate will trigger a bloodbath. This theory has to be taken seriously because it is extremely important to minimize further bloodshed. Clashes, riots, and interethnic antagonisms in Kirkuk's past, notably during the early days of the Iraqi Republic, support the theory. Saddam's policies have left poisonous residues and easy targets for unscrupulous demagogues. But care should be taken not to presume the worst, although it is sensible to take steps to prevent the worst.

A bad history in a bad neighborhood does not guarantee a bad future. Two questions decisively matter in deeply divided places. One is whether there can be a fair process to resolve major disagreements, one that provides cushions and assurances for the minority who feel they are losers. The second is whether there is effective control over security in the divided place. Without effective security it is easy for deep divisions to be trip-wired into intense intergroup violence by very small events. With effective security even deep animosities can be regulated, if not completely suppressed.

There are two fair processes available. One is to follow the Constitution's Article 140 and hold a referendum based on a normalized electoral register within the historical boundaries of Kirkuk province. A second would be to use the 2005 votes throughout the districts and subdistricts of what was the Kirkuk governorate to allocate them either to the Kurdistan Region or not. What matters for political stability is whether the likely losers from the referendum (or an allocation of districts and subdistricts of the kind described above) can be given sufficient assurances that they will be able to live decently and securely within the KRG.

Under Article 140 of Iraq's Constitution, the political status of the "governorate" (province) of Kirkuk, the city, and of other disputed territories was scheduled to be resolved by the end of December, 2007. According to Article 140:

> (1) The executive authority shall undertake the necessary steps to complete the implementation of the requirements of all subparagraphs of Article 58 of the Transitional Administrative Law.
>
> (2) The responsibility placed upon the executive branch of the Iraqi Transitional Government stipulated in Article 58 of the Transitional Administrative Law shall extend and continue to the executive authority elected in accordance with this Constitution, provided that it accomplishes completely (normalization and census and concludes with a referendum in Kirkuk and other disputed territories to determine the will of their citizens), by a date not to exceed the 31st of December 2007.[20]

Article 140 was necessary because the Coalition Provisional Authority and the Iraqi transitional government failed to perform their duties under Article 58 of the Transitional Administrative Law (TAL), let alone rectify the relevant injustices "expeditiously." Key provisions of Article 58 read as follows:

> (A) The Iraqi Transitional Government...and other relevant bodies, shall act expeditiously...to remedy the injustices caused by the previous regime's

practices in altering the demographic character of certain regions, including Kirkuk, by deporting and expelling individuals..., forcing migration in and out of the region, settling individuals alien to the region, depriving the inhabitants of work, and correcting nationality.[21] To remedy this injustice, the Iraqi Transitional Government shall take the following steps:

(1) With regard to residents who were deported, expelled, or who emigrated; it shall...within a reasonable period..., restore the residents to their homes and property, or, where this is unfeasible, shall provide just compensation.

(2) With regard to the individuals newly introduced to specific regions and territories, it shall...ensure that such individuals may be resettled, may receive compensation from the state, may receive new land from the state near their residence in the governorate from which they came, or may receive compensation for the cost of moving to such areas.

(3) With regard to persons deprived of employment or other means of support in order to force migration out of their regions and territories, it shall promote new employment opportunities in the regions and territories.

(4) With regard to nationality correction, it shall repeal all relevant decrees and shall permit affected persons the right to determine their own national identity and ethnic affiliation free from coercion and duress.

(B) The previous regime also manipulated and changed administrative boundaries....The Presidency Council...shall make recommendations to the National Assembly on remedying these unjust changes in the permanent constitution. In the event the Presidency Council is unable to agree unanimously on a set of recommendations, it shall unanimously appoint a neutral arbitrator to examine the issue and make recommendations. In the event the Presidency Council is unable to agree on an arbitrator, it shall request the Secretary General of the United Nations to appoint a distinguished international person to be the arbitrator.

(C) The permanent resolution of disputed territories, including Kirkuk, shall be deferred until after these measures are completed, a fair and transparent census has been conducted and the permanent constitution has been ratified. This resolution shall be consistent with the principle of justice, taking into account the will of the people of those territories.[22]

Article 140 plainly authorizes the federal executive (the Presidency Council, the prime minister, and the Council of Ministers) to fulfill its obligations without federal or regional legislation. Implementing the article was extended, by agreement, for six months, until the summer of 2008, and then again by agreement for another six months. The obligation to fulfill the article remains a constitutional imperative. A small number of Iraqis and Joost Hiltermann of the International Crisis Group maintain that the article is null and void because the timetable has slipped. (Usually, however, the very same people want other amendments to the Constitution to be made in which the relevant timetable is much further behind!) No responsible member of the High Committee of the federal government of Iraq charged with Article 140's implementation holds that the article is dead. They are conscious of what it means to the Kurdistan Regional Government. Without Article 140 Kurds would have voted down the Constitution. President Mas'ud Barzani has declared, "If any side thinks this article is dead, let it know that the death of Article 140 means the death of the Constitution."[23]

The views of the non-Kurds of Kirkuk governorate on unification with the KRG are mixed. Some are ardently opposed; others are anxious; others are persuadable. There are non-Kurds who are elected on the Kurdistan party lists. There are some intermarriages with Kurds, and some non-Kurds sensibly believe that their security and prosperity will be better within the KRG, the most stable part of Iraq. Most, when pressed, recognize that the Kurds have suffered injustices. The city's Assyrians, mostly Christians affiliated with the Catholic Church, usually privately believe they will be better off under the KRG, which has treated its Christian minorities well, despite what you may read on the web sites of the Assyrian diaspora in the United States.

In the highly segregated city, Arab districts are materially much better off to the naked eye. The Baathists manipulated planning regulations to prevent Kurds and Turkomen from maintaining their properties, which means that many are now beyond repair. Large parts of the city need to be rebuilt, which leads some to favor unification with Kurdistan, where the three major cities of Duhok, Erbil, and Sulaimania are thriving amid construction booms. In Kirkuk governorate council, the Kurdistan list, 26 out of 41 members, includes non-Kurds, and the Kurdistan parties have made efforts to reach a power-sharing accommodation with the non-Kurdistan lists but have repeatedly been rebuffed, leading many analysts to predict worse to come.

When I visited Kirkuk in 2004 and 2005, some Arab politicians told me that the Peshmerga were organizing the expulsion of Arabs. This contention was denied by Kurdish spokesmen and was not then supported by Assyrian and Turkomen politicians. I found no credible evidence, other than a rumor mill, which still continues. (That there have been some private expulsions or retaking of homes and flight seems possible, but they have not been authorized by the KRG or by Kurdish parties.) At interfaces in the segregated city, ugly episodes have occurred, and jihadists have carried out suicide attacks. Kirkuk is not about to be a city of brotherly love. Turkomen politicians privately conceded they were no longer the largest group in the city, although they invariably argued that Turkomen founded the city. The Sunni Turkomen Front, sponsored by the government of Turkey, fared dramatically less well in elections in 2005 than the Front itself, commentators, or the government of Turkey expected. The Turkomen

Shia have sought alliances with Shia Arab politicians and some reject the idea that they are a national diaspora of the Turks.

Calling Kirkuk city a powder keg is exaggerated if it implies that the slightest provocation will lead to protracted and deeply vicious violence of the kind that has occurred in other mixed Iraqi cities. Since 2003 the city has been comparatively quiet in relation to most commentators' expectations. This is because the Kurdistan security blanket now, most of the time, extends to much of governorate—after the United States reversed its initial and misjudged decision to ask the Peshmerga to withdraw, a policy apparently pursued out of deference to Ankara. Al-Qaeda in Iraq has been unable to provoke sustained national or sectarian violence in Kirkuk, though not for want of trying. Kurdistan's security blanket has prevented them from establishing effective bases—though they have had support in al-Hawija. The city has also been relatively quiet because most Kurds have patiently awaited justice rather than taking the law into their own hands. From a policing perspective, there are good reasons to believe that the Peshmerga would be able to manage the unification of Kirkuk governorate and the KRG with relative ease. What will matter in the long run therefore is whether the KRG can provide credible and sufficient assurances to the minorities in Kirkuk that will be joining the Kurdistan Region.

The existing Kurdistan Region is the safest place in Iraq. Internally displaced people have fled there from the Arab civil war. Not a single U.S. soldier has been killed there in combat. That is significant testament. The Kurdistan Region is now unified. It is spending its money on economic development and professional security, albeit with the usual complaints about corruption that are normal in developing countries. The two major parties of Kurdistan, the KDP and the PUK, have operated an effective deal in which the PUK leads for Kurdistan in Baghdad while the KDP leads within Kurdistan. Both the major parties know that after unification it is vital to have sustained power-sharing and proportional representation arrangements in Kirkuk city—and a representative police service. They have made good faith efforts with partial success in these directions. They have members from all minorities on their federal Iraqi lists. They know that proportional representation has worked well within the KRG to give the major and minor parties a stake in the political system. Therefore they will extend these arrangements to the new minorities. Within the existing Kurdistan Region, inclusive policies have operated for all nationalities, and ethnic, linguistic, and religious minorities—creating a tolerant climate very different from that of the rest of Iraq. KRG Prime Minister Nechirvan Barzani knows the KRG will be judged by how it treats all the nationalities and religious communities of

Kirkuk and is ready for the challenge—promising that Kurdistan's regional constitution will be exemplary in its protections for minorities.[24]

The unhappiness of the city at present flows from its unresolved status; neither the federal government nor the KRG (which has no legal standing yet) provides the city or the province with appropriate financial support. The Property Claims Commission must return properties or compensate those who lost out, although it is not necessary that its work be completed before the status of districts and subdistricts is resolved. Reports from Kirkuk suggest that thousands have signed up to relocate voluntarily.

National and international counsel and mediation should focus on protecting minorities after Kirkuk becomes part of the KRG. In the controversies that will doubtless occur after this book goes to print, bear this analysis in mind. Profound instability is more likely to arise from the failure to implement Article 140 in Kirkuk, to the letter or in spirit, than from its implementation. One source has suggested that KRG President "Mas'ud Barzani...has warned that 'if Article 140 is not implemented, then there will be a real civil war'."[25] Failure to implement the article will render both the KDP and the PUK vulnerable to their Kurdish nationalist critics and encourage Saddam's victims to take matters into their own hands. By contrast, with appropriate mediation, the minorities who will lose out can be assured of their security and equal citizenship through legal and institutional arrangements within the Kurdistan Region—or through individual compensation if they wish to leave the region. The unification of Kirkuk with the rest of Kurdistan can occur with much less international and domestic resistance than is predicted at present, especially if some appropriate precautions are taken by the KRG and its Shia allies in the federal government.

Proposals will shortly be made by a UN mediator, Staffan di Mistura, to assist the federal government of Iraq and the KRG in resolving Kirkuk and the other disputed territories. The proposals of the technical United Nations Assistance Mission in Iraq (UNAMI) will be advisory, not binding. If the federal government fails to fulfill its obligations or to follow recommendations made by UNAMI that have the support of the KRG, then it is possible that the Kurds in the KRG and governorate council of Kirkuk would organize a referendum to enable Kirkuk to integrate with Kurdistan.[26]

The KRG is prepared for a referendum in Kirkuk, according to the President of the Kurdistan National Assembly Kemal Kerkuki, and the KRG's Minister of Extra-Regional Affairs Mohammed Ihsan, who is also a member of Iraq's High Committee dealing with Article 140.[27] The KRG has the knowledge and data to organize a fair electoral register.

It would be for the best if the federal government acts appropriately and is appropriately advised by the UNAMI team. The latter's initial reports have focused on a small number of allegedly uncontroversial disputed territories but appear to be following no consistent principles and to be making recommendations beyond its assignment, which may not augur well for its legitimacy. But it is an illusion in which American policymakers have indulged Arab Iraqis and Turkomen to believe that infinite delay of these issues is possible. Kurds have political and security powers that they may use in the event of a manifest failure to fulfill the letter or the spirit of Article 140. Their leaders are under profound pressure from their public, especially those forcibly displaced from their homes by Saddam. They have waited with immense patience for five years precisely because their leaders have argued that the constitutional process will work.

UNAMI needs to exercise great care. Some of its officials are quoted as saying that everyone should agree on a settlement. That is impossibly pious. UNAMI has no authority to give veto powers that are not in Iraq's Constitution to Turkomen, Arabs, or any other group. By contrast, there is every reason to assist a generous postunification settlement and to encourage negotiations on the terms of a postunification settlement—including rights of opting out for Arab majority or Turkomen majority subdistricts at the perimeters of the new KRG border.

A well-managed unification will extend the zone of peace and stability within Iraq, provided the KRG lives up to its promises to its prospective new influx of minorities. A fourth large urban center will add to the region's infrastructural construction boom and increase its proportionate entitlement to Iraq's shared oil revenues. The Kurds will only have themselves to blame if they mishandle the minorities of Kirkuk within an expanded KRG.

Knowing that change is going to come will break the solidarity of those opposed. The minorities of Kirkuk governorate are already divided. The Sunni Arabs of Kirkuk cannot hope to govern the city or to bring Kirkuk into a Sunni Arab region. The same is true of Shia Arabs. The Arab vote in the future will be split both along sectarian lines and among numerous parties. Many Shia Arabs are taking the compensation funding on offer and leaving—amid much local rumor and gossip about corruption. The Turkomen, divided as they are between Sunni and Shia, no longer the second largest ethnicity in the governorate, constitute a small minority in Iraq. Only the foolhardy among them aspire to being delivered by a Turkish conquest, while their relatives know that no better event could be designed to endanger their lives. The Kurds are reaching out to local Sunni Arabs and to Arabs in general. The elected Arabs have recently gone back onto the governorate council in an accommodationist deal. They agreed to end their boycott in return for a power-sharing compromise: the post of deputy governor, and an agreement to split civil posts equally: 32 percent to each of the three major groups, with 4 percent reserved for the other minorities—although Turkomen continue to boycott the council. It is therefore possible to see the outlines of a local power-sharing settlement with numerous nationalities who are not cohesively opposed to the KRG's territorial ambitions. Their leaders should be internationally as well as domestically encouraged to bargain now for appropriate guarantees and rights within the Kurdistan Region.

The peaceful accession—not the annexation—of Kirkuk to the Kurdistan Region is a constitutional and democratic imperative, and it need not precipitate a new major round of bloodshed or generate new injustices. What is required, within Kurdistan and Iraq and internationally, is determined planning to make the referendum or territorial allocation process fair, accompanied by credible commitments by the KRG to protect the minority nationalities. The city might have a power-sharing governmental form entrenched in Kurdistan's regional constitution. The city may be made trilingual or quadralingual. It could be the established site of the KRG's highest court *and* the established site of Iraq's future supreme court.

In August 2008, President Mas'ud Barzani of the KRG toured the city and declared "I have come to send a message of peace to Kirkuk which is both a city of Kurdistan and of Iraq."[28] The ideas promoted here, with international support and American government encouragement, would create meaningful versions of special status for Kirkuk—within the KRG and within Iraq, and fit President Barzani's portrait of the dual status of the city. None of this is beyond the wit of the region's leaders. The KRG is working to make Iraq's Constitution work, not to have the region secede. Helping it achieve its constitutional rights on the Kirkuk question will stabilize the region. Blocking Kurds' constitutional rights will return Iraq to the world before the Baathists, in which Baghdad governments fought Kurdish rebels only to make promises to them which they would later betray when they recovered their strength. A return to that cycle is best avoided.

The Other Disputed Territories

Most maps used in the European and American media usually fail to draw the March 19, 2003, internal border of the existing KRG accurately. They often fail to indicate that parts of Ninevah, Kirkuk, and Diyala governorates are already within the KRG's jurisdiction, and that, at least nominally, not all of Dohuk and Sulaimania governorates are within the existing KRG. These are practical reasons why the status of the disputed territories needs to be resolved. The boundaries of the KRG and the existing governorates do not coincide. The maps presented in Western media reports usually fail to specify that the March 19, 2003, internal border of the KRG was established unilaterally by Saddam, not by the KRG. It does not follow the lines of the 1970 Autonomy Agreement between the Iraqi Government and the KDP—when Mulla Mustafa Barzani negotiated on behalf of Kurdistan. The existing boundary is the result of a maneuver by Saddam; it is neither the product of local wishes nor of democratic and constitutional negotiations.

Almost all of the affected areas in Map 7 have Kurdish majorities or supermajorities—and where they do not some of the dilution of Kurdish

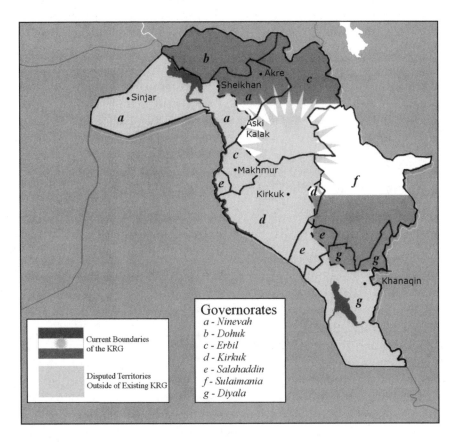

Map 7. The disputed territories in the north.

demographic strength is the outcome of recent movements of internally displaced people. No sensible person contests the presence of strong Kurdish majorities in places such as Akre, Sheikhan, Zimmar, Sinjar, Makhmur, Aski Khalak, or Knanaquin. Almost all of these areas either have strong links to the major Kurdish parties or have benefited from emergency support from the KRG, but plainly all the affected citizens would benefit from the regularization of their relationship to the KRG.

There are reasonable principles that might guide others, including UNAMI, in facilitating the resolution of the territories in dispute between the KRG and the rest of Iraq. First, the Kurdish majority governorates of Dohuk, Sulaimania, and Erbil should be wholly incorporated within the KRG (modified where necessary to their pre-Baathist boundaries). Second, *all of Kirkuk governorate* should be subject to normalization based on the 1968 boundary—that is, the districts or subdistricts of Chamchamal, Kifri, Kalar, and Tozkhurnato should return to Kirkuk governorate. Third, consideration should be given to the right of districts or subdistricts to opt out of the KRG after the referendum (or on the basis of an agreement between local parties based on 2005 election results). There is no Kurdish resistance to the idea that al-Hawija or al-Zab should be allowed to leave Kirkuk governorate. Fourth, the allocation of the districts of Akre, Sheikhan, Sinjar, Tel Afar, and Qarquosh should be informed by UN evaluation of local preferences. Where there are significant doubts about local preferences, there can be a local plebiscite. These districts or subdistricts should be covered under the provisions for the relevant minority rights in the KRG constitution. It is very likely that Tal-Afar will want to opt out of the KRG, and the KRG will let that happen. The same policies should apply to the districts or subdistricts of Zammar, Bashiqua, Aski Kalak, Khanaqin, and Mandali. Last, if the KRG pursues the claims made by some Kurds on Badra and the subdistrict of Jassan, which seems doubtful, then they should be subject to a principle of democratic reciprocity. If there are to be votes to determine territorial status here, then Kurds should, in return, accept those who vote to opt out of districts or subdistricts of Kirkuk governorate that are adjacent to the rest of Iraq.

UNAMI and others should avoid obvious or tempting mistakes. One would be to propose a pacing recommendation, going for the allocation of easy districts first, leaving more difficult cases to later dates, especially if such proposals amount to accepting the gerrymandered status of Kirkuk. The pre-1968 boundaries of Kirkuk have to be restored to what they were before the Baath came to power. The KRG will accept a Kirkuk that excludes al-Hawija and al-Zab, but that has to be negotiated. It is far better to resolve uncertainty by creating a clear road map on all the disputed territories so that all can know their likely future status. Abiding by the principle of "normalization," the return to pre-Baathist boundaries, and letting the restored Kirkuk become part of the KRG are the major priorities.

If the resolution of the disputed territories outside of Kirkuk as well as of Kirkuk itself are sensitively handled, there will be a significant expansion of the territory of the KRG but not such a significant rise in its population, because many of the wide expanses of territory are sparsely populated. What would be the consequences? It may give added impetus to those inclined to form regions elsewhere in Iraq. Most importantly, it will resolve the decades old Kurdish-Arab national question in Iraq by demarcating the borders of the Kurdistan Region in a manner commensurate with local democratic preferences and historical and geographical realities. That will make the KRG a satisfied party within Iraq. The federation will work better because its obligations toward the KRG will have been met. The KRG will then be able to work as a full partner with Arab-dominated Iraq, either in an asymmetrical federation in which it is treated as a special federacy or as one large region amid other larger regions. These are not fantasies.

What is fantastic is to imagine that one can stabilize Iraq by postponing the resolution of the status of Kirkuk and the disputed territories. Deepening tension flows from the failure of Iraq's federal government to fulfill its constitutional obligations. Protracted delays are making Kurds suspicious that they will be cheated of the opportunity to rectify Saddam's injustices. Justice delayed is justice denied. If the federal government fails to deliver or to follow recommendations made by the United Nations supported by the KRG, many Kurds will regard the Constitution as worthless. The next U.S. administration can help avoid that prospect. Defending Iraq's territorial integrity and Iraq's Constitution are integrally linked. If the constitutional provisions on Kirkuk and the disputed territories are not followed to the letter or in spirit, then the Constitution will have been violated and the secession of Kurdistan will become far more likely, with all the attendant risks to regional stability that might pose. A wise U.S. administration therefore stands to gain from fully supporting Iraq's Constitution.

Chapter 8
Informing, Calming, and Working with the Neighbors

> Let us never negotiate out of fear. But let us never fear to negotiate.
> —John F. Kennedy, Inaugural Address, January 20, 1961

In 1948, Arshak Safrastian, an Armenian scholar, wrote an accessible short guide to *Kurds and Kurdistan*. He observed in his first footnote to his discussion of the term *Kurd*: "As to the general attitude of the two neighboring Empires of Turkey and Persia towards the Kurdish race, no better illustration could be found than a play of words on the very racial name, Kurd. By a strange coincidence the word '*Koort*' means 'wolf' in both Turkish and the new Iranian languages; the learned etymologists of the two Empires have not failed to discover an original identity between their word '*Koort*' and the generic name 'Kurd.' The hypothesis is entirely false. Yet this faked etymology sums up a political theory which is in no way out of tune with the actual practice as understood, and periodically put into effect, by Turkey."[1]

Today's Kurds are not above repaying these compliments. They often refer to "the four dogs," or indeed "four wolves," that bully the Kurds, namely, Turkey, Iran, Syria, and Arab Iraq. Of these, the Kurds of Iraq express the greatest fear of the Turks, although they also worry about Iran. The Kurdish stereotype of the Turk is that of a blunt but predictable bully; the Kurdish stereotype of the Iranian is that of a cunning manipulator. But the Kurds are not alone among Iraqis in fearing their geographic neighbors. Sunni Arabs fear—and often detest Persians. (Khairallah Tulfah, Saddam's uncle, foster-father, and father-in-law, infamously published a booklet with the title *Three Things God Should Not Have Made—Persians, Jews and Flies.*[2]) The Shia

Arabs of Iraq know that the Arab states to their west, with the intermittent exception of Syria, backed the Baathist regime because it kept the lid on the Shia, and they also know that Syrian, Jordanian, and Saudi governments have scarcely stirred themselves to stop Sunni jihadists from reaching Iraq. Each major set of Iraqis therefore has reasons—rational and emotional— to be profoundly nervous toward at least one of Iraq's neighboring states. Their rational fears aggravate the extreme xenophobia that Arab Iraqis (and Kurds to a much lesser degree) have been found to display in public surveys (see Appendix 2).

The last part of the case for organizing a withdrawal from Iraq with integrity can now be advanced. Iraq's constitutional and territorial integrity, I have suggested, should be supported as long as that is what a majority of Iraqis want. But any such policy must be accompanied by a coherent and effective U.S. foreign policy in Iraq's immediate vicinity. Iraq's neighbors need to be given every reasonable incentive not to destroy the positive institutions that have emerged from the horrors of the last five years. Such a foreign policy is feasible. Although some of the ideas advanced here will be shocking to some, they should be less surprising than some of the adventurism in U.S. foreign policy of recent years.

Turkey's New Neighbor, Kurdistan

Since the U.S. intervention in March 2003, commentators have warned of the possibility of a Turkish invasion of northern Iraq,[3] especially to prevent Kirkuk's accession to the KRG.[4] Some exploit this fear. They argue that Turkey can only be prevented from invading if the United States squeezes the KRG into indefinitely postponing its ambitions to unify with Kirkuk. That was the counsel of the Baker-Hamilton Report.

Regrettably, there is some evidence for the thesis of "the terrible Turk." In 2003, Turkish special operatives were caught by American troops on their way to assassinate the Kurdish governor of Kirkuk. Their arrests caused outrage in Turkey, but the Turkish public that is not Kurdish did not seem much interested in reflecting on the murderous mission of the Special Forces. Since the 1990s the Turkish Army has occupied Iraqi land, with a military base, in the Kurdistan Region, near the Turkey-Iraq border. It is, of course, not the sole foreign government to have occupied Iraq or to have established bases. But in the Turkish case it was Saddam who encouraged the intruders when he was not especially concerned about preserving his sovereign prerogatives in Kurdistan. During the Iran-Iraq war (1980–88), when Saddam had lost control of Kurdistan, he gave permission to Turkey, on four occasions, to engage in hot pursuit of the Kurdish Marxists of the PKK, whose recruits almost invariably come from Turkey. In "Operation Steel," in the spring of 1995, some 35,000 Turkish troops were deployed in Iraq against the PKK.

In May of that year President Süleyman Demirel of Turkey, in interviews with Turkish journalists, suggested that he wanted to revise his country's border with Iraq. He explained why he thought it was wrong that Great Britain had prevailed at the League of Nations during 1926, when it successfully incorporated the former Ottoman *vilayat* (province) of Mosul into Iraq over Turkish objections. The *vilayat* of Mosul included the present-day KRG, Kirkuk, and the Arab-dominated sections of northwestern Iraq.[5] Demirel retracted his remarks in the same month, but they have not been forgotten in Iraq. A fear of Turkish irredentism persists because few Arabs or Kurds have any nostalgia for the Ottoman Empire (which they now recall as a Turkish tyranny even if some of their great-grandparents thought differently).

In 2002, U.S. National Security Advisor Condoleezza Rice thought it would be helpful to have the Turkish army join the U.S.-led intervention in Iraq because the Turkish Army would be composed of Muslim soldiers. She apparently did not know that the Arab revolt in World War 1 showed that some Muslims had opposed Ottoman rule; or she did not know that the doctrines of Kemal Atatürk, calcified as "Kemalism," had made Turkish and Kurdish nationalists into implacable enemies since the 1920s.[6] If Rice's counsel had been tested, another war would have been added to those triggered by the March 2003 intervention—one between Turkey and the Kurds of Iraq. No one, fortunately, offers this counsel any longer. The current government of Turkey has, however, authorized limited military incursions into the Kurdistan Region, with the approval of the Ankara parliament, to pursue pockets of the PKK in inaccessible locations in the KRG, including the Kandil mountains. The Bush administration facilitated the Turkish military efforts with intelligence during the winter of 2007–8, enabling their air and ground forces to know the locations of PKK encampments, even though the U.S. government is supposed to be responsible for protecting Iraq's sovereign air space.

We should, however, be hardheaded in appraising "the terrible Turk thesis." Turkey has strategic interests in its relations with Iraq. First, it wishes to protect the territorial integrity of the existing Turkish state, its famous "rectangle."[7] That is why it is determined to crush the PKK. That is also why it has failed formally to recognize the Kurdistan Region—either during its period of isolation from the rest of Iraq (between 1992 and 2003) or since. Turkish nationalist leaders fear that an independent Kurdish state, although built in former Iraqi territory, will inevitably ignite or reignite secessionist sentiment among the Kurds of Turkey. That is also why they fear Kurdish control of the oil of Kirkuk (which Turkish ultranationalists describe as the oil of the lost province of Mosul). Turkey has shown intermittent interest in the fate of the Turkomen minority in northern Iraq, concentrated in Kirkuk province. This, however, is not a deep pan-nationalist commitment. When Iraq's Baathists were repressing Turkomen, and when Turkomen were emigrating to Turkey in the 1970s and 1980s, Ankara was effectively silent. It is only when Kurds seem likely to unify with Kirkuk that Turkish politicians play the Turkomen card with obvious and ruthless cynicism—including ludicrous estimates of the size of the Turkomen population. Ankara used to claim the Turkomen numbered 3 million of Iraq's denizens, when they compose, at most, 300,000, of whom only one-half are Sunni Turkomen empathetic to Turkey.

Turkey's strategic interests led its political elite to express strong views on Iraq's internal affairs during the making of the Transitional Administrative Law in 2004. Those views were at the top of Turkey's agenda during a January 2004 visit of Turkish leaders to Washington, on the eve of which Turkish Prime Minister Recep Tayyip Erdogan warned the Kurds not to play with fire and threatened that Syria, Iran, and Turkey had agreed to intervene if a breakup of Iraq looked imminent. Turkish General Ilker Basbug warned that an ethnically-based Iraqi federation would be "difficult and bloody."[8] Former U.S. Secretary of State Henry Kissinger speculated, "If Kurdish autonomy goes beyond a certain point, there is a not negligible threat of a Turkish military intervention, perhaps backed by Iran."[9] He did not, however, specify the point at which that would occur.

These are the fears and the threats. They remain on the table. Can they be managed, or must they simply be appeased? And are there any sound grounds for thinking that the threats are exaggerated? Turkey is neither united nor the sole player with any leverage in these matters. Some of Turkey's elites want to join the European Union. Others do not. Turkey's Islamists seek alliances with Kurds. The democratic Islamists, less preoccupied with Turkey's national ethos than the Kemalists, try to appeal to Kurds as Muslims. With up to one-fifth of Turkey's electorate being of Kurdish origin, huge voting dividends are at stake. Turkey's Kemalists cannot appeal so easily to Kurds, at least not without revising Kemalist doctrine and recognizing Kurds as a nation within a nation.

Turkey's management of its relations with the Kurdistan Region of Iraq, as well as with its domestic Kurds, is already being used by members of the

European Parliament to assess Turkey's standing as a peaceful democracy that respects human rights, and in which civilians have control over the military.[10] Since the European Parliament has co-decision-making rights on EU membership applications, its power in this respect is not trivial. Any invasion of Iraq to block the outcome of a referendum (or any other fair process) to determine internal boundaries within a neighboring state will terminate Turkey's prospects of joining the European Union. A future U.S. administration should make clear to the government of Turkey that any such violation of Iraq's Constitution would lead to Turkey's expulsion from NATO. It would violate NATO's emergent status as an alliance of democracies. In the eventuality of a Turkish occupation of Kirkuk, some European member states will put it to the United States that the NATO alliance can include the Canadian and European democracies, or Turkey, but not all together. Post-Communist East Europeans now number over a third of EU member states, and most are NATO members. The southeastern Europeans have no nostalgic recollections of the Ottomans and monitor Turkey's development closely. One can invade and occupy other people's countries when one is a member state of the European Union, but candidate members have no such privileges! This international military and alliance leverage can and should check Turkish adventurism with respect to Kirkuk, provided it is exercised with reasonable decorum and addresses reasonable Turkish concerns (which I shall treat shortly).

Other strategic considerations may cause a rational Turkish government or military to stand back from the risks of an invasion and occupation. No one should doubt President Barzani's determination to protect the Kurdistan Region militarily. A Turkish invasion of Kirkuk would add no less than 100,000 combat-trained KRG Peshmerga to those prepared to fight the Turkish military through guerrilla warfare in Turkey. The KRG would withdraw all Peshmerga currently on loan to the Iraqi federal government and the U.S. military and deploy them in defense of Kurdistan. President Barzani has already signaled that he can cause as much trouble for the Turkish government in Diyarbakir as the Turkish Government can cause the KRG in Kirkuk. In short, Turkey's threat capacity is not as overwhelming as it is often portrayed, and no U.S. administration should feel obliged to succumb to Turkish blackmail on Kirkuk. The correct response of any U.S. administration is that the resolution of Iraq's internal provincial and regional boundaries is a matter for Iraqis to resolve under their Constitution.

A Turkish invasion and occupation of Kirkuk would utterly destabilize Turkey's current democratic and economic prospects. To undertake an invasion over Kirkuk, the military would probably have to topple Turkey's elected government—and that would ensure Ankara's isolation from both the European Union and the United States. If the governing party supported an invasion to avoid being deposed by the military or in return for concessions on some other policy questions, it would face the problem that it would no longer win Kurdish votes in southeastern Turkey. Any protracted military intervention would produce volcanic Kurdish eruptions within Turkey and send Turkey's stockmarket plunging. It would smash Ankara's relations with Washington and Brussels and leave a much worse mess than its leaders helped to create in Cyprus. Why would they take such risks?

A full Turkish invasion makes geostrategic sense only if the Turkish political elite are utterly convinced that the Kurds are intent on using the Kirkuk oil field to finance the formation of an independent state, *and* if they believe that the formation of such a state would be an existential threat to their own state. The first belief is false. The next U.S. administration, which will have a fresh start with Turkey, may be able to communicate the falsity of that belief with better conviction. The falsity of the first belief makes the second totally misplaced—and many Turks recognize this. Arguably what Turkey needs most is another secular democratic entity on its borders, interdependent with it in trade and foreign investment and ensuring the passage of oil supplies. These elementary considerations need to be spelled out by the United States, in cooperation with the European Union, to Turkish diplomats, politicians, and generals—and to the Turkish public. The next U.S. administration should also offer assurances, perhaps in a multilateral treaty, to respect the existing border between Iraq and Turkey. Such a treaty would calm Turkey's anxieties, admittedly misplaced, about a Greater Kurdistan originating in Erbil, and, conversely, calm fears within Iraq that Turkey still harbors irredentist ambitions toward the old *vilayat* of Mosul.

A U.S. administration determined to withdraw from Iraq with integrity should ensure that the government of Turkey shows scrupulous respect for Iraq's Constitution. That will only be persuasive, of course, if the United States is showing similar respect. The Iraqi Constitution confines the status of Kurdistan to that of a regional government; it is not an independent state. The Constitution locks in a reasonable deal over the revenues from Kirkuk's oil fields, which should benefit the local Turkomen and provide a boost to the economy of southeastern Turkey. It is appropriate for the government of Turkey to express reasonable concerns for the Turkomen. Ankara's diplomatic attention should be focused on human and minority rights for the Turkomen within the KRG. But then Ankara must expect to be asked to grant reciprocity by permitting foreign governments to express concern for the human and minority rights of Kurds, Armenians, Alevis, and Christians in Turkey. Turkish governments cannot credibly insist on federal rights for Turkish Cypriots but deny the rights of the Kurds of Iraq to a similar form of self-government.

These issues do not need to be discussed solely in the brutal language of leverage or military capacities. The threats from allegedly "terrible Turks" should not be exaggerated, and it should be acknowledged that Turkey is showing significant signs of welcome organic change. Turkey's Constitution of 1980 entrenched the military and a secular Kemalist judicial elite as its guardians. The Constitution banned both religious and ethnic parties and absolutely forbids proposing amendments to some of its key provisions—including, for example, proposals that might threaten Turkey's indivisibility, such as autonomy or federalism. This 1980 Constitution is, however, palpably collapsing. The military's special status, embodied in a national security council that entrenched what the Turks call "the deep State," has been modified, and it will have to be modified further if Turkey wants to become an EU member state. Turkish President Turgut Ozal, before his premature death, opened the Kurdish question up in the 1990s in ways that the guardians of the latest Kemalist Constitution have found very difficult to close down. Ozal was also a party to what became the Kurdish safe haven and to enabling British and American aircraft to enforce the no-fly zone over Saddam's Iraq.

The Turkish government has, on paper, started to lighten its repression of Kurdish culture. It has legalized the Kurdish language, Kurdish publications, and Kurdish broadcasting, but much remains to be done to make these rights meaningful. On all my trips across the border from Turkey to the Kurdistan Region between 2002 and 2005, any publications with the words "Kurd," "Kurdish," or "Kurdistan" printed on them were summarily confiscated by military personnel at checkpoints. Having been warned of this practice, I used to send copies of all these materials electronically to my own e-mail address before my encounters with Turkish officials at the Habur (Turkish) border post that faces the Ibrahim Khalil (Kurdish) border post.

The Justice and Development Party, known by its Turkish abbreviation as the AKP, decisively won the last two general elections in Turkey.[11] It is a socially conservative but economically liberal party that has to be shy about its soft Islamism because of the 1980 Constitution. It is precisely the type of Islamic party that European and American governments should want to see coming to power in Muslim-majority countries because it is committed both to democracy and a modernizing version of Islam.[12] Turkey's Kemalists have so far seen the AKP as bent on undermining the state's secularism by stealth, but they face a problem since Turkey's European Union application and the AKP's electoral strategy both point toward full Kurdish emancipation.

The AKP wins significant votes from socially conservative Kurds in Turkey precisely because its Islamist agenda is compatible with recognizing Kurdish ethnicity.[13] The AKP has, however, been utterly reluctant so far to allow teaching in Kurdish in schools or to permit the establishment of Kurdology in universities—partly because it fears that the Kemalist military would treat that as an attack on the ethos of the Constitution. The AKP, which won just over one in eight of its seats in the Kurdish-dominated southeast in the July 2007 parliamentary elections, believes it can undermine Kurdish nationalism through economic development or through withholding investment from areas that support the PKK. Kurdish nationalists, by contrast, vote for independents and other parties, including ones that stand as disguised fronts for the PKK. Kurdish politicians and parties cannot openly identify themselves as having an ethnic rights agenda. When they do so, or in some cases before they do so, the courts ban them. Banning peaceful and democratic religious and ethnic parties would be impermissible if Turkey were to become an EU member state. Turkey is serious about its European destiny. It has to be for multiple reasons, both geopolitical and economic. Its historic rivalries with Russia and its inability to lead the Turkic peoples of central Asia point its elites toward deepening rather than ending their alliances with the European Union and NATO. But if it is to become an EU member state, it will have to register that Belgium, Spain, and the United Kingdom function with multiple democratic nationalist and secessionist parties and that continental European democracies usually have a religious party (of Christian Democrats) in office more often than they do not.[14] Some Turks have spoken for some time of the Kurdish "reality," and some of them actually want to be realistic about accommodating that reality on Kurdish as well as Turkish terms.

Kurdish nationalism in Turkey will not be stopped by economic development or by any fearsome repression that falls short of genocide. Nationalism is not susceptible to any known or straightforward economic explanation.[15] Neither will an inclusive form of Sunni Islam, whether promoted by the AKP or any other agency, ever permanently smother Kurdish nationalism in Turkey. But Kurdish nationalism can be democratically accommodated without Turkey's breakup, provided that its constitutional order is restructured. Unless Turkey's political class makes determined efforts to accommodate democratic Kurdish nationalism—minimally through broad-ranging cultural rights and meaningful decentralization—it will be intermittently faced with violent Kurdish nationalism, as it has been since the 1920s, and it will also face the possibility that some Kurdish nationalists will morph into jihadists. The coming crisis of the Turkish state therefore points toward deepening democratization and EU membership as the best means of resolving Turkey's Kurdish and Islamic questions.

The Turkish parliament avoided participation in the U.S.-led removal of Saddam in 2003 for wise though contingent reasons. For similar reasons, it may avoid an invasion and occupation of Kirkuk, but it will need to be steered into that position by orchestrated and co-coordinated U.S. and EU diplomacy in the course of the U.S. withdrawal from Iraq. Changes in the territorial status of Kirkuk should be supported provided that they are fair, and the United States should advocate that fair commitments should be made in Kurdistan's regional constitution to the Turkomen—more generous ones than Turkey has so far made toward its own Kurds. The Kurds of Iraq would likely comply with any such request.

Turkey has legitimate fears about the PKK, which need to be treated seriously by both the United States and the KRG. Originally a Marxist-Leninist party, the PKK became a deeply violent Stalinist cult under its leader, Abdullah Ocalan ("Apo"), who looks like a made-over version of the Georgian tyrant who ran the Soviet Union. The PKK fought from 1984 until 1999 to create a Greater Kurdistan. Its war led to the loss of over 30,000 lives, mostly Kurds, and was estimated to have cost the Turkish government $10 billion per year at its peak.

The PKK's central committee meetings were held in Turkish because that was the language in which its leaders had been (coercively) educated. Its heavily Turkish provenance was one reason the PKK had little resonance among Kurds who were not from Turkey. The exceptions to this pattern were some Kurds from Syria, encouraged by the Damascus government. Syria was a Soviet ally and had territorial and water disputes with Turkey and therefore provided a base for the PKK. Damascus was happy to allow its Kurds to cause problems for Syria's regional rivals provided they raised no serious difficulties with their "home" regime. Until 1999, the PKK's operations were directed by Ocalan from a safe base in Syria. But the end of the Cold War weakened the Syrian government, which had been heavily dependent on the Soviet Union. Turkey eventually assembled an army on its border with Syria and gave Damascus an ultimatum. Ocalan's Damascus sponsors backed down. He left the country, and after a meandering trip across places unwilling to grant him asylum, he was eventually kidnapped in Kenya—allegedly with the aid of the CIA. Under arrest and trial, the PKK's leader soon proved much less hard line when it came to the subject of his own life—and his demoralized and subservient party ordered a cease-fire.

The PKK had initially won extensive support among the poor downtrodden Kurds of southeastern Turkey. But its authoritarian nature, its killings of Kurdish civilians—including teachers who taught in Turkish, as they were legally compelled to do—and its ruthless disposition toward all other autonomous Kurdish organizations rapidly dissipated the popularity it had won for challenging the Turkish state.[16] Mas'ud Barzani ended KDP cooperation with the PKK in the 1980s because it had "earned the hatred and disgust of all the Kurdish people"—which was true of most Kurds both inside and outside Iraq, including a high proportion of the Kurds of Turkey. The KDP would go on to cooperate with Turkish governments against the PKK in the 1990s.

The PKK's extremism was in one sense a scream of rage at the Kemalist program of "nation-building"—that is, Turkey's literal nationalizion of its populations into a single ethos, ethnos, and language. Turkey has had no patience for dual or multiple identities, and its governments mandated not just the definitional but also the cultural and even physical destruction of other nations within its borders. Late Ottoman, Young Turk, and Turkish regimes assaulted, expelled, exterminated, or coercively assimilated Armenians, Greeks, and Kurds. On one careful estimate 1,883,000 were murdered in genocidal or ethnic purges by twentieth-century Turkish regimes.[17] The Armenians and the Greeks of Turkey now have nation-states and have settled some scores with their former masters, but the survivors of "Ottoman hospitality" live outside their ancient homelands of Asia Minor and Eastern Anatolia. The Kurds of Turkey have not been so lucky. The revolts led by Sheikh Sai'd in 1925, the Koybun insurrection of 1929–30, and the Dersim rebellion of 1937–38 were all crushed.[18] The Turkish army "found control of Kurdistan to be its prime function and raison d'être. Only one out of 18 Turkish military engagements during the years 1924–38 occurred outside Kurdistan. After 1945, apart from the Korean War, 1949–52, and the invasion of Cyprus, 1974," all Turkish army operations have been against the Kurds[19]—until the NATO operation in Afghanistan. The Turkish military has done nothing more frequently since the Republic was founded than repress Kurdish rebellions. The PKK insurrection was put down through the destruction of thousands of Kurdish villages—draining the guerrilla's sea—and the successful countermobilization of village guards, recruited among Kurds opposed to the PKK. After its leader's arrest in 1999, the PKK's campaign seemed to be effectively over.

Under the implacable pressures of Kemalism, some Kurds in Turkey assimilated, and some have tried to forget their Kurdish roots. Educated Kurds speak and write Turkish in public; for them, Kurdish has become a language of the home.[20] In his trial, the PKK leader Ocalan defended himself—if that is what he did—in Turkish, not Kurdish. Sustained, concerted pressures on the Kurdish identity in schools, workplaces, and public media, the pulverization of Kurdish villages, and the deliberate dilution of areas of Kurdish concentration have been devastating. The Kurds of Turkey are now less culturally Kurdish than they once were. They are also now much more dispersed; Kurds are said to constitute 3 million of Istanbul's residents. They migrate within Turkey to the west, to its European shore, and from Turkey to Europe, where they sometimes blend, especially in Germany, into the Turkish community.

With the PKK's leader imprisoned,[21] and the PKK having renounced its ambitions to achieve independence or even federal status for the Kurdish-majority zones of Turkey, and with the PKK's military prowess no longer what it was, why is there a PKK question at all? Largely because the government of Turkey has refused to provide an amnesty to the surviving guerilla bands—and fighting for an amnesty seems the only way to understand the PKK's current behavior. Cynics suggest the Turkish military has used the PKK as a pawn in its campaign against the AKP government. In support of this thesis are multiple episodes in which Turkish special forces operatives have been caught carrying out bombings or killings that were intended to be blamed on the PKK.[22] But the PKK is not just a figment of Turkish paranoia, or a bogey constructed by recalcitrant members of the Deep State. It still exists; it has some encampments (rather than bases) in militarily inaccessible mountain ranges within the KRG; and it has been able to kill or capture both Turkish soldiers and village guards. I have been to the lower slopes of many of the mountains within the KRG. No one needs to be a general to see why they form a perfect guerrilla habitat. They are inhospitable in winter and have the kind of topography and microclimates that render fairly useless the helicopters used in high-tech counterinsurgency.

It is entirely appropriate for the United States to mediate between the government of Turkey and the KRG on the subject of the PKK. The former needs to be encouraged to recognize the KRG's security powers under Iraq's Constitution; the latter needs to show greater willingness to do what is necessary to prevent the PKK from using KRG soil to launch attacks on Turkey. It is true that the PKK question, as the KRG insists, should be handled politically; and that amnesties for the PKK rank and file will achieve the organization's dissolution. The KRG can help with the demobilization, and with the cooperation of the Baghdad government, provide asylum status for those PKK leaders willing to abandon violence. Having made peaceful overtures to the PKK on its soil, the KRG should not hesitate to engage in tougher action if necessary—the PKK did not hesitate to attack the KDP when the latter was suffering brutally at the hands of Saddam, so there is no debt of gratitude owed. The public of the Kurdistan Region does not want to assist Turkey or any other neighboring power in the repression of Kurdish guerillas, but in this case the PKK's activists are deliberately jeopardizing the safety of the KRG.

The Kurds of Iraq will put their own security first, knowing that most of the Kurds of Turkey will consider that a sane choice. Iraq's Kurds should use their influence in favor of those Kurdish politicians and movements prepared to work for peaceful and democratic change in Turkey while arguing for political and amnesty measures to tackle the PKK's surviving activity. Kurdish voters and their potential politicians in Turkey now shift between seeking cultural rights, working with soft pan-Islamists who recognize them as fellow Muslims and as Kurds, and hoping that Turkey's possible entry into the European Union will bring relief. Having been disorganized, repressed, and partially assimilated, they are hopeful that a democratic and Europeanizing Turkey may eventually become a proper home for them. They hope to bring the border of the European Union to Kurdistan. That is a worthy project. U.S. diplomacy should assist it, sensitively—Europeans do not take kindly to suggestions from Washington as to who should be members of their Union, and jihadism in Europe has aggravated those European publics wary of opening their confederation to Turkey.[23] The Turkish-KRG border, which could one day mark the border of the European Union, is at present the site of extensive trade and investment flows. The KRG has welcomed Turkish business to develop its airports, roads, and cities. Settling the PKK question will enable that border to have multiple access points and to become a series of civilian bridges rather than military lines.

Iran: The Case for Détente Rather Than Cyanide

Détente is a diplomat's word. The French noun describes the relaxation of strained relations between states. Since the 1979 revolution that toppled the Shah of Iran and brought the Ayatollah Khomeini to power, détente has not been a prominent feature of American-Iranian relations. Indeed, since 1979 Americans have tended to demonize Iran and Iranians even if they did not all concur with President Bush's thesis of an "axis of evil" linking Iran's ayatollahs, Iraq's Saddam Hussein, and North Korea's hereditary Communist despotism. Among the most prominent episodes that explain American public hostility toward Iran's government are, first, its indulgence and then exploitation of the Islamist revolutionary students who held diplomats and other Americans hostage at the U.S. Embassy in Tehran for 444 days between November 1979 and April 1981. The hostages were maltreated,[24] and the Carter administration was humiliated. Second, Americans are correctly taught that Iranian governments have sponsored organizations that have used terrorist methods—including Hezballah in Lebanon and Hamas in Palestine. This sponsorship led directly to the killing of U.S. Marines in Beirut in 1983 and other fatal attacks on Americans and on America's allies, including Israel. Last, President Ahmedinejad's deliberately provocative questioning of the Holocaust and of Israel's right to exist is considered especially outrageous—and not only among American Jews concerned for the security of Israel.

Tehran and Washington have not had formal diplomatic relations since the hostage crisis. But just as there were times when it was appropriate to pursue détente with the Soviet Union and Communist China, so there is a case for détente with Iran, especially if such a policy best serves American interests. Many agree that U.S. policy toward Iran needs a diplomatic surge, but most seem to think that the direction should be the same as before: to squeeze Iran into following U.S. demands, especially on Iran's prospective manufacture of nuclear weapons and its support for organizations that use terrorism in Lebanon, Palestine, and Iraq. The squeezing proposed is usually heavy-handed, though not always as unsubtle as that commended by Benjamin Netanyahu, the former prime minister of Israel and the Likud Party leader who hopes to hold executive office again in Tel Aviv. In 2006, Netanyahu argued that the time is 1938, and that Iran is Germany—and that it is getting nuclear weapons. In response to this threat, he declared, "All ways must be considered"[25]—including, it would appear, bombing Iran. A candidate for the U.S. presidency has sung that argument to the tune of "Barbara Ann" by the Beach Boys, though he robustly maintains he did so in irony.[26] Martin Woollacott, the seasoned English journalist, thinks these are no laughing matters. For President Bush and Vice-President Cheney to suggest that air attacks and the bombing of Iran's nuclear facilities should be "on the table" is like saying that so should a bucket of cyanide.[27]

The negative fallout that might flow from U.S. (or Israeli) air attacks on Tehran's nuclear facilities is easy to envisage.[28] There might be large-scale civilian casualties in the built-up areas where the facilities are supposed to be located. That is, assuming that the intelligence on their precise locations is correct and that the facilities have not been moved since they were first identified. There might have to be repeat missions, especially if such actions are as unsuccessful as was President Jimmy Carter's "Operation Eagle Claw" in April 1980. (This operation to liberate the hostages at the U.S. Tehran Embassy had to be abandoned amid technical failures, crashes, and adverse weather.) Bombing Iran would almost certainly lead the price of oil to go through the ceilings established in 2008, both because of fearful reactions in the futures markets and likely Iranian production and marketing decisions. America's partiality toward Israel would be more globally condemned than it is normally: Israel, after all, has nuclear weapons, unlike any of its regional adversaries. Moscow (or Beijing) would seek to forge an alliance with Tehran, and Tehran might be receptive. Iran would almost certainly retaliate violently against the United States, immediately and bloodily, or it would serve its revenge later, and with cunning. It would not confine its efforts to encouraging provocations by Hezballah and Hamas. It would be able to hit U.S. targets in Iraq: its officials have publicly declared that they know the location of all the American bases, which are within Iranian missile ranges. Iran would also cause trouble in any European countries that supported raids to take out Tehran's facilities. It is an altogether unpleasant prospect. There is surely room for a more considered U.S. policy with less drastic side effects.

A considered policy is required for a successful substantive U.S. withdrawal from Iraq. Effective policymakers should always put themselves in their adversaries' shoes. Strategic effectiveness rarely occurs if regimes or their peoples are treated as mere parameters. American policymakers must conduct elementary appraisals of Iran—and Iran's relations with Iraq. Being described as "the Great Satan" every Friday in Tehran's mosques reminds Americans that Iranians unreservedly demonize them—along with Israelis. But they need to understand why America is demonized. Self-hatred is not required, and Iranian renditions of history do not have to be swallowed whole. To understand does not mean to forgive all. To understand is simply good strategy.

Under Point 1 of the Algiers Accords of January 1981, which ended the hostage crisis, the United States made a pledge to the government of the Islamic Republic of Iran "that it is and from now will be the policy of the United States not to intervene, directly or indirectly, politically or militarily, in Iran's internal affairs."[29] That it was Point 1 was no accident. The Iranian regime feared for its survival. It still does. Khomeini's guardianship of the jurists was established and confirmed in a constitutional referendum during the hostage crisis, the same year that Saddam Hussein declared war amid the chaos of the revolution and disorder within Iran's army. That war lasted eight years and bled Iran dry. Washington's tilt toward Saddam under the Reagan administration prevented Iran, despite having three times the numbers of Iraq's population, from achieving the victory it might otherwise have secured. Khomeini eventually had to swallow poison—as he put it—and accept a UN-brokered truce. (He did so shortly after the U.S. Navy shot down, in a still disputed incident, an Iranian passenger plane—killing all those on board—in the Persian Gulf.)

The ayatollahs' regime emerged in opposition to Iran's monarchy, which the United States had reestablished and supported. The theocratic regime sought to expand in self-defense. It survived Saddam's onslaught, although at tremendous cost in lives and finances—and despite losing some of its theological luster in the curious Iran-Contra affair.[30] The point is that the Tehran regime owes its domestic legitimacy not just to Shia Islam but also to Iranian patriotism.[31] That patriotism—both among the regime's supporters and its domestic opposition—is deeply rooted in the rejection of previous and present American efforts to accomplish regime change. In 1953 America and Britain reinstalled the Shah of Iran. In doing so, they overthrew a popular and honest democrat and a liberal constitutional nationalist, Mohammad Mossadegh, the prime minister of Iran. His crime had been the lawful nationalization of Iran's oil industry (with compensation).[32] Communism was suggested, risibly. The Americans and the British thereby irredeemably stamped themselves as neocolonial imperialists in Iranian eyes. The English-speaking powers have done more than any other foreigners to damage Iran's otherwise quite reasonable prospects of emerging as a liberal, constitutional, and parliamentary state.[33] Those charged with diplomatic engagement with Iran need to be familiar with this history because it shapes Tehran's behavior now and will do so in the future.[34]

Since its revolution Iran has been both a champion of international Islam and Shia Islam, which earned it enemies among all the secular regimes of the Sunni Arab-dominated world. That was one reason why Saddam Hussein went to war against Ayatollah Khomeini and why he was eventually backed by the Reagan administration. Iran also inspired fear among overtly Sunni Islamic regimes. Saddam's bloody draw with Iran halted the export of the Iranian revolution, as his Western and Sunni Arab backers had hoped. And after Khomeini's death, Iran stood to one side as a U.S.-led coalition gave it belated satisfaction by removing its deadly rival Saddam from Kuwait, although not from office. After 1992 the United States, rather than taking the risk required to build fully constructive relationships with post-Khomeini Iran, adopted a policy of dual containment and dual sanctions toward Iraq and Iran,. The scale of that lost opportunity is apparent in one detail that is often lost sight of. Ayatollah Khomeini disbanded the Shah's nuclear weapons program because he deemed it incompatible with Islamic ethics. His successors restarted it, not because they have different ethics but because they were more fearful of their regime's survival.

In Chapter 2, I argued that the Bush administration lost a possible opportunity to try to seek Iran's cooperation in the overthrow of Iraq's Baathists. Both the United States and Iran stood to gain, as the Iranians recognized better than the Americans. In May 2003, when President Bush was celebrating the defeat of Saddam, Iranian officials contacted the Swiss ambassador and asked him to convey proposed subjects for negotiation with Washington.[35] The Iranians offered to freeze their nuclear program. They elaborated: they would support a democratic and nonreligious government in Iraq, meaning that they would not encourage the export of their own regime, which they had advocated during the Iraqi-Iran war. They also offered to cooperate fully in the war on terror and not just against the Sunni fanatics in al-Qaeda. They would stop provisioning Hamas.

What did the Iranians want in return? To be assured that they would not be the subject of attempted regime change; to come off the list of state sponsors of terror; and not to be treated as part of the axis of evil. They asked the United States to repatriate to Iran the members of the Mujahideen-e-Khlak (the MEK), who were living in bases in Iraq. This group of Iranian oppositionists was an ally of Iraq's Baathists. It helped Saddam crush Kurds in 1991, but that is not the only proof of its repulsive nature. The MEK is on the U.S. list of terrorist organizations, but because it works for regime change in Iran, it has been lightly treated by the Bush administration. The Iranians also wanted an end to all international and U.S.-ordered sanctions, support for war reparations in the course of an anticipated U.S. resolution of Iraq's national debt, and the resolution of questions related to frozen Iranian assets in the United States. They also sought nuclear energy technology for economic rather than military purposes.

The Bush administration turned down this remarkable opportunity to trade favors without entering into any evaluation of the credibility or integrity of the Iranian proposal. It was a moment of complete hubris, which cost America dearly in lives and resources, when Iran subsequently made America's occupation of Iraq resemble hell. American commentators sometimes observe that Iranians think they are "the center of the universe."[36] Others complain that Iranians have an inflated view of their civilization and its global importance. Others think they ask for too much when they demand "respect."[37] Americans, however, need to be reminded that humility has not been the strongest suit of their own diplomacy in the Middle East. The Bush administration's arrogant refusal to explore the Iranian offer in 2003 needs to be seared in the memory of every official who may engage with Iran on behalf of future U.S. administrations.

Instead of a mutually convenient grand bargain, there has been a one-sided exchange. The United States has removed the Baathist government in Baghdad. That has left Iran as the dominant regional power in the Persian Gulf.[38] Iran is very happy to see the Baghdad government led by its allies in ISCI and Da'wa. But to inhibit any American ambitions to achieve regime change in Iran and to make an each-way bet, Tehran aided Iraqi insurgents and Sadrist actions against the United States—through supplying arms, and explosives, and subtly exploiting multiple factional rivalries.

Iran's strategy has been successful. The United States, if it is rational, is now in no position to follow up the Iraq wars with either an armed intervention against Iran's nuclear ambitions or with a policy of regime change in Tehran. The United States cannot have an Iraqi government that is anti-Iranian—because the United States supports a democratic Iraq, which means that friendly Shia Arab parties whose leaders lived in exile in Tehran are in power. The full consequences of these realities need to be fully absorbed by Washington's policymakers.

The United States, if it is sensible, has to adapt to and try to steer with rather than against Iran's new domination of the Persian Gulf. It was once U.S. policy to support a strong Iran, under the Shah. Thirty years later, it should become U.S. policy to build détente with the Shah's successors—if they are still open to persuasion, as they were in 2003, some time before President Ahmedinijad was elected in a four-way split of the candidates approved to run by Iran's Expediency Council.

Some believe that leaving Iraq will make it easier for the United States to get tough on Iran. Perhaps so. But at what cost? The United States will be leaving behind a Baghdad government dominated by Shia Arabs that is well disposed to Iran. The KRG's leaders have all at some juncture had good relations with Iran's leaders. The United States and Iran backed the same side in the retaking of Basra in the spring of 2008: Iran's ambassador to Iraq called the Sadrists "outlaws."[39] Iran mediated in the fights between the Iraqi government and the Sadrists in Sadr City.[40] Obtaining an anti-Iranian government in Iraq is a lost cause: the United States cannot bring back Sunni Arabs to power in Baghdad. A U.S. attack on Iran after an irresponsible exit from Iraq will simply mean that Iran will have every incentive to dominate Iraq even more.

The United States should learn from its recent strategic incoherence. It should leave Iraq and Iran to resolve all of their difficulties arising from the Iran-Iraq war and their previous legacies of conflict. A fully sovereign Iraq will be able to settle Iran's security anxieties. The two countries have outstanding border questions to resolve. They also each need completely to dissolve support for organizations that use armed violence against their respective regimes. The Baghdad government will want Iran to withdraw all its direct and indirect investments in the Sadrists—something that America also wants. With the U.S. departure, the Tehran government will be well disposed toward the Baghdad government because the Sadrists are the most Arabist and the least pro-Iranian among the major Shia factions in Iraq. It is not in Iran's interests to see the Sadrists come to power or to become sufficiently strong to destabilize the strength of the ISCI and Da'wa. The Iranians will be more helpful to their Iraqi allies when the United States leaves.

The United States would not be an especially welcome mediator or arbitrator at meetings between the sovereign governments of Iraq and Iran. The United States can, however, be helpful to Iraq through its own separate engagement with Iran. The United States should unilaterally end efforts to organize regime change in Iran by not supporting armed opposition to the Tehran government and subsidizing other opponents of the Tehran regime, especially its discredited royalists. Such activities merely destabilize Iraq because they encourage bad behavior in response from Tehran. Having done so, the United States will be in a better position to do what it can with its European allies in order to facilitate an Iranian step back on nuclear weapons development. All U.S. public intelligence estimates issued to Congress in December 2007 unanimously concluded, with high confidence, that Iran halted its nuclear weapons development in the fall of 2003. That freeze date is important. It may have owed far more to the end of the existential threat to Iran's security posed by Saddam's regime that it did to fear of the United States. Washington should move to reestablish full diplomatic relations with Iran, creating forums to address past differences. It may not be too late to bargain for a better outcome than a nuclear-armed Iran. The use of soft power and exchange may work or they may not; but no one should imagine that Iranian nuclear disarmament will be accomplished through bellicose threats from the United States.[41]

There is a moral difference between Saddam's Baathists and Iran's ayatollahs. The former were genocidal and twice invaded other countries to start major wars. Iran's ayatollahs have been deeply repressive—of minorities, of democrats, and of women—but their human rights abuses have never been on anything like the same scale as that of the Baathists. They govern with rather than against a Shia majority in their country. Starting détente with Iran does not mean that the United States should cease to advocate human rights improvements in Iran—Iran is a signatory to these international standards, and the next U.S. administration will be seeking to reestablish its own credibility on the nonuse of torture and "extraordinary renditions," in which suspects are handed over to foreign governments known to practice torture.

The United States does not, of course, publicly have to favor theocratic government in Iran any more than Tehran can be expected to endorse America's Constitution as the best hope of mankind. All that the United States needs to do publicly and privately is to cease trying to destabilize Iran's government. There are two negative reasons to do so: the United States has not been very good at the task, and this policy has jeopardized and continues to endanger America's mission in Iraq, whether it is staying or leaving.

There is also a positive reason. The regime in Tehran is more likely to reform—liberalizing both its economy and its society—and move toward a full democracy that will displace the tutelage of the guardians, if it is not under sustained U.S. military pressure.[42] The depth and intensity of U.S. pressure on Iran fit all patriotic Iranian narratives about American imperialism. To be heard in Iran the Iranian opposition often has to distance itself from the United States. Iran is surrounded to its east and north by Sunni Muslim majority states. The United States is in Afghanistan and Iraq, which border Iran, and has alliances with many of the post-Soviet Central Asian Republics in Iran's neighborhood. The United States is an ally of Israel, and of Turkey, which Iran fears may exploit its (largest and Turkic-language speaking) Azeri minority's nationalist sensibilities.[43] If one is an Iranian, one sees an Iran surrounded by the United States and its clients. This geopolitical pressure makes it easier for Iran's hard liners to win public support and close ranks.

Détente with Iran will therefore not only benefit American policy in Iraq but will also give Washington a better chance of achieving endogenous and voluntary regime change within Iran. But will détente enable Tehran to deepen its repression of its national and religious minorities? Not necessarily. Détente will lower the likelihood that Iran's minorities will be seen as national security risks by the current regime. The smaller nationalist minorities of Iran—the Kurds especially, but also other groups—have had a very grim twentieth century.[44] In some respects the Kurds of Iran were treated better than the Kurds of Iraq: Iran early on recognized a province called Kurdistan (*Kordestan* in Farsi pronunciation). But successive regimes in Tehran (both royalist and religious) and Baghdad (both Baathist and pre-Baathist) exploited the other side's Kurdish minority. In the twentieth century, Iran made alliances with Kurds from Iraq and used them to attack the Kurds of Iran. Iraq followed the same policy, seeking alliances with Iranian Kurds and engaging them to attack Iraqi Kurdish organizations. They also usually divided the Kurds within their own regime. The Baathists and the ayatollahs both successfully exploited intra-Kurdish rivalries within their respective territories.

The Kurds in particular have much to gain from détente between the United States and Iran and between Iraq and Iran. It will partly desecuritize their position. The Kurds of Iraq have won most of the freedoms they sought and control their own domestic security. Just as they do not want a Turkish intervention to jeopardize their gains, so the Kurds of Iraq do not want to antagonize the Iranian government. For that reason, they have no good cause to support armed Kurdish guerrilla movements against Tehran. Such movements have failed before and do not seem likely to succeed in the future. Periodic attacks by PJAK, the branch of the PKK recruited among Iranian Kurds, encourages Iran to bomb Kurdish villages in the province of Sulaimania inside the KRG. No one profits much from this—not even PJAK, which the media often misidentifies. The Iranians suspect the Americans (and the Turks!) of supporting PJAK. The KRG has every reason to cooperate with Iran to restrain PJAK, and they have a joint interest in hunting down Sunni jihadists who seek to establish themselves in the mountainous terrain that separates Iranian Kordestan from Iraqi Kurdistan.

It is also not all obvious that the Kurds of Iran stand to gain from armed struggle against the Pasdaran, the Iranian revolutionary guards. The chances are that the Kurds of Iran will do better for themselves through following a peaceful, civil-rights based strategy—even though that will lead to periodic and severe hardships. They will likely achieve far more politically if they build alliances within Iran—peaceful alliances—rather than seeking unreliable American sponsorship for revolutionary action. In so doing, they would also be less likely to endanger the achievements of their co-nationals in Iraq.

No one is going to give the Kurds a Greater Kurdistan, either by diplomacy or by armed force. The road to a Greater Kurdistan will certainly not start with armed military struggle against Iran's revolutionary guards. Kurds will achieve cultural rights and autonomy much more effectively, in each part of historic Kurdistan (in Turkey, Iraq, Iran, and Syria), if they are not entrapped in armed struggles that work against one another's feasible political projects. Serious Kurdish strategists know this. An American withdrawal from Iraq does not therefore have to involve any betrayal of the Kurds—if executed along the lines proposed here. American détente with Iran would not betray the Kurds of Iraq or Iran, but it will need a complete reengineering of America's Middle East policy.

The Kurds of Turkey, Syria, Iraq, and Iran have one common functional resource and need: water. Turkey and Iran have both built huge dams for irrigation projects, which have reduced the flows into the Tigris and the Euphrates and have thereby adversely affected the Kurds of Iraq, the Arabs of Iraq, and traditional Kurdish habitats in Turkey, Iraq, Syria, and Iran. Kurdish nationalists will enrich international empathy for their cause if they highlight these ecological questions.[45] Helping Iran, Turkey, and Iraq, directly or indirectly, to modernize their energy infrastructures will improve regional and intergroup relations within each state, and head off water fights. A strategic and high-minded American foreign policy should number that among its indirect objectives.

The Arab Neighborhood

Europeans and Americans typically tend to focus most on Iraq's Arab neighborhood and on the Arab world when they review the external impact of the repercussions of the U.S.-led intervention in Iraq. That is partly because of a series of usually unquestioned assumptions—for example, that Iraq is an Arab nation, that the intervention in Iraq is the latest in a series of European and American imperial interventions in Arab countries, and that Sunni jihadism has been exponentially encouraged by the U.S. intervention in Iraq, with spillovers and blowback among the populations of "Eurabia" (as some have unpleasantly and inaccurately described the Arab and Muslim migrant peoples of the European Union).

Iraq, however, is not an Arab nation—or, it is less an Arab nation than the United Kingdom is an English nation. Although the Arabs are the largest nation in Iraq, its largest Shia Arab component is much better disposed to Iran than it is to the Arab states to the west and south of Iraq, which supported the historical repression of the Shia. The Kurds of Iraq are not Arabs. They detest European and American "Arabists," whether they be scholars or diplomats, because they see them as apologists for successive Iraqi and Arab dictatorships and as cultural relativists, who support democracy at home but not in countries with large Arab populations and

Kurdish minorities (like Syria and Iraq). Kurds have often observed to me that many champions of Palestine never publicly championed the cause of Kurdish national self-determination against Saddam's Iraq.[46] There is also a more than nominal case for questioning whether the March 2003 intervention was conceived as a colonial venture. There are no settlers; and there was no plan for a long-term occupation of Iraq. The intervention had multiple motivations, as we have seen, but direct rule of Iraq was not one of them. And a democratic state is not a client state of traditional elites, as favored by imperialists.

Last, Salafi jihadism had its origins outside of Iraq—in Egypt, in Pakistan, in Afghanistan, and in Algeria. Jihadists went to Iraq in large numbers from Arab-majority countries after 2003—both to perform suicide missions and other anti-American or anti-Shia or anti-Kurdish terrorist operations. But the movement was already in existence. Iraq simply became its latest cause. Al-Qaeda in Iraq is now being defeated, mainly by Sunni Muslims turning on its members. That is to the advantage of Iraqis and to the vast majority of Europeans and Americans who wish to see al-Qaeda extinguished. Likewise, the self-starting leaderless jihadists in Europe, analyzed so well by Marc Sagemen, have presented what has happened in Iraq as a justification for their activities, but had it not been Iraq it would have been Afghanistan, Kashmir, Israel, China, or anywhere where Sunni Muslims are in conflict with other states and civilizations.[47]

The present atypical perspective of a European (and U.S. permanent resident) author explains the much shorter treatment to be allotted to the Arab neighborhood of Iraq in what follows when compared with the pages just devoted to Turkey and Iran. A comparatively briefer treatment does not suggest that Arab citizens or peoples are any less normatively important than any others, in the neighborhood or worldwide. It does suggest that the neighboring Arab states and peoples will have much less influence on the future of Iraq than Turkey and Iran. The latter two are regional powers, with large populations (of 72 and 66 million people, respectively) and formidable militaries (by local standards).

Table 8.1 provides estimates from multiple sources of the military and economic capabilities of Iraq's major neighbors. Turkey's and Iran's punching power looks far more formidable than that of Iraq's Arab neighbors, especially since their militaries have had extensive recent experience—unlike Saudi Arabia's. The offensive capabilities of Saudi Arabia's, Syria's, and Jordan's militaries are not given high estimates by foreign military experts. (To put matters in comparative perspective, Jordan's military expenditures are only slightly higher than those of my country of origin, Ireland, a neutral

TABLE 8.1   Estimates of the Military and Economic Capabilities of Iraq's
Neighbors, 2008

| | Population (millions) | Armed Forces (1,000s)[1] | | GDP[2] | Military Expenditure | | Active Troops (per 1,000 citizens) |
		Active	Total		$U.S. billion	World Ranking, 2008	
Turkey	71.9	515	1,044	888	25.4	12	7.0
Iran	65.9	545	12,585	753	6.3	25	11.7
Syria	19.7	296	537	87	0.9	67	15.9
Saudi Arabia	28.2	199	235	565	31.1	9	6.8
Jordan	6.2	101	146	28	1.3	56	17.4

[1] Including reserves and paramilitaries.
[2] $U.S. billion purchasing power parity.
Sources: Adapted from on-line data for 2007–8 published by Center for Strategic and International Studies, Washington, D.C., Stockholm International Peace Research Institute, and Central Intelligence Agency.

and pacific European democracy.) These considerations are put forward to emphasize a basic point. Strategically, getting U.S. foreign policy toward Turkey and Iran right, as part of a U.S. withdrawal from Iraq with integrity, is far more important than getting policy right toward Iraq's immediate Arab neighbors. That is not, however, to suggest that policy toward the Arab world can or should be neglected. It is just of less importance for Iraq than Europeans, Americans, and Arabs typically claim.

An America executing a substantive withdrawal from Iraq will appease (or elate) pan-Arab sentiment in Jordan, Syria, and Saudi Arabia, provided that the withdrawal is substantive, that any remaining American military presence is genuinely advisory, and that any U.S. bases in Iraq are a function of the will of elected Iraqi governments, federal and regional. In such circumstances it will be more difficult for the neighboring Arab regimes to continue to talk of an American occupation. Some of the Arab states will hope that the American withdrawal will be succeeded by sufficient stability in Iraq to enable the return of significant numbers of Iraqi refuges, which have caused serious humanitarian crises in Syria, Jordan, and Lebanon. Since Iraq's territorial integrity will be intact, the neighbors will hardly be able to claim that America has partitioned Iraq—although that will not stop many (Sunni) Arab nationalists from saying otherwise. What America cannot give the pan-Arabists is what it took away: a Sunni Arab-dominated Iraq.

The Gulf States are already engaging the new Iraq. The United Arab Emirates, Kuwait, and Bahrain have already reestablished their embassies in Baghdad.[48] Kuwait, of course, is happy not to be talked about as Iraq's nineteenth province by the new Baghdad government. Gulf business organizations are investing in the Kurdistan Region. King Abdullah of Jordan visited Iraq in August 2008. He has repudiated his frightened talk in 2004 of a Shia crescent under Iranian hegemony, claiming that he was misunderstood. He has sought to reestablish supplies of Iraqi oil to his country—at a discount, and he has advised his fellow Arab leaders to reestablish diplomatic ties with Baghdad. Jordan is therefore signaling that it can live with the new Iraq. It appears to want other Arab governments to engage with Baghdad if only to limit Iran's influence. Jordan will therefore cooperate with any well-organized American withdrawal from Iraq.

That leaves two major immediate Arab neighboring states to consider— Saudi Arabia and Syria. The former is a formidable financial and oil power, but its offensive military capabilities are unproved and much doubted. Its regime is virulently fearful of Iran—and of its potential ability to win ideological support among the Shia Arabs of the eastern provinces of Saudi Arabia (where the country's major oil fields are located). Saudi Arabia's official version of Islam is Sunni, its version of jurisprudence is Hanabali, and it is doctrinally Wahhabi, treating Shiism as idolatry and apostasy.[49] Its official intolerance is exported in Saudi missionary work. Saudi Arabia is a tribal monarchy for its aristocrats, a Wahhabi theocracy for its subjects, and the prime exporter of the theological intolerance in which Salafi jihadism flourishes. But it is also going through a distinctive and unresolved modernization.[50] We all know that nineteen of its citizens executed the attacks of 9/11—compared with no Iraqis. But the Saudi regime is not itself jihadist in the contemporary sense. The United States relations with Saudi Arabia are complex, and they are not captured by any simple model of neocolonialism or a client state.[51]

Throughout the two terms of the Bush II administration, Saudi Arabia has indicated that its formal foreign policy priority is the comprehensive settlement of the conflict between Israel and Palestine.[52] It wants to achieve this goal partly to avoid Iran's becoming the main external patron of Palestinian nationalism. The U.S. intervention in Iraq in March 2003 was not causally linked to the Israel-Palestine question. Its neoconservative proponents sometimes suggested that peace in and over Jerusalem would be advanced by a regime change in Baghdad. Its opponents sometimes claimed that the U.S. intervention in Iraq was against America's strategic interests and was enacted on behalf of hard-line Zionism (in Israel and within the United States), and that the intervention in Iraq would aggravate the Israeli-Palestinian conflict. Both the proponents and the opponents, it is fair to say, exaggerated their arguments. Matters may, however, develop in stranger directions than either side anticipated.

There is "linkage" between a successful U.S. withdrawal from Iraq and the question of Israel and Palestine, but of an indirect kind. A U.S. administration that actively seeks to establish a Palestinian state—that is, a meaningfully sovereign state with just borders and contiguous territory—will be different from recent U.S. administrations. If Washington overtly promotes a just resolution of the well-known final status questions (on Jerusalem/ Al-Quds, the right of return or compensation of Palestinian refugees, and the Israeli settlements in the occupied territories), it will be able to win back some trust in the Arab states and will certainly be well regarded in Saudi Arabia. In so doing, Washington may ease the difficulties that Arab states and their peoples might be able to pose to a U.S. withdrawal from Iraq. The principal threat capacities of the Arab neighboring states are obvious. They may continue to provision Sunni Arab insurgents in the hope of returning a Sunni-dominated regime to power, and they might turn a blind eye to the provisioning of al-Qaeda with money and recruits.

An America that is not seen to be Israel's attorney will have considerable leverage over Saudi Arabia—including the Saudis' current refusal to settle Iraq's debts (from the wars it fought against Iran and Kuwait, the first with the Saudis' full support). Saudi diplomats and intellectuals would appear still to entertain naïve hopes that federalism in Iraq can be reversed and that Iran's regional rise can be averted.[53] American diplomats intent on organizing America's withdrawal from Iraq will be able to offer them no assurances of either a recentralized Iraq or of a Sunni Arab restoration in Iraq. If the Saudis care about Sunnis as opposed to Arabs, they should be advised to encourage Iraq's Sunni Arabs to compromise with Sunni Kurds on federalism and the disputed territories, but the Kurds will not be holding their breath.

Syria's priorities are different from Saudi Arabia's. Its regime looked to be on its last legs when it was evicted from Lebanon under popular pressure and when it was caught red-handed in assassinations in the state it considers its lost province. Damascus is full of Baathists from Iraq—Saddam's defeat has led to a certain rapprochement between Syrian and Iraqi Baathism, but the Syrian regime must know that the Iraqi Baathists will only secure a return to power in Iraq, if at all, at a provincial level and under new colors. Damascus has cooperated very fitfully in securing Iraq's western borders, where Arab tribes, as in Jordan, are divided by the modern demarcations. The Syrian government maintains good relations with Iran. Some would say, it is a disguised (secular) Shia dictatorship, but the principle that the enemy of my enemy is my friend is sufficient to explain its conduct. Syria cosponsors Hezbollah in Lebanon and Hamas in Palestine. It is, in some respects, the last holdout of militant secular pan-Arabism.

How might a United States intent on a well-organized withdrawal from Iraq manage its relations with Syria? The Baker-Hamilton Report suggested that the United States should encourage Israel to return the Golan Heights to Syria as part of its plan to stabilize Iraq. The report in general won widespread congressional approval, but this particular proposal was not deeply explored.[54] Unlike Iran, the United States has less motivation to engage in détente with Syria because Syria's wrecking capacities are less than Iran's, and the United States has many ways of exercising leverage over Syria. But, that said, the Golan Heights are not part of historical Palestine, and Israeli governments have intermittently indicated that their return to Syria is negotiable. It will be an interesting surprise if American diplomats work more vigorously to accomplish normalization of relations between Syria and Israel and to promote a Palestinian state as a byproduct of a well-organized withdrawal from Iraq. Any U.S. administration embarked on this course may find itself at odds with hard-line Israeli politicians. The United States should pursue these goals in any case—as the best way to stabilize Israel and Palestine—rather than because of any uncertain pay-offs in the stabilization of Iraq. If there is less regional Sunni Arab hostility toward the transformation of Iraq, that will be welcome; it cannot be guaranteed or engineered by any feasible U.S. policies.

Chapter 9
Cleaning Up Without Ruling

We do not wish for anything outside the constitution and do not want anything more than what the constitution gives us.

—Mas'ud Barzani, President of the Kurdistan Regional Government, September 1, 2008

You never know where you are going to end.

—George Kennan on Iraq, 2002

The "i-Rack" is a satirical sketch that can be found online at YouTube.[1] It shows the founder of Apple Computers, Steve Jobs, announcing his latest invention, the "i-Rack," a play on the standard American mispronunciation of Iraq. The "i-Rack" is to succeed the i-Phone, the i-Mac, and the i-Book, but it is a shaky contraption, with three rickety shelves. Jobs is presenting this new "product" to an audience of Apple's stockholders. They remonstrate with increasing anxiety that the i-Rack is unstable, to which Jobs responds with "trust me." He maintains it can work without directions or plans, and that the mission is accomplished. He then places an increasing number of Apple products on the shelves of the "i-Rack," causing smoke and fire to emerge. When the audience suggests that things should be taken out of the "i-Rack," he refuses, because he knows what's best, and starts throwing dollars at the mess. As the stockholders start to panic at the fire he announces he will send 21,000 more items into the "i-Rack" (that is, "the surge"). The stockholders try to quit the building, but he tells them there is no "exit strategy." They should stop focusing on the "i-Rack" and instead focus on his next product, the "i-Ran." The video ends amid screams of shock and horror.

What Has Been and Is Being Claimed

Although it is not the i-Rack, the new Iraq is still in many ways a shaky contraption. It will not successfully stabilize through direct American governance or from the supply of more resources toward the same policies. Neither more sustained use of U.S. troops in counterinsurgency, nor more American oversight of the recentralization of Iraq's institutions, is in order. A consensual recentralization of Iraq (with broad-based majority support among all of its three major communities) could conceivably work in the long run, but that project is not this, or the next decade's, feasible task.

Unilateral Arab recentralization will make much more likely a return to armed conflict between Kurdistan and Arab Iraq. As I write a clash has just been averted between Iraqi federal forces and Kurdish Peshmerga over Khaniqin, a Kurdish-majority city in northern Diyala—one of the disputed territories. There appears to have been no consultation with the KRG by the federal forces, and the Arab commander of the federal forces did not consult the Kurdish Chief of Staff of the Iraqi army. The episode led KRG President Barzani to issue warnings in an interview with a London-based Arabic newspaper with an English-language edition. As he put it, "The consequences of monopolizing authority are well known."[2] If a strengthened Baghdad decides not to fulfill the constitutional promise to enable the disputed territories to be resolved largely in Kurdistan's favor, and if it contests control of security within the KRG's expected zone of unification, and, last, if it seeks a monopoly over the oil industry and its revenue allocation, then renewed civil war is certain. We will then be returned to Iraq before the Baath, with an alienated Kurdistan and with two places and peoples in antagonism: Kurdistan and Iraq al-Arabi. Any federation in Iraq has no chance of stabilization unless Kurdistan is satisfied on its southern boundaries, on its resource-allocation entitlements, and on its freedom to develop its oil and gas in unexploited fields—that is, unless Iraq's Constitution is implemented. If Kurdistan is not satisfied, then contests for power within Arab Iraq will spill over into conflicts with the KRG, and vice versa. If the United States wants a federation to work in Iraq, then it should do what it needs to do and steer its hard and soft power toward supporting the Kurdistan Region, the federacy that is the best byproduct, so far, of America's intervention in Iraq.

A multiunit federalized Iraq has much better prospects of achieving wider and sustained stability than a two-unit federation. That stands a good chance of creating a satisfied Kurdistan Region along with satisfied Arab majority regions and (largely self-governing) provinces. That will generate a multipolar Iraq, in which power-sharing over limited federal functions has a decent prospect of success. That vision is made possible in Iraq's Constitution, under existing Iraqi legislation on region formation, and under currently stalled draft legislation (approved by the KRG and some in the Iraqi federal executive) that would allocate oil revenues proportionally across all of Iraq but would keep the federal government from controlling the pot. The United States has not properly supported the vista of a multipolar Iraq because of its wish to reincorporate Sunni Arabs into Iraq, on the terms of the Sunni Arab agenda of recentralization (primarily because that agenda coincides with the U.S. desire to have a strong Iraq to balance against Iran). Existing U.S. policy simply rekindles Kurdish fears, strengthens the Shia determination never to be resubordinated, and encourages Iran to provoke mayhem (in perceived self-defense). If the United States wants a more stable Iraq after its exit, its favored policy of recentralization must be abandoned.

U.S. policy must be reoriented on the way out, not just because that is the right thing to do but also because it has a greater chance of being successful than the existing policy. Under federalization, Sunni Arabs can recover self-government, facilitated through the existing possibilities for provincialization. They will be able to do so on terms acceptable to Shia Arabs, who will not be obliged significantly to incorporate the Awakening and Sons of Iraq personnel into the federal forces. Provincialization is also fully acceptable to Kurds, provided that the northern borders of the Arab-majority provinces are resolved largely in the Kurds' favor—as they should be if the Constitution is implemented, if democratic preferences are respected, and if Saddam is not to dictate the border of Kurdistan from his grave.

This analysis has an important implication. One argument that we often hear about a U.S. withdrawal within the United States—that it should not take place until the Baghdad government is in control of the country— is simply invalid. A withdrawal before a new Baghdad government has full control of the country is in fact far better for Iraq's largest and small minorities and for the policy advocated here. Provided U.S. diplomacy shields Iraq from its neighbors along the lines suggested in the previous chapter, then Iraq will achieve much better progress in federalization with an unsteady Baghdad government. That is because the Shia-dominated Baghdad government will have to make deals with both Kurdistan and the Sunni Arab-majority provinces rather than try to dictate terms to them.

Current American policy is in severe danger of overshooting in three ways, which are not typically appreciated. On the one hand, U.S. policy may be fostering restorationist illusions among Sunni Arabs, expectations that are certain to be dashed. On the other hand, U.S. policy may be enabling the Green Zone's government to overestimate its powers. Prime Minister Maliki and the Da'wa party's centralists are beginning to show signs of delusion, believing they can achieve a unitary Iraq under Shia dominance: Ramadi and Basra yesterday, Khaniqin and Kirkuk tomorrow. Such expectations and fantasies must be nipped in the bud. The third form of overshooting is less noticed. The new Iraq requires a military that is not a threat to its people or its neighbors. The stronger the Iraqi federal forces are becoming, the greater the prospects that the army will be used to abuse minorities —and the lower the chances of successful civilian control of the military. An unsteady Baghdad government, by contrast, will be one in which the agenda of the Hakims of ISCI, based on an alliance with Kurdistan and the Iraqi Islamic Party, or the regionalist vision of Mowaffak al-Rubaie, will have better prospects of being realized. Under an unsteady Baghdad government Sunni Arabs can bargain but not dictate. For similar strategic reasons, U.S. policy should in the future promote policing and intelligence improvements among the regions and governorates rather than further strengthening of repressive central institutions that might again be a threat to Iraq's citizens and Iraq's neighbors.

The U.S. role should be to try to protect a productive internal balance of power within Iraq—as is embedded in Iraq's Constitution—not only because this is the best way to protect Iraq's national and religious minorities, but also because it is in U.S. strategic interests. Chapter 7 explained why partition should be resisted in favor of federalization, but rejecting partition does not make a case for recentralization. It should also be axiomatic that any thoroughgoing coercive domination of Iraq by either Shia or Sunni Arabs is undesirable. The United States should not waste any more time in pursuit of the chimera of a secular and cross-sectarian Arab nationalism. There is not sufficient support for such a program. It would be equally unwise to back the centralists within Da'wa. They will lose if they try a thoroughgoing unitarism, as has every Baghdad government since 1920. Already some Sunni Arabs in the northern provinces are turning toward the KRG to balance against Shia Arab aspirations.

U.S. policymakers need to focus on facilitating and deepening the de facto power sharing that currently exists and that underpins the possibility that Iraq's Constitution will in the future describe both how it functions as well as how it should function. U.S. generals need to ensure when they act that federal security policy is the joint policy of Iraq's federal coalition—and not just the goals of the prime minister's immediate coterie. They should fully consult with the KRG and any other regional or provincial government on security policies within their jurisdiction and respect their share of Iraq's sovereignty. U.S. military, policing, and intelligence training and assistance, if requested, should in the future be allocated to the regional and provincial governments because these are the institutions that need to be built to make Iraq work as a multinational and multireligious federation. Existing or previous military bases could be converted into such assistance centers, again when sought.

There is now a five-party council that displays sustained power-sharing potential at the federal level. It consists of the ISCI and Da'wa among the Shia, the KDP and the PUK among the Kurds, and the Islamic Party among the Sunni Arabs. The last is the weakest component, and in the longer run Iraq will require all three of its ethnic and sectarian legs to stabilize its central seat of government. The long-run stabilization of power sharing requires greater Sunni Arab cooperation and incorporation, but that can easily happen only after the Sunni Arabs have revised their "restorationist" ambitions. If and when they make such revisions, they will have Kurdish partners who share their desire to prevent a tyranny of the Shia Arab majority and have roughly the same numbers of voters. Sunni Arabs would prefer it to be the other way around—that Kurds would be their partners in a recentralized Iraq. But that is not a strategy that any representative of the Kurds is any longer willing to consider. There are too many betrayed promises and mass graves for that. The Kurds have frequently felt excluded from major decisions by the three Shia Arab federal prime ministers since 2004, even when consultation is mandatory or appropriate under the Constitution. So power sharing has a long way to go before mutual trust characterizes intergroup and interleader relations. But it is power sharing, not centralization, that the United States should be promoting both now and after its departure.

Readers of this book probably selected it because of its title. They may have an ethical conviction that the United States cannot simply walk away from Iraq, or they do not want to blame Iraqis for what follows after a U.S. departure. They may fear catastrophe, and therefore they want a responsible departure. They rightly ask those who chortle at the prospects of democracy, federation, and constitutionalism in Iraq what they would recommend instead. They usually find them to be silent. Occasionally they find apologists for dictatorship. Sometimes they find advocates of partition. This counsel, I have shown, can be reasonably rejected without having to indulge in blasé optimism.

Ethical Americans know it will be unhelpful to have a debate that blames a new U.S. administration for not "staying the course" if things go wrong.

The course set under the Bush administration—a recentralized Iraq—cannot work in the long run. It promises only the peace of more graves. That is not to disparage some of the recent security gains won by U.S. troops, but it is to suggest that a different political course will better exploit the advantages created by the surge and other recent positive changes in the security situation. Americans, Republicans or Democrats, do not have to resign themselves to hopelessness. The course set by Iraq's Constitution can work for both Iraqis and Americans, and it will work better if the U.S. withdrawal is designed along the lines proposed here.

Americans know that the new Iraq has no weapons of mass destruction, and it will not develop them—if it abides by its Constitution. Jihadist terrorism has taken a heavy blow, partly because of al-Qaeda's conduct in Iraq. It has turned its own core constituency of Sunni Muslim believers against it. The new and recuperating Iraq will include many people who will want to attack U.S. personnel and interests, but after a successful disengagement they will be controlled by Iraqi governments (federal, regional, and provincial) that are more likely to have local legitimacy and that could in extremis call upon U.S. military support.

A democratic Iraq will have been accomplished provided that Iraq's Constitution holds and that scheduled provincial and federal elections go ahead within the next eighteen months. As long as the elections do not deliver power to parties determined to replace democracy with theocracy or autocracy, Iraq will have begun the walk toward regime consolidation. The creation of a federal and democratic Iraq will be of immense long-run benefit to all its peoples. It can be better shepherded to consolidation by America's withdrawal from efforts to directly govern Iraq. Such an Iraq will correspond with America's reasonable interests and will have met the goal of what many have argued America owes Iraq, a new state strong enough and legitimate enough to stand on its own and not to be a threat to others.[3]

America's intervention in Iraq has been domestically and internationally controversial. That is a deliberate understatement in the interests of a calm hearing from both those who supported and those who opposed the intervention. Those who supported the intervention can rightly claim—"no intervention, more Saddam." Those who opposed the intervention can rightly claim, "with intervention, chaos in Arab Iraq." This book is inspired by the conviction that there is a general strategy that America can follow if it wishes to end its intervention with integrity irrespective of people's fundamental judgment on the origins of the intervention. Instead of focusing on the justice of the intervention, we need to focus on a just departure.

This then is the reappraisal that should shape American policymaking in its withdrawal from Iraq. The United States should respect Iraq's sovereignty and its Constitution and work to facilitate power sharing in the federal government while making the decentralization of security and resource allocation among regions and provinces work as effectively as possible. This strategy can and should be pursued by the new administration, in conjunction with America's allies in Iraq, Iraq's neighborhood, and the European Union. The strategy requires respect for Iraq's sovereignty and for Iraq's Constitution, both to ensure that there is no form of imperial government over Iraq and to respect Iraq's democratic and constitutional transformation.

What has been advanced here is not an instruction manual on how to get out of Iraq, complete with logistical planning for the military,[4] detailed treaty provisions, and the minutiae of useful constitutional amendments and power-sharing institutions. Nor does this book provide extensive diplomatic talking points. Instead, what has been offered is a set of arguments for a major strategic reorientation, which, in principle, can be converted into detailed operational security and diplomatic instructions and appropriate institutional design and support. This strategic reorientation has far-reaching implications and will enable an honest and morally responsible withdrawal.

This resteering of U.S. policy toward Iraq would be compatible with a surprising number of the original goals of the Bush II administration and the more mainstream goals of key figures in the U.S. Congress. Some of these absurdly ambitious goals cannot be met, such as immediate and wider democratization of the region. Other goals that cannot be met should not occasion despair but a rethinking of the issues. Détente with Iran, considered disinterestedly, offers surprisingly good prospects for regional stabilization. If a U.S. president could go to Maoist China, a U.S. president can go to Tehran. The trickiest reorientation will be required in foreign policy toward Turkey. Here the United States has to work with Turkey's democrats and restrain its Kemalist military. The United States and Turkey stand to gain immensely from stabilizing a satisfied Kurdistan Region, which is secular, has no irredentist claims on Turkey, and will play its part to make Iraq work as a federation. Turkey will need to end its strategic manipulation of the Turkomen and focus on coexistence with the Kurdistan Region.

As for the imputed goals of the Bush II administration, some of these have been (fortunately) shown to display hubris and to be infeasible or immoral: imperial unilateral demonstrations, establishing a client state, or constructing an Iraq whose oil is owned by U.S. corporations. What is salvageable in

Iraq is what was worth considering in the intervention in the first place—the replacement of a genocidal regime by a loose, pluralist federation.

Respecting Iraq's sovereignty will require that any continued American military presence in Iraq in 2009 and after should rest on the explicit authorization of Iraq's governments in freely negotiated agreements or treaties. The Iraqi federal government is responsible for Iraq's national security policy and, so far, is responsible for the domestic security forces of Iraq outside of much of the KRG. The KRG, by contrast, is the lawful authority for domestic security in the Kurdistan Region and the de facto authority in most of the disputed territories outside the rim of the existing KRG. A policy of rapid withdrawal of U.S. and Coalition combat troops to bases and the withdrawal of American forces from major built-up areas in Arab Iraq is likely to be sought by the Iraqi federal government within the next year, with negotiable adjustments on timing. Such requests should be accepted and respected.

Respect for Iraq's Constitution, and for its sovereignty, will impose several obligations on American foreign policy. These entail decisive shifts from current expedients, which I have elaborated in the preceding chapters. Respecting Iraq's Constitution does not mean that America has to accept every reading of that document given by officials in Baghdad, especially in the absence of an established and authoritative Iraqi federal supreme court. Iraq is now a federation in progress, but it is a far more decentralized federation than most in the records of constitutional history. The United States respects the European Union but knows that EU policy is a function of its many members' interactions, and the United States has separate and distinct external relations with all the members of the Union. It should act in the same manner with Iraq. Under its Constitution, its regions are entitled to independent diplomatic representation on any matters outside of the exclusive competence of the federal government. At this time only the Kurdistan Region has availed itself of that right, but others may join it if other Iraqi provinces exercise the right of region formation.

Respect for Iraq's sovereignty and Constitution will require the United States to use its leverage to ensure that Turkey, Iran, and Saudi Arabia and other Arab states respect Iraq's sovereignty and Constitution—including its borders, its federal entities and regions, and any border adjustments that are made to the KRG's southern borders under Article 140 of Iraq's Constitution. Chapter 8 advanced reasons to believe that such a policy has some prospects of success.

The new policy orientation would, of course, have implications for how the United States helps, rather than dictates, Iraq's institutional development. Assistance in public administration and governance—*if sought*—should be focused on regional and provincial governments—aiding the building of workable, transparent, and effective institutions. Help at the federal level of government—*if sought*—should be focused on drawing from the constitutional and institutional experiences of other pluralist federations and meaningful power-sharing systems. Iraq could never be a mini-America, and it will be very difficult for it to become a big Belgium, or a big Switzerland, or another Canada, but the latter are better targets of policy ambition. Advice at federal level, *if sought*, should focus not on how to make the prime minister more powerful but on how to make the Council of Ministers more effective and collegial, on how to make the prime minister work collegially with his deputy prime ministers, how to form and manage coalition cabinets, and how to coordinate policymaking among multiple parties. In short, advice, *if sought*, should focus on how to make coalition governments work—on how to make Iraq more like the power-sharing European parliamentary democracies.

The new policy should be accompanied by a shift in U.S. resources toward logistical and diplomatic support for humanitarian relief efforts. Assistance in the care, resettlement, and relocation of refugees and the internally displaced is badly needed. This will also assist in constructive relations with the neighboring Arab states. The U.S. Defense and State Departments owe debts of honor to the numerous Arabs and Kurds who have served them as interpreters—or indeed as informants. They will have to be given asylum or citizenship or helped in relocating within Iraq.

The new policy orientation mandates a downsized U.S. embassy. The gargantuan scale of the existing embassy symbolically spells out imperial hubris and temptation. It invites persistent Arab Iraqi nationalist discontent. If it is feasible to share the embassy with all the Western democracies, including the European Union, and all the offices of international organizations, including the World Bank and the Arab League, well and good. If not, a major downsizing is in order. The existing Embassy might usefully be sold to the Baghdad governorate council.

The new policy orientation would also have commercial implications: The U.S. Departments of State and Commerce should stop sanctioning or threatening U.S. or foreign firms that prospect and work within the KRG according to the provisions of Kurdistan's Investment Law and Kurdistan's Petroleum Law. These are lawful activities under the KRG's rights within Iraq's Constitution. The relevant legislation was deliberately drafted to be compliant with Iraq's Constitution. The State Department often discourages such U.S. investors because it supports the centralizing objective of making the federal government the major agent in the management of Iraq's oil and gas policies. Other Iraqis are, of course, entitled to have that as their policy goal, but they will need to change the Constitution if they wish it to be the universal law of the land. This is another example of how the United States can best protect its ally, the Kurdistan Region, by respecting Iraq's Constitution, even when not all the Iraqis in the federal government are doing so.

Will there be any strategic benefits to a U.S. military withdrawal from Iraq? Yes, if Iraq is not left in chaos and does not immediately suffer from a rekindling of its civil war. U.S. strategic needs in the neighborhood can be met. They are preventing any regional or other global power from developing a monopoly or chokehold over oil and gas supplies to the Western economies before they have changed their energy consumption and production policies, and preventing threats posed by jihadist terrorists and the habitats that might support them. Both of these goals can be met by nurturing rather than trying to control the new Iraq, and by adopting a new foreign policy toward Iran and in the wider Middle East. Iraq will not have a federal hydrocarbons law soon that will rapidly and dramatically improve U.S. energy supplies, but an agreed-upon law is more likely when the pressure to have one will be stronger. But all Iraqis and all Americans stand to gain from a rational power-sharing settlement over natural resources as I argue in Chapter 6—and the making of that agreement is more likely to occur under the pressure of a substantive U.S. withdrawal. Whether there will be U.S. bases in Iraq, and on what terms, will be decided, appropriately, by Iraqis rather than by Americans, but it seems highly likely that Iraqis will minimally provide full-scale intelligence cooperation against Sunni jihadists. Over time, there may also be other long-run and less tangible strategic benefits. A democratic federal Iraq that works will have a positive influence on its wider neighborhood. The United States will have more of its hard power freed for other needs—including deterring renewed authoritarianism in Russia and regulating the geopolitical ambitions of China.

Iraq Is Not Vietnam, Germany, Japan, Korea, or Bosnia

In thinking about America's prospective withdrawal from Iraq, it is helpful to think comparatively about what it will not be like, and what it should not be like. Four comparative paradigms are strongly inappropriate (Vietnam, Germany, Japan, and Korea), but they are instructive. A last paradigm, Bosnia-Herzegovina, has the most parallels, but it also is replete with warnings as to what should not be done. Let me deal with each comparison briefly.

Forty years ago John Kenneth Galbraith wrote a short, influential and impressive pamphlet, *How to Get Out of Vietnam.*[5] I read it as a teenager in 1975. It came to mind when I selected the title for this book, even though I believe that Vietnam and Iraq are strongly different examples of American interventions. Galbraith's central argument was that America was not fighting Communism in Vietnam, even if it thought it was. It was fighting Vietnamese nationalism—and it could not win that fight, except at unacceptable costs. Last, he claimed correctly, America had no fundamental strategic interests at stake in Vietnam. There would be no significant domino effect in favor of global communism, and he predicted, correctly, that the Chinese and the Vietnamese would not get on after the United States left.

It is easy to see how one might replicate Galbraith's argument today, and people have, knowingly or unknowingly.[6] They maintain that America has not been fighting al-Qaeda but against Iraqi nationalism, in a fight that could not be won, except at unacceptably high costs, in a place where the United States has no fundamental strategic interests at stake. Some also predict that Iran and Iraq will not get on after the United States leaves Iraq. It is not necessary to list advocates of each of these positions because there is no need to personalize what is at stake. But the arguments are not compelling, whatever their origins.

America has not been fighting Iraqi nationalism in any sense that is analogous to Vietnam. America has been fighting Baathist pan-Arab Iraqi nationalists, but these have overwhelmingly been drawn from the Sunni Arab population, a minority of Iraq's population of approximately one-fifth— and they have never had unanimous support within that minority. America has fought racist and genocidal fascists in Iraq, and irreversibly removed the Baathist variety from power in Baghdad. Iraq's largest community, Shia Arabs, is mostly Iraqi Arab nationalist, but it has been the victim and enemy of Baathist nationalism. The Shia Arabs have nearly all cooperated with the United States in the overthrow of Baathist nationalists. Sadrists have since fought against Americans, but not in significant coordination with the Baathists or with other Sunni Arab insurgents. The most powerful Shia Arabs, in their religious institutions and religious parties, have allied with America and the Kurds to overturn Baath nationalism, which Kurds classify as fascism and Shia Arabs as sectarianism. Kurdish nationalists are not Iraqi nationalists, they are Iraqi federalists, but they have fought for their own nation. Vietnam had no large territorial compact national minority that resembles the Kurds, and had no centuries-long religious and political division among the Vietnamese. Iraq is just not a nation, unlike Vietnam. Iraq is at most a binational entity, but there is a case for arguing that the Iraqi nationalisms of Sunni Arabs and Shia Arabs are as opposed to each other as they are to the United States.

In Vietnam, America replaced a French colonial regime, sought to maintain a partitioned country, supported a coup (at least in outcome) in the South, and fought left-wing nationalists and Communists who had widespread public support. In Iraq, the United States encouraged Kurdistan to rejoin the state, to remake it as a federation, rejected partition, and fought right-wing pan-Arab fascists and sectarian theocrats.

America has strategic interests in the Persian Gulf that transcend any that were claimed in Vietnam. America has an interest in preventing anti-American powers from establishing a chokehold or a monopoly over energy supplies and supply routes that remain vitally important to the United States and the world economy. One may argue that the United States has not guarded its strategic interests well or appropriately, but that it has them neither its friends nor its critics deny.

Comparisons between al-Qaeda and Communism require more nuanced rebuttals. Al-Qaeda or Salafi jihadism, whether in the world of Islam or amid the Muslim minorities of the West and Asia, poses nothing like the strategic threat to the United States and its allies that was once posed by Marxist-Leninist regimes or by Communist parties in other regimes. The Sunni Salafists have had only brief moments of ascendancy, mostly in weak states such as Afghanistan and Sudan. They perhaps had a prototype in Libya that is now being repudiated by the man who brought it into being. Were Sunni Salafi to capture state power in oil-rich Iraq or Saudi Arabia, then they could pose a much more profound strategic danger than at present. This is why it is important that al-Qaeda and Salafi jihadism be extinguished—militarily and ideologically, but as yet they neither have significant states nor weapons of mass destruction.

A high proportion of Western liberals and leftists either sympathized with or directly supported the victory of Vietnamese nationalism under a Communist banner. They saw the victory of the Vietnamese as an anticolonial struggle for self-determination. Only a self-hating minority would similarly celebrate the defeat of America in Iraq under the banner of Sunni Salafi jihadism or Sadrist theocracy. A victory for the Baathists, ex- or otherwise, would be a victory for a species of fascism. A victory for either the Sunni jihadists or the Sadrists would be a victory for neofundamentalist Islam with ethnic colors but with strikingly opposed views on the future of Iraq. And in any case, they are not going to win. The United States, on leaving Iraq, will not be negotiating a treaty in Paris with a government with which it has been directly at war, and with other great powers as signatories. The United States will be leaving Iraq at the request of Iraq's elected governments, not at the point of Arab guns or bayonets. There will not be helicopters leaving the U.S. Embassy in Baghdad with people hanging on for fear of retribution. In Iraq, the United States has brought a genocidal regime to an end; in Vietnam the United States executed major war crimes that led directly or through collateral damage to mass civilian deaths.

The U.S. occupations of Germany, Japan, and Korea were apparently required reading for neophytes in the Coalition Provisional Authority bent on "nation-building" and "state-building" in Iraq. Whatever guidance these cases may have provided in dealing with war-torn and devastated economies or in occupations organized through the Pentagon, they were inept for guidance on Iraq's past and future. Germany, Japan, and Korea, like Vietnam, were homogeneous nation-states (and more homogeneous at the end of World War II than they had been before). Germany, Korea, and Vietnam experienced partition because of the Cold War, not because of internal ethnic or sectarian divisions. Germany, as it happened, was rebuilt in its west as a model federal democracy, but around a homogeneous people eager to avoid incorporation within the Soviet bloc. Japan was reconstructed with some of its old institutions, including its Emperor, and embarked on a long march to economic success. Germany and Japan had experienced modernization and fascism and had aggressively sought to carve out regional empires. In these respects they resembled Saddam's Iraq, but the latter had never developed a comparable industrial economy. Korea remains partitioned to this day, but much of its postwar history was under military dictatorship—hardly a model for what the United States should seek to pursue in Iraq. Above all, none of these cases warranted reconstruction as multinational or multireligious entities (Catholic-Protestant relations in Germany were nowhere near as venomous as those between Shia and Sunni factions in Iraq). Altogether these comparisons are not fruitful—except in reminding us that Iraq is primarily composed of three peoples, not one.

The United States intervened in the Balkans in the mid-1990s and restored the external boundaries of Bosnia-Herzegovina, which had seceded from Yugoslavia only to have its secession militarily contested both by Bosnian Serbs and by Serbia. After extensive ethnic expulsions and genocide, a three-way war was brought to an end through American military and diplomatic power, with some help from a divided European Union. In the Dayton Accords, American diplomats and lawyers forged a constitution for Bosnia-Herzegovina. They had earlier created a federation between the Bosniaks (Bosnian Muslims) and the Croats, and they combined this federation with Republika Srspka (the Serbian Republic). Three peoples were united in a confederation of two entities. One entity was a federation, the other a unitary state of Serbs. Power-sharing institutions and quotas for public office were established. Each entity had its own security powers. Implementing the settlement was to be overseen by an international High Representative, backed up by the armed might of NATO.

On the face of it Iraq and Bosnia have some similarities. Both have three major peoples. In each case the U.S. intervention was (eventually) supported by two peoples but enforced on a third (eventually). Genocide and ethnic expulsion (past and present) were used to justify the two interventions, directly in one case (Bosnia), indirectly in the other (Iraq). Some have also suggested that a confederal division of Iraq might make sense and might even be stable if it were to be produced through negotiations among the major participants and enforced by foreign military power. Bosnia suggests this possibility. And it has been nonviolent since 1995.

But there similarities may end, although not necessarily instructive comparisons. The establishment and maintenance of the Dayton Accords have required a huge NATO troop presence in a small country (whose total population is less than that of the Kurdistan Region). Even if such an agreement could be engineered in Iraq, partition to create a three-unit confederation would not necessarily accomplish what most American advocates of partition want: a substantive withdrawal of American troops. As the conservative writer Max Boot has argued, "a serious partition plan of this kind would require an indefinite, long-term presence by our forces—at least 450,000 soldiers, if we are to have the same troop-to-civilian ratio as in Bosnia. Despite claims to the contrary by Henry Kissinger and others, it is hard to imagine that India or Indonesia would volunteer sizable numbers of their own troops to lessen our burden. They certainly have not done so in the past, notwithstanding considerable American pleading and arm-twisting. Yet without such outside supervision, any de facto partition would result not in less violence but in a great deal more, at least in the short run."[7] We are not likely to see a test of Boot's claim in the last sentence.

The most important instructive lesson from the Balkans is this: Bosnia is still governed as an international protectorate, in which none of the entities enjoy fully meaningful self-government. In fact, Bosnia has all the global and European international organizations of a multilateralist's dreams present within it and directly engaged in its governance. Successive high commissioners have sought to recentralize in order to create what they invariably call a common state. In the process they have stripped each of the entities of their sovereignty and of their autonomy in security affairs. If they were free to reject this process the Bosnian Serbs would, and so might the Bosnian Croats. There are two reasons why the High Representative is obeyed. One is the sheer power of the foreign troop presence after an exhausting civil war (which on a per head basis almost certainly exceeded the scales of violence in postintervention Iraq). The other is the promise of admission to the European Union if Bosnia meets standards of compliance spelled out by the High Representative. Neither the stick nor the carrot to sustain this kind of system is available in Iraq, even if we were to conclude that it would be desirable.

There is another instructive lesson to be extracted from this comparison. In Bosnia an external partition was prevented, but its internal partitions were broadly respected. The Bosniaks and the Croats had wanted to secede from Yugoslavia, whereas the Serbs did not. So Bosnia obtained its independence through a contested secession and descended into a deep war because the losers from its secession sought to secede themselves—and used expulsions and genocide to clear their path. No directly comparable process has yet occurred in contemporary Iraq. Far from seceding, the Kurdistan Region has relinked with Iraq after Saddam, and neither Sunni nor Shia Arabs have sought to secede from Iraq. Iraq is being fought and struggled over, but so far no entity has sought to secede. Kurdistan reserves the right to secede in extremis. It will not do if its constitutional rights are implemented and respected. That is another reason the United States in its withdrawal should seek to protect Iraq's Constitution—and Kurdistan's rights. In so doing it will be heading off the dangers that might otherwise occur from a contested secession.

Neither Hopeless Nor Forlorn, and Without Illusions

It is for readers to judge whether these arguments have been compelling. They amount, in sum, to a defense of Iraq's new constitutional order and the claim that the best way for the United States to defend that new order is through a well-organized withdrawal, first to military bases within Iraq and then comprehensively at the request of Iraqi authorities. Any U.S. bases in Iraq should be for a set period of time, present at the will of authorized Iraqi governments, federal or regional, and soon confined to training and any joint external alliance role that might be agreed upon. It is best to withdraw substantively sooner rather than later because that offers the best way to stabilize the prospects of the Constitution. Substantive withdrawal should occur while the Baghdad government is still weak enough to be obliged to negotiate with all the major communities of Iraq and before the newly resurgent Baghdad government poses a threat to Iraq and its neighbors. The argument is, finally, that the United States must use its diplomatic and other forms of power to stabilize Iraq's neighborhood to give the new federation a chance to work.

This argument is made without illusions. No effort has been made to suggest that the new order in Baghdad, Erbil, and Basra is perfect. Its democratic imperfections are obvious, although they are difficult to redress amid intense contention and civil strife. Its liberalism is limited, especially in Arab Iraq. Everyplace in Iraq would benefit from more accountable, more transparent, and less corrupt government. But the new order is in major part a function of arrangements made by elected Iraqi leaders and endorsed by their voters. Democracy and liberalism should not be confused: Iraq as a whole has much more of the former than the latter; the Kurdistan Region has an adequate and rising share of both.

Any decision to withdraw from Iraq must avoid illusions and not be based on feeble excuses. It is not true that Iraqis simply want theocracy: the Kurds want democracy and the Arabs democracy with Islamic characteristics (see Appendix 2). Not all Iraqis want the United States to leave—the Kurds are most fearful of a U.S. departure, which is another reason the United States should support Iraq's Constitution, which if implemented, amply satisfies Kurdistan's historical aspirations. If the United States leaves Iraq, it is an illusion to pretend that the United States will stand ready to go back to fight al-Qaeda. Unless by some strange route al-Qaeda takes power within a major territory of Iraq, that scenario will not happen: Shia Arabs, Kurds, and indeed the Sunni Arabs of Iraq will take care of al-Qaeda with the assistance of U.S. intelligence. It is an illusion to pretend that the United Nations can or should replace the United States in Iraq by providing security or governance, although it can assist in development and humanitarian work and in constitutional and electoral advice (functions it performs quite well). It is an illusion to pretend that the United States can promote or deliver a substantial modification of Iraq's Constitution on behalf of Sunni Arabs, now or later. Such changes as may arise will come from bargaining among Iraq's parties, not from U.S. diktats. It is an illusion and contemptuous of Iraq's sovereignty to require its elected politicians to meet U.S. benchmarks and deadlines that confirm to conventional U.S. expectations of what would be good for Iraq.

It is also an illusion to pretend that a U.S. withdrawal from Iraq will necessarily promote reconciliation. If Arab governing parties in Baghdad do not honor the constitutional commitments they have made to Kurdistan, that will make a breakup of Iraq likely—but that judgment merely underlines the importance of U.S. support for the Constitution made under its protection though not under its instructions. But it is not an illusion to suggest that a withdrawal along the lines proposed here will make reconciliation between Arab and Kurd and between Sunni and Shia Arab more feasible. And it is not an illusion to argue that the United States has the capabilities to sustain the kind of foreign policy that is required to give the Iraqi federation a chance to breathe. How these capabilities will be used will determine historians' judgments on the president who takes office on January 20, 2009.

Appendix 1
On Difficulties in
Counting Deaths in Iraq

The Iraq Body Count, which sponsors the web site of the same name, is an independent group. Its founders opposed the intervention in Iraq. It counts deaths using numerous public sources. It thinks, fairly, that its figures are likely to be underestimates, although not major underestimates. It rightly criticizes the failure of the U.S. government and its allies to organize an official body count. Its web site is headlined with a quotation from U.S. General Tommy Franks—the commander of U.S. forces during the Iraq intervention—that "We don't do body counts." Despite the political origins of Iraq Body Count, it is criticized by far left critics of the U.S. intervention, who prefer to extrapolate from survey studies done by Les Roberts and colleagues, two of which have been published in the UK's *The Lancet* medical journal. These studies seek to estimate all "excess deaths," subsequent to the intervention, that is, they include combatants, infant deaths, deaths from disease, and so on. They do so in relation to a presumed death rate that would have occurred without the intervention.

My previous primary empirical research domain was conflict in Northern Ireland. When I was on the faculty of the London School of Economics and Political Science I worked with the Irish Information Partnership, which was the first organized multiperson group to try to report all public data on violence related to that conflict. It is for that reason that I am strongly inclined to respect the working methods and caution of the Iraq Body Count group. It also partly explains my agreement with the skepticism that group has expressed about Roberts's work. Roberts's politics may not have contaminated his surveys, but it has colored his extrapolations from them.

The published studies in *The Lancet* appear to be classic examples of unrepresentative samples. The Iraq Body Count writers and researchers observe that among the implications of Roberts's and coworkers October 2006 study published by *The Lancet*, which estimated, through survey methods, that over 650,000 excess Iraqi deaths had occurred since March 2003, are the following:

- On average, a thousand Iraqis were killed every day in the first six months of 2006, with fewer than one-tenth of them being noticed by any public surveillance mechanisms—including health authorities, security personnel, and mass media;
- Over 800,000 Iraqis suffered blast-wounds and other serious injuries in 2004–6, but fewer than 80,000 of them received any hospital treatment—which would be bizarre behavior by injured people and their relatives;
- Over 7 percent of Iraq's adult male population has been violently killed, with not less than 10 percent killed in the worst affected areas of central Iraq. This would mean a literal decimation of Sunni Arab males (not just those of combat age); and
- Half a million death certificates were received by families that were never officially recorded as issued.[1]

The methodology of the published *Lancet* studies, in principle, is fine, provided that the samples are representative and not biased toward zones of conflict, and provided that procedures and data collection are fine. There are, however, multiple difficulties on all these fronts. How does one get a representative sample in a state with no reliable census since 1947 and that has been racked by internal repression and external wars since 1979? The 1997 census was rigged by Saddam to inflate the numbers living outside the KRG—to maximize revenues under the UN oil-for-food program. Flight-based demographic estimates, as in South Africa, have been shown to overestimate populations. How does one get reliable responses from people in a highly conflictual space? How does one measure "excess deaths" because of war without highly controversial counterfactuals? Estimates of infant-mortality rates before and after the March 2003 intervention are highly problematic (and some of the same surveyors, it has been suggested, have used conveniently different estimates over time to measure the impact of the UN-authorized sanctions in the 1990s and the March 2003 intervention). Is it reasonable to attribute all "excess deaths" (based on some extrapolation of the regime's likely performance in public health) to the American and British dominated intervention? Would life chances have got worse or better or stayed the same under Saddam? (And whose fault would that have been?)

There are no "addresses" in the American or European sense in Iraq, at least not when I was last in Kurdistan and northern Iraq. Getting a properly stratified probability sample is therefore difficult. The method used was a grid, a geographical information system, followed by cluster sampling. The results, it has been suggested, may have been contaminated by "main street" and major "cross-road" bias; that is, oversampling may have occurred in areas likely to have higher levels of violence. The teams whose work was published in *The Lancet* failed, according to their own evidence, in giving appropriate time per interviewee—questionable conduct, not on the part of the organizers, but likely on the part of the possibly scared interviewers. The cluster sampling proceeded by word of mouth in order to inhibit suspicions, but that may have led to overconcentration on those who lost family members. (I give the teams the benefit of the doubt on family structure—that they have not, for example, over-reported the death of the same "brother" who is in fact a cousin of many but called a "brother" by many in the vicinity, as might happen among both Arabs and Kurds.) Last, the estimates published in *The Lancet* vastly exceed all others, including those of the Iraqi Living Conditions Survey (to May 2004), which had a much larger and better distributed sample.

The published estimates in the two *Lancet* studies suggested death tolls even higher than those who have had an interest in exaggerating them. Before the reports were published, neither critics of the war nor armed opponents of the U.S. intervention suggested figures in these ranges. Now, sadly, they are treated as authoritative, especially in the European press and among critics of the intervention. The *Lancet* reports are also often cited elsewhere without their confidence limits, which are exceedingly wide. The October 2006 report expresses 95 percent confidence that the excess deaths are between 300,000 and 900,000. If these estimates are right and everyone else is wrong, then the daily deaths are both grossly underreported and undernoticed by both reasonable and highly partisan people who have an interest in reporting mass horrors. To put it rhetorically: Why does anyone think that United States, the United Kingdom, and the new Iraqi governmental officials have been competent in covering up genocidal massacres when they have been so incompetent in every other respect?

A more recent household survey, this time published in the January 31 issue of the *New England Journal of Medicine*, estimated that 151,000 violent deaths occurred in Iraq between March 2003 and June 2006.[2] The Iraq

Family Health Study Group's 95 percent confidence intervals are between 104,000 and 223,000. These figures are just one-fourth of the point figure in Burnham and colleagues' estimates published in *The Lancet*. They are also three times that of the Iraq Body Count in the same period—though the latter does not count combatant deaths, which would have been picked up in the surveys. The Iraq Family Health Survey Group had a much larger sample size, with more than a thousand separate clusters. Its quality control measures appear to have been much better, and it is much more convincing for these reasons than the reports published in *The Lancet*.[3]

The Iraq Body Count therefore seems to provide a reliable lower bound estimate of the number of violent civilian deaths that may have occurred, and the IFHSG's study provides a good estimate of the highest number in the period it surveys. It is also reasonable to assume that the Iraq Body Count provides a good portrait of trends in violence, even if it does not capture all violence-related deaths.

In April 2008, Professor John Sloboda, the Executive Director of the Oxford Research Group, director of the ORG's project on Recording Casualties in Armed Conflicts, and a member of the Iraq Body Count, made an eloquent appeal entitled, "Can There Be Any 'Just War' If We Do Not Document the Dead and Injured?"[4] He correctly observed that it is now much easier to record deaths during armed conflicts than it used to be and rightly suggested that it should be a governmental and military obligation. He cites the *Bosnian Book of the Dead* as an example of what can be done. That book records all the details of 97,207 individuals killed there during 1992–95. Another example is *Lost Lives*, which records all the details of those killed in the conflict in and over Northern Ireland since 1966.[5] But, surprisingly, Sloboda does not reference *Le Livre noir de Saddam Hussein (The Black Book of Saddam Hussein)*.[6] The subtitle of this book, edited by the indomitable Chris Kutchera, is *Two Million Victims*. It marks a first step toward an equally necessary but still unfinished, task to that commended by Sloboda. The lamentable task of composing a full *Iraqi Book of the Dead* remains to be fulfilled. The Iraq Body Count is to be commended for starting the assignment for the period after April 2003.

Xenophobia, Sexism, In-Group Solidarity, Traditional Religiosity, and Democratic Dispositions in Iraq

Social scientists have long argued that existential insecurity—fear of death —makes people more likely than they might otherwise be to express xenophobia, hatred, and intolerance toward foreigners and other out-groups. Existential insecurity also makes them strengthen their commitments to their traditional culture, their in-group (a variation of this thesis is sometimes called the "terror-management hypothesis" by social psychologists). An important study published in 2007 by Ronald Inglehart, Mansoor Moaddel, and Mark Tessler, based on the World Values Survey (WVS), allows us to consider Iraq's public (and its three major communities, Shia Arabs, Kurds, and Sunni Arabs) in a truly comparative and revealing perspective on these subjects.[1]

They show that at the end of 2004 the Iraqi public as a whole expressed higher levels of intolerance of foreigners than any other of the more than eighty publics surveyed in the WVS. It also showed an exceptionally strong tendency to disrespect lower status groups (women, for example) or out-groups (such as homosexuals), and very high levels of in-group solidarity (demonstrated both in pride as Iraqis and with respect to solidarity within each of three main communities).

There are two obvious explanations of these patterns. One would suggest that Iraqis have always been extraordinarily xenophobic, intolerant, racist, patriarchal, sexist, and sexualist. (One implication would be that Iraq is truly barren soil for democratic pluralism.) The major problem with this hypothesis is that it does not conform with most reports of Iraq before the Baathists, whether issued by anthropologists, travelers, historians, or

Iraqis. Even if they were not Swedes, Iraqis were just not regarded as the world leaders in these negative respects. The second explanation and that favored by Inglehart, Moaddel and Tessler is that it has been the extreme existential insecurity engendered by the genocidal and repressive Baath regime, followed by the extreme insecurity of postintervention Iraq, that has generated these intensely negative attitudinal responses.

There were obvious reasons why in late 2004 Arab Iraqis would reject having Americans or British as their neighbors, one of the survey questions posed. But despite the fact that the French government had strongly opposed the U.S. intervention in Iraq, fully 90 percent of Arab Iraqis said they would not like to have someone from France as a neighbor. This is in contrast with 51 percent of Kurds, who perhaps disliked the French for not supporting the intervention but disliked them half as much as Arabs. In the case of every named group of foreigners in the survey, Kurds were more tolerant than were Arab Iraqis, but they were not especially tolerant by global standards. A full 61 percent of Iraqis as a whole did not want Turks as neighbors, and 55 percent did not want Iranians. Arab Iraqis are the global outliers in the WVS in not wanting to have foreigners as neighbors. The Kurds of Iraq are nearly half as much as likely to display xenophobia but still figure in second place among the global publics.

As for patriarchal views, 93 percent of Iraqi Arabs agreed that men make better political leaders than women by contrast with 72 percent of Kurds. When asked the values that should be encouraged at home in the development of children, Iraqi Arab respondents were among the lowest in the world in selecting "independence"; by contrast, Kurds ranked slightly above the international median. Iraqi Arabs were, however, world leaders in emphasizing "obedience"; Kurds followed them, but not as intensively. Iraqi Arabs were joint top among the eighty publics surveyed (with Indonesians) in emphasizing the importance of religion in their lives; Kurds, by contrast, fell well short of their Arab peers. Iraqi Arabs came second only to Pakistanis in considering atheists unfit for public office; by contrast, the Kurds of Iraq were significantly less likely to endorse this view but were among the higher-ranked publics of the world in low tolerance of atheists in government.

Fully 86 percent of Arab Iraqis were "very proud" to be Iraqi at the end of 2004—they were sixth in the world in national pride (the five nations above them are also besieged, so national pride seems higher amid adversity rather than during periods of serene prosperity). Only a third of Kurds felt the same way as Arab Iraqis. With respect to in-group solidarity the rankings of Iraq's major communities were different: 96 percent of Kurds said they would trust other Kurds "a great deal"; 86 percent of Shia Arabs said that of Shia Arabs; and 68 percent of Sunni Arabs felt that way about their fellows. Even the last figure, however, is exceptionally high among the global publics. Insecurity generates both high out-group hostility, and high in-group solidarity. Inglehart, Moaddel, and Tessler report that both dispositions increased in 2006—when all, rationally, should have felt more insecure. For example, the percentage not wanting Turks or Iranians as neighbors went up to 71 and 61 percent, respectively.

These data are highly suggestive. The greater security of the Kurds (because of their longer freedom from Saddam and the greater internal security in the KRG) may explain their higher tolerance toward out-groups. The deep insecurities of Arab Iraqis, pre- and post-Baathist rule, powerfully explain their currently very deep xenophobia, intolerance, and emphasis on traditional values. There is an implication that Inglehart and his colleagues rightly allow their readers to entertain—namely, if security can be established in Iraq, then these intensely negative dispositions will fall and Iraq will have much better democratic prospects.

They report that the WVS survey shows that 85 percent of the Iraqi public agreed that "democracy may have problems, but it is better than any other form of government." Kurds affirmed this proposition more than Shia Arabs, and Shia Arabs more than Sunni Arabs, but all affirmed it at supermajority levels of support. Iraqis were also asked, however, to respond to the following question, "I am going to describe various types of political systems and ask you what you think about each of them as a way of governing this country. For each one would you say it is a very good, a fairly good, fairly bad, or very bad way of governing this country?" Among five options the two leading preferences were for "Having a democratic system" and "Having an Islamic government, where religious authorities have absolute power." The results are shown in Figure A.

The results show that Kurds are strong exponents of democracy (92 percent thought democracy was "very good" or "fairly good"). The Shia Arabs concur (at 90 percent), and Sunni Arabs are not far behind (with 85 percent giving positive affirmations). But they also show that a supermajority of Shia Arabs, a bare majority of Sunni Arabs, and a minority of Kurds also favor Islamic government (phrased in a strongly theocratic form). These figures are highly suggestive. A high proportion of Arab Iraqis see no contradiction between democracy and religious government, whereas a majority of Kurds do. Arab Iraqis are more likely, it would appear, to want to

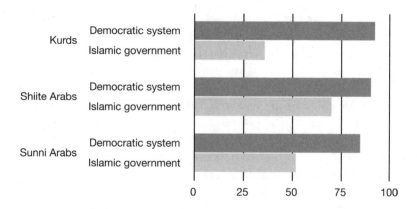

Figure A. Support for democracy as opposed to Islamic government (percentages) among Iraq's three major communities (December 2004). Adapted from Ronald Inglehart, Mansoor Moaddel, and Mark Tessler, "Xenophobia and In-Group Solidarity in Iraq: A Natural Experiment on the Impact of Insecurity," in *Values and Perceptions of the Islamic and Middle Eastern Publics,* ed. Mansoor Moaddel (New York: Palgrave Macmillan, 2007), 311.

combine Islam and democracy, whereas most Kurds would want to subordinate Islam to democracy. That may be because Kurdish culture is more tolerant than Arab culture; alternatively, it may be because Kurds have had longer experience of nondictatorial government; and there may, of course, be truth in both of these explanations.

Notes

Preface

1. I remained a salaried member of the faculty of the University of Pennsylvania while the Kurdistan Government paid my university for my time. The other members of the team in 2004 were Khaled Salih of the University of Southern Denmark, a Kurd and Swedish citizen and later the KRG Spokesman, and Peter W. Galbraith, the former U.S. Ambassador to Croatia. In 2005 the advisors included the Polish American Professor Karol Soltan of the University of Maryland and later Jonathan Morrow, an international lawyer.

2. The word is often mistranslated; e.g., Aaron Glantz, *How America Lost Iraq* (New York: Penguin, 2005), 90, has it as "after-death men." To judge by his book, he would prefer it if the Peshmerga were ghosts.

3. See Middle East Watch, *Genocide in Iraq: The Anfal Campaign Against the Kurds* (New York: Human Rights Watch, 1983), and Joost R. Hiltermann, *A Poisonous Affair: America, Iraq and the Gassing of Halabja* (Cambridge: Cambridge University Press, 2007). Hiltermann and I disagree about Iraq's new Constitution (which he insisted should be immediately scrapped), on Kirkuk (which he thinks the Kurds should cease to aspire to unify with the Kurdistan Region), and on appropriate international policy toward Iraq, but his data collection on the Anfal campaign will always remain important. Hiltermann seems to prefer Kurds as victims rather than as exercisers of their rights.

Part I Introduction

Epigraphs: President Bush quotation from http://www.whitehouse.gov/news/releases/2003/05/20030501-15.html; Bush made these remarks on board the U.S.S. *Abraham Lincoln*, dressed as a fighter pilot, off the coast of San Diego, under the banner "Mission Accomplished." Ambassador Crocker quotation from http://armedservices.house.gov/pdfs/FC040908/Crocker_Testimony040808.pdf, Testimony to the Senate Armed Services Committee, 13.

1. Aaron Glantz, *How America Lost Iraq* (New York: Penguin, 2005), published his book before the making of the Iraq Constitution (he chides the Kurds both for being realists and for expecting too much). David L. Phillips, *Losing Iraq: Inside the Postwar Reconstruction Fiasco* (New York: Westview Press, 2005), makes some telling observations on failures in U.S. planning and administration, but he does not consider whether any reversals or improvements in policy might be possible. Larry Diamond, *Squandered Victory: The American Occupation and the Bungled Effort to Bring Democracy to Iraq* (New York: Owl Books, 2005), has an important afterthought toward the end: "Despite the litany of blunders we have committed, Iraq may yet emerge slowly from

the political chaos, first into a troubled semi-democracy, and then, gradually, into a democracy. But the costs will be much greater than we had imagined, or than were necessary" (305). While I would criticize his lack of knowledge of the Kurds and of their preferences and disagree with his criticisms of consociational democracy (317), Diamond's afterthought accurately describes the most optimistic tenor in the book before the reader. My friend Peter Galbraith's book, *The End of Iraq: How American Incompetence Created a War Without End* (New York: Simon and Schuster, 2006), which is required reading, is infinitely better than its title, which prematurely predicted the death of Iraq and what fortunately has never happened, "a war without end." Galbraith's book is far more sophisticated than his publisher's marketing strategy, and at most points is compatible with what is argued here. Jonathan Steele, *Defeat: Why America and Britain Lost Iraq* (London: I.B. Tauris, 2008), 2, advances what he calls a more fundamental thesis, namely, "No matter how efficient, sensitive, generous, and intelligent the U.S.-led Coalition Provisional Authority had been, it could not have succeeded....The occupation itself was the mistake." I agree, as does Galbraith, that the formal occupation, especially through the establishment of the CPA, was a critical mistake. But I disagree with many of Steele's other arguments, as I will occasionally observe in the notes below. Steele treats Iraq as just an Arab country and assimilates Kurds and minorities into his assessments of all Iraqis. If he treated the English as equivalent to all the inhabitants of the United Kingdom, he would be rebuked by his editors at *The Guardian*. Steele neglects how unintended good luck can emerge from chaos, the merits of Iraq's Constitution, and the wisdom of Churchill's observation that America can always be trusted to the do the right thing after exhausting all the alternatives. If Iraq pulls through, he will be another author with an embarrassing book title in libraries. Charles Ferguson, *No End in Sight: Iraq's Descent into Chaos* (New York: Public Affairs, 2008), the book accompanying his important documentary film, is a splendid series of interviews with participants in the U.S.-led occupation and may stand as the "verbatim" record of the "what went wrong literature," but there may yet be an end in sight that is better than chaos.

2. I use the plural "wars" in order not to forget that there was a first American war against Saddam's Iraq in 1991—to compel Saddam's withdrawal from Kuwait. This was followed by two civil wars—another war of the Iraqi state against Kurdish rebels and a war between the Baathists and the spontaneous and badly organized Shia Intifada uprising. From 1992 until 2003, there was a cold war between Iraq and a U.S.-led coalition—bent on enforcing UN Security Council resolutions that Iraq completely dismantle its weapons of mass destruction programs. "No-fly" zones were imposed and enforced by the United States against Saddam's forces, protecting an experiment in Kurdish autonomy, which was marred by an intra-Kurdish civil war. The second American war against Saddam took place in 2003. It was succeeded by a Sunni Arab-led set of insurgencies against the U.S. occupation and the successor Iraqi governments. It was also succeeded by an intra-Arab civil war between Sunni and Shia militias and the Iraqi federal government—in which more people died than in the earlier wars. Last, there has been an intermittent war for influence launched by the Sadrists, both against the Americans and against the Sadrists' nominal partners in the Baghdad government. That makes eight wars since 1991—and arguments could be made for more.

Chapter 1

1. "Background briefing" by White House Officials to the Press, White House, January 1, 2003.

2. For key documents on weapons of mass destruction until February 2004, see National Security Archive Electronic Briefing Book 80, "Iraq and Weapons of Mass Destruction," ed. Jeffrey Richelson, at http://www.gwu.edu/~nsarchiv/NSAEBB/NSAEBB80/. See also David Albright, *Iraq's Aluminum Tubes: Separating Fact from Fiction* (Washington, D.C.: Institute for Science and Security, December 5, 2003); Joseph Cirincione, Jessica T. Matthews, and George Perkovich, *WMD in Iraq: Evidence and Implications* (Washington, D.C.: Carnegie Endowment for International Peace, January 2004); Anthony Cordesman, *Intelligence and Iraqi Weapons of Mass Destruction: The Lessons from the Iraq War* (Washington, D.C.: Center for Strategic and International Studies, July 1, 2003); Barton Gellman, "Iraq's Arsenal War Only on Paper," *Washington Post* (January 7, 2004): A1, A14–15; International Institute for Strategic Studies, *Iraq's Weapons of Mass Destruction: A Net Assessment* (London: IISS, September 2003); Kenneth M. Pollack, "Spies, Lies, and Weapons: What Went Wrong," *Atlantic Monthly* 293 (1) (2004): 78–92; and Thomas Powers, "The Vanishing Case for War," *New York Review of Books* 50 (19) (December 4, 2003): 12–17.

3. CIA Director George Tenet was not alone in telling President Bush that it was "a slam dunk" that Iraq possessed WMDs; see Bob Woodward, *Plan of Attack* (New York: Simon & Schuster, 2004), 249.

4. See Hans Blix, *Disarming Iraq* (New York: Pantheon, 2004).

5. In speaking to the House of Representatives Armed Services Committee on September 18, 2002, Donald Rumsfeld said, "*We do know that the Iraqi regime currently has chemical and biological weapons of mass destruction, and we do know they're currently pursuing nuclear weapons*, that they have a proven willingness to use those weapons at their disposal and that they've proven an aspiration to seize the territory of and threaten their neighbors, proven support for and cooperation with terrorist networks and proven record of declared hostility and venomous rhetoric against the United States. Those threats should be clear to all" (my emphasis); http://transcripts.cnn.com/TRANSCRIPTS/0209/18/se.01.html.

On March 16, 2003, three days before the start of the U.S. intervention, Vice-President Dick Cheney was interviewed by Tim Russert on *Meet the Press*. He said, "in the late '70s, Saddam Hussein acquired nuclear reactors from the French. In 1981, the Israelis took out the Osirak reactor and stopped his nuclear weapons development at the time. Throughout the '80s, he mounted a new effort. I was told when I was defense secretary before the Gulf War that he was eight to ten years away from a nuclear weapon. And we found out after the Gulf War that he was within one or two years of having a nuclear weapon because he had a massive effort under way that involved four or five different technologies for enriching uranium to produce fissile materiel. We know that based on intelligence that he has been very, very good at hiding these kinds of efforts. He's had years to get good at it and we know he has been absolutely devoted to trying to acquire nuclear weapons. And we believe he has, in fact, reconstituted nuclear weapons. I think Mr. El Baradei frankly is wrong. And I think if you look at the track record of the International Atomic Energy Agency and this kind of issue, especially where Iraq's concerned, they have consistently underestimated or missed what it was Saddam Hussein was doing." See http://www.mtholyoke.edu/acad/intrel/bush/cheneymeetthepress.htm.

6. Fouad Ajami is among those who maintain that "the claims about Iraq's weapons of mass destruction were to prove incorrect, but they were made in good faith." "Why We Went to Iraq," *Wall Street Journal*, June 4, 2008. See Mark Danner, *The Secret Way to War: The Downing Street Memo and the Iraq War's Buried History* (New York: New York Review of Books, 2006), for the now orthodox view of critics of the Bush administration, namely, that reporting of intelligence was fixed to support a predetermined policy of invasion, to paraphrase a British official. There is now a more

recent claim from public and off-the-record sources that British and American intelligence personnel successfully turned the head of Saddam's head of intelligence, Tahir Jalil Habbush, immediately before the intervention. From him they are said to have learned that Saddam had no weapons of mass destruction but needed Iran's government to believe that he had. Such information was, however, unwelcome to senior officials in the Bush administration, who may have been intent on disinformation—or simply suspicious of the source. Outlined in Roy Suskind, *The Way of the World: A Story of Truth and Hope in an Age of Extremism* (New York: Harper, 2008), the story is accompanied by another remarkable claim, namely, that the White House forged a letter from Habbush that linked Saddam's Iraq to the attacks on September 11. However, two of Suskind's sources, one of them Rob Richard of the CIA, deny that a fake document was ordered or produced.

The literature on "threat inflation" by the Bush administration and the Blair government shows no signs of abatement. For a fluent statement, see Chaim Kaufmann, "Threat Inflation and the Failure of the Marketplace of Ideas," *International Security* 29 (1) (2004). See also Michael Isikoff and David Corn, *Hubris: The Inside Story of Spin, Scandal, and the Selling of the Iraq War* (New York: Crown, 2006); John Prados, *Hoodwinked: The Documents That Reveal How Bush Sold Us a War* (New York: New Press, 2004); and Paul R. Pillar, "Intelligence, Policy, and the War in Iraq," *Foreign Affairs* 85 (2) (2006): 15–27.

7. Article 9(E) of Iraq's 2005 Constitution reads: "The Iraqi Government shall respect and implement Iraq's international obligations regarding the non-proliferation, non-development, non-production, and non-use of nuclear, chemical, and biological weapons, and shall prohibit associated equipment, materiel, technologies, and delivery systems for use in the development, manufacture, production, and use of such weapons."

8. The opponents of the intervention in Iraq usually like to emphasize its illegality and its preemptive nature. I think they cannot so easily have it both ways. How preemptive can a war have been that was formally intended to apply a numerously affirmed set of Security Council resolutions?

9. In its latest annual report, for 2007, the University of Heidelberg's conflict barometer, which measures conflicts and codes their intensities, classified Iraq as one of a small number of full-scale wars in the world for the fourth year in a row. See http://www.hiik.de/en/konfliktbarometer/pdf/ConflictBarometer_2007.pdf.

10. See http://www.iraqbodycount.org/. The precise estimate on August 5, 2008, was between 86,456 and 94, 328 documented civilian deaths from violence. See Appendix 1.

11. Bremer's decision making and his liaison with his principals in Washington have been the subject of much debate. His defense may be found in his memoir, L. Paul Bremer, III, *My Year in Iraq: The Struggle to Build a Future of Hope* (New York: Simon & Schuster, 2006), 57–58, 223–24. See Chapters 6 and 7 of Charles Ferguson, *No End in Sight* (Washington, D.C.: Public Affairs, 2008), for revealing interviews with key decision makers. One thing is certain: Kurds and Shia Arabs in general were happy with the dissolution of an army that had become identified entirely with the regime.

12. Interview in *Asharq al-Awsat,* January 5, 2005.

13. The Iraq Study Group subsequently identified four core problems with governance arrangements in the new Iraq: (i) biased government by the Shia-led federal government, (ii) insecurity, (iii) rampant corruption, and (iv) problems caused by missing technocrats lost in de-Baathification. See James A. Baker III, Lee H. Hamilton, Lawrence S. Eagleburger, Vernon E. Jordan, Jr., Edwin Meese, III, Sandra Day O'Connor, Leon E. Panetta, William J. Perry, Charles S. Robb, and Alan K.

Simpson, *The Iraq Study Group Report: The Way Forward—A New Approach* (New York: Vintage, 2006). Who would not favor unbiased government, security, clean government and technocratic competence? But Baathists never provided impartial, secure or clean government.

14. It is conventional to refer to a "Sunni triangle" with its three points lying at (1) Tikrit in the north, (2) east of Baghdad in the central southeast, and (3) west of Ramadi in the central southwest. There is truth in the description, but the expression omits Mosul, the historic epicenter of Sunni Army officers, and tends to suggest that Baghdad is majority Sunni, which it has not been for a very long time.

15. An Iraqi general, Ahmed Rahal, said the regime did not even prepare for guerrilla warfare adequately: "We should have mined the roads and bridges. We should have planned a guerilla war. We were crippled by a lack of imagination," cited in Ahmed S. Hashim's *Insurgency and Counter-Insurgency in Iraq* (Ithaca, N.Y.: Cornell University Press, 2006), 12.

16. See Mohammed M. Hafez, *Suicide Bombers in Iraq: The Strategy and Ideology of Martyrdom* (Washington, D.C.: U.S. Institute of Peace Press, 2007), Appendix 1. The number 56 incorporates numerous claims by separate brigades within these groups. Hafez's generally well-focused study is complemented by the extended treatment of the Sunni-dominated insurgency groups in Hashim's *Insurgency and Counter-Insurgency in Iraq*.

17. Hafez, *Suicide Bombers in Iraq*, 53.

18. For a discussion of Zarqawi of varying quality, see Loretta Napoleoni, *Insurgent Iraq: Al Zarqawi and the New Generation* (London: Constable and Robinson, 2005). The Jordanian Abu Musab al-Zarqawi had been an Afghan jihadist. Zarqawi and his colleagues fled to Iraq in 2002–3 after the Americans toppled the Taliban regime. They initially were hosted by Ansar al-Islam, the Islamic jihadists of Kurdistan, which was shortly after crushed by American troops and Kurdish Peshmerga. Zarqawi emerged soon after as the leader of the Tawhid wal-Jihad in Iraq—specializing in brutal Internet-broadcast beheadings and the organization of suicide bombings. In October 2004, he renamed his organization al-Qaeda in the Land of the Two Rivers (Mesopotamia or Iraq) and received Osama bin Laden's public imprimatur some two months after.

19. Sadiq al-Sadr had been the cousin of a previous Grand Ayatollah, Mohammed Baqir al-Sadr (Sadr I), whom the regime executed in 1980. His sister, Amina Sadr bint al-Huda, was raped in front of him, and he had a nail driven through his head before both were killed. For an intrepid and illuminating investigation of the Sadrs and the Sadrists, see Patrick Cockburn, *Muqtada: Muqtada Al-Sadr, the Shia Revival, and the Struggle for Iraq* (New York: Scribner, 2008).

20. The Mahdi army lost far more men than did the Coalition forces. The ratio of losses may have been ten to one, showing fierce commitment from the Sadrists. They disrupted American supply lines so extensively that Bremer had to consider rationing the food of the CPA's staff; see Galbraith, *The End of Iraq*, 10–11.

21. For a memoir of a British CPA official who had to cope with the Sadrist uprising in Wasit Province, see Mark Etherington, *Revolt on the Tigris: The Al-Sadr Uprising and the Governing of Iraq* (London: Hurst, 2005).

22. For a page-turning account of life as an obligatory friend of Saddam by a plastic surgeon and artist, see Ala Bashir, *The Insider: Trapped in Saddam's Brutal Regime* (London: Abacus, 2005).

23. See Marc Sageman, *Leaderless Jihad* (Philadelphia: University of Pennsylvania Press, 2008), and his previous *Understanding Terror Networks* (Philadelphia: University of Pennsylvania Press, 2004), for the most compelling analyses of the jihadist networks.

24. My own view at the time, published later in 2005, and not changed since, was that an appalling genocidal regime was removed, but for the wrong reasons: Brendan O'Leary, "Afterword: Vistas of Exit from Baghdad," in *The Future of Kurdistan in Iraq*, ed. Brendan O'Leary, John McGarry, and Khaled Salih (Philadelphia: University of Pennsylvania Press, 2005), 288–89.

25. Fouad Ajami, "No Surrender," *Wall Street Journal*, March 19, 2008.

26. For anticipation that al-Qaeda in Iraq's vulnerable moment would come through its attacks on its own constituency of Sunni Muslims, see Brendan O'Leary and Karin Von Hippel, "Winning the War of Ideas," *Washington Times*, December 1, 2005. For comparative reflections on what works in policy toward insurgents that use terrorism, see Brendan O'Leary and Andrew Silke, "Conclusion: Understanding and Ending Persistent Conflicts, Bridging Research and Policy," and Brendan O'Leary and John Tirman, "Introduction: Thinking About Durable Political Violence," in *Terror, Insurgency, and the State: Ending Protracted Conflicts*, ed. Marianne Heiberg, Brendan O'Leary, and John Tirman (Philadelphia: University of Pennsylvania Press, 2007), 1–17, 387–426. For different criticisms of the Bush administration's global approach to terrorism, see Ian S. Lustick, *Trapped in the War on Terror* (Philadelphia: University of Pennsylvania Press, 2006), and Stephen Holmes, *The Matador's Cape: America's Reckless Response to Terror* (New York: Cambridge University Press, 2007).

27. See Juan R. I. Cole, *The Ayatollahs and Democracy in Iraq*, ISIM Paper 7 (Leiden: International Institute for the Study of Islam in the Modern World, Amsterdam University Press, 2006). Sistani still holds an Iranian passport and needed a visa to return to Iraq after recent medical treatment in the United Kingdom.

28. The text may be found as Appendix 2 to O'Leary, McGarry, and Salih, eds., *The Future of Kurdistan in Iraq*. My commentary may be found in the same volume, "Power-Sharing, Pluralist Federation, and Federacy," 47–91.

29. It is against international law for an occupation authority to draft another country's constitution—so it was inappropriate for the CPA advisors even to talk of drafting Iraq's Constitution.

30. "(a) Islam is the official religion of the State and is to be considered a source of legislation. No law that contradicts the universally agreed tents of Islam, the principles of democracy, or the rights cited in Chapter Two of this Law may be enacted during the transitional period. This Law respects the Islamic identity of the majority of the Iraqi people and guarantees the full religious rights of all individuals to freedom of religious belief and practice," from Article 7 of the Transitional Administrative Law; see Appendix 2 of O'Leary, McGarry, and Salih, eds., *The Future of Kurdistan in Iraq*, 317.

31. It is nice to report a successful empirical prediction in this respect; see Karna Ekland, Brendan O'Leary, and Paul R. Williams, "Negotiating a Federation in Iraq," in *The Future of Kurdistan in Iraq*, ed. O' Leary, McGarry, and Salih, 116–42, written in the spring of 2004.

32. For the elections and their outcomes, see Liam Anderson and Gareth Stansfield, "The Implications of Elections for Federalism in Iraq," *Publius: The Journal of Federalism* 35 (3) (2005): 1–24.

33. Fouad Ajami, "Blind Liberation: Review of Ali A. Allawi, *The Occupation of Iraq: Winning the War, Losing the Peace*," *New Republic Online*, April 23, 2007.

34. See John McGarry and Brendan O'Leary, "Iraq's Constitution of 2005: Liberal Consociation as Political Prescription," *International Journal of Constitutional Law* 5 (4) (2007): 670–98, reprinted in *Constitutional Design for Divided Societies: Integration or Accommodation?*, ed. Sujit Choudhry (Oxford: Oxford University Press, 2008), 342–68.

35. See Brendan O'Leary, "Federalizing Natural Resources in Iraq's Constitution," in *Iraq: Preventing a New Generation of Conflict*, ed. Markus E. Bouillon, David Malone, and Ben Rowswell (Boulder, Colo.: Lynne Rienner, 2007), 189–202.

36. The fall in the seat-share of the Kurdistan Alliance was also caused by an adverse change in the election law. List proportional representation was maintained, but in December 2005 it was organized by lists in each of the governorates, not in Iraq as a whole. And because the compensatory seats, introduced to correct disproportionality, were also organized by governorate and not across Iraq as a whole, it meant that Kurds were not rewarded for their higher turnout. In an Iraq-wide electorate, Kurds would have won more seats because their core governorates had the highest turnouts.

37. Jonathan Steele narrates witnessing the visit by Condoleezza Rice and Jack Straw to persuade Ja'afari to resign: *Defeat: Why America and Britain Lost Iraq* (Berkeley, Calif.: Counterpoint, 2008), 227–29. He uses the moment as his opening story for a chapter labeled "The Farce of Sovereignty." They did try to get him to resign after a long delay in government formation after the election, but Steele fails to emphasize that it was the Kurds and the newly elected Sunni Arabs who had made Ja'afari's position untenable by refusing to support his re-election. Though Steele notes that al-Maliki emerged from the same party to replace Ja'afari, he does not reflect on the fact, which he registers, that the preferred candidate of the Americans and the British, Adel Abdel Mahdi, now Iraq's vice president, was not the successor. In short, Iraqi sovereignty was not farcical even if it was not yet fully restored.

38. See Andrew Cockburn, *Rumsfeld: His Rise, Fall, and Catastrophic Legacy* (New York: Scribner, 2007), for a well-documented indictment of Bush's Secretary of Defense. He deliberately used his enthusiasm for the "revolution in military affairs" to prevent any feasible long-term planning for the reconstruction of Iraq—including sufficient troops to provide public order. He treated Iraq as an experiment in military strategy, divorced from politics and basic human needs, rather than a place which had suffered three decades of a totalitarian dictatorship, two major external wars, genocide, and severe sanctions. See also Fred Kaplan, *Daydream Believers: How a Few Grand Ideas Wrecked American Power* (Hoboken, N.J.: John Wiley, 2008).

Chapter 2

1. British commentary typically derides Prime Minister Tony Blair as George Bush's or America's "poodle" on Iraq matters. The diplomatic sophisticate's version of the claim may be found in Christopher Meyer, *DC Confidential: The Controversial Memoirs of Britain's Ambassador to the U.S. at the Time of 9/11 and the Run-up to the Iraq War* (London: Phoenix, 2006), but his case is no more compelling than his habit of wearing red socks. Blair, however, had a history as a humanitarian interventionist—in Kosovo, Sierra Leone, and Liberia as well as Iraq. He was more interventionist than Clinton on Kosovo and unilateralist in Sierra Leone. He also sought to make the intervention in Iraq more multilateral and to win UN support for principled as well as pragmatic reasons, and he may have been responsible for Garner's replacement by Bremer.

2. Richard Lugar, "Key GOP Senator, Richard Lugar, Blasts Bush Iraq Strategy," *America Blog*, June 25, 2007, http://www.americablog.com/2007/06/key-gop-senator-richard-lugar-blasts.html.

3. Senators Warner and Luger's failed amendment declared U.S. vital interests in Iraq and the Middle East to be: "the prevention of Iraq or any piece of its territory from being used as a safe haven or training ground for terrorists or

as a repository or assembly point for weapons of mass destruction; the prevention of acts of violence and disorder that upset wider regional stability, undermining friendly governments, expanding refugee flows, impairing the international shipping lanes in the Persian Gulf, or destroying key oil production or transportation facilities; the prevention of Iranian domination of or aggression toward nations or areas of the Middle East, which would have potentially serious consequences for weapons proliferation, terrorism, the security of Israel, and the stability of friendly governments; and the protection of U.S. credibility in the region and throughout the world." See http://warner.senate.gov/public/index.cfm?FuseAction=PressRoom.StatementsSpeeches&ContentRecord_id=b22a2cb6-7e9c-9af9-7e69-7e80cdb4c6e3&Region_id=&Issue_id=.

4. My criticisms of this report may be found in Brendan O'Leary, "Iraq's Future 101: The Failings of the Baker-Hamilton Report," *Strategic Insights* 6 (2) (March 2007).

5. See Marion Couldrey and Tim Morris, eds., *Iraq's Displacement Crisis: The Search for Solutions* (Oxford: *Forced Migration Review*, June 2007). These estimates are, of course to be treated with caution. The same issue of *Forced Migration Review* quotes rather different estimates and from different time periods. Since then there have been reports of significant numbers of persons returning home or moving back to Iraq—partly because of increased security and partly because of a lack of welcome in neighboring states and refusals of asylum applications in numerous countries.

6. On the PKK see Aliza Marcus, *Blood and Belief: The PKK and the Kurdish Fight for Independence* (New York: New York University Press, 2007). On Turkish perspectives on boundaries and the PKK, see Ümit Cizre, "Turkey's Kurdish Problem: Borders, Identity and Hegemony," in *Right-Sizing the State: The Politics of Moving Borders*, ed. Brendan O'Leary, Ian S. Lustick, and Thomas M. Callaghy (Oxford: Oxford University Press, 2001), 222–52.

7. See Chapter 8, pp. 184–89.

8. Peter Galbraith, *The End of Iraq*, 6. Galbraith's incisive criticisms of the lack of strategic foresight on the part of Bush administration are compelling. They are largely accepted here; see especially 6–7, 10–11, 71–75.

9. Andrew Kohut and Richard Wike, "All the World's a Stage," *National Interest Online*, May 6, 2008.

Chapter 3

1. John Mearsheimer, "Hans Morgenthau and the Iraq War: Realism Versus Neo-Conservatism," *openDemocracy*, 2005, http://www.opendemocracy.net/node/2522/pdf. See also his article with Stephen M. Walt, "An Unnecessary War," *Foreign Policy* 134 (January–February 2003): 51–59.

2. See Edward Luttwak, "The Logic of Disengagement," *Foreign Affairs* 84 (1) (January–February 2005): 26–36, and "To Help Iraq, Let It Fend for Itself," *New York Times*, February 6, 2007. Much the same position was articulated shortly after by Daniel Pipes, "Salvaging the Iraq War," *New York Sun*, July 24, 2007.

3. For the strongest statement of this belief, see Elie Kedourie, *Democracy and Arab Political Culture* (London: Frank Cass, 1994, 2nd posthumous edition), an essay composed during the first Gulf War by the most famous Anglophone conservative to emerge from Baghdad's Jewish community in modern times.

4. In the *National Interest* (November/December 2006), Pipes argued that "The occupying forces should have sponsored a democratically-minded strongman to secure the country and eventually move it toward an open political process; see

http://www.danielpipes.org/article/4112. He was consistent; Pipes had argued for exactly this in April 2003, "A Strongman for Iraq?" *New York Post*, April 28, 2003. Pipes has consistently commended strongmen for Iraq. Laurie Mylroie and Daniel Pipes once openly backed Saddam's regime, near the height of its genocidal activities, for strategic reasons, to balance against Iran; see their "Back Iraq: Why Iran's Enemy Should Be America's Friend," *New Republic*, April 27, 1987. They also perceived "a degree of moderation" in the Baathist regime.

5. Nikolas Gvosdev and Ray Takeyh, "Mr. President, This War Is Over," *International Herald Tribune*, January 11, 2007.

6. Neoconservative foreign policy perspectives may be found in Robert Kagan and William Kristol, eds., *Present Dangers: Crisis and Opportunity in American Foreign and Defense Policy* (San Francisco: Encounter Books, 2000). Neoconservative advocacy to remove Saddam may be found in Lawrence Kaplan and William Kristol, *The War over Iraq; Saddam's Tyranny and America's Mission* (San Francisco: Encounter Books, 2003). Critics of the neoconservatives include Ivo H. Daalder and James M. Lindsay, *America Unbound: The Bush Revolution in Foreign Policy* (Washington, D.C.: Brookings Institution Press, 2003); Stefan Halper and Jonathan Clarke, *America Alone: The Neo-Conservatives and the Global Order* (Cambridge: Cambridge University Press, 2004); Gary Dorrien, *Imperial Designs: Neoconservatism and the New Pax Americana* (New York: Routledge, 2004); James Mann, *Rise of the Vulcans: The History of Bush's War Cabinet* (New York: Viking/Penguin, 2004); Jeffrey Record, *Dark Victory: America's Second War Against Iraq* (Annapolis, Md.: Naval Institute Press, 2004); Ian S. Lustick, *Trapped in the War on Terror* (Philadelphia: University of Pennsylvania Press, 2007); and John J. Mearsheimer and Stephen M. Walt, *The Israel Lobby and U.S. Foreign Policy* (New York: Farrar, Straus and Giroux, 2008). The 1997 "Statement of Principles" of the Project for a new American Century may be found at http://www.newamericancentury.org/statementofprinciples.htm. For a repudiation of neoconservatism by a self-styled conservative who supported the intervention in Iraq, see Francis Fukuyama, *America at the Crossroads: Democracy, Power, and the Neoconservative Legacy* (New Haven, Conn.: Yale University Press, 2006).

7. See Tariq Ali, *Bush in Babylon: The Recolonisation of Iraq* (London: Verso, 2004).

8. See Susan Watkins, "Editorial: Vichy on the Tigris," *New Left Review* 28 (July–August 2004): 5–17. Are we to understand that the Baathist Republic resembled the French Third Republic, the Americans are the Nazis, and that the Sunni jihadists (both Iraqi and foreign) are analogous to the Free French and the French resistance, with the equivalents of Jean-Paul Sartre, Albert Camus, and Samuel Beckett working for their cause? The analogy is shameful and stupefying.

9. See Emmanuel Todd, *After the Empire: The Breakdown of the American Order*, trans. C. J. Delogu (London: Constable, 2004), 209.

10. Noam Chomsky, *Transcript: Why Is Iraq Missing from the 2008 Presidential Race? Democracy Now! The War and Peace Report*, 2008. Available from http://www.democracynow.org/2008/2/26/noam_chomsky_why_is_iraq_missing.

11. Naomi Klein, *The Shock Doctrine: The Rise of Disaster Capitalism* (New York: Picador, 2008).

12. Rashid Khalidi, *Resurrecting Empire: Western Footprints and America's Perilous Path in the Middle East* (Boston: Beacon Press, 2005), x–xi. Another Middle East scholar, and my colleague at the University of Pennsylvania, also made the argument that this was a war of choice, and prioritized this explanation: the intervention in Iraq was a "supply-side war"; there was little demand and no necessity for it. The impact of 9/11 provided an opportunity to fulfill the "fantasies" of a "small but powerful group of neoconservative hawks" who wanted to use the "glory and dangers of overseas adventures" to reinvigorate and morally rearm American foreign

policy. This "cabal" could not prevail until 9/11 gave them their opportunity and the necessary military and political capital. Ian S. Lustick, "Storm Warnings for a Supply-Side War (Review of Kenneth A. Pollack, *The Threatening Storm: The Case for Invading Iraq*)," *The Nation*, March 4, 2003.

13. The neoconservative "cabal," according to Lustick, had "an unstated but powerful objective to transform the Arab countries…from states putatively obsessed with irrational hatreds of a wholly innocent Israel into rational, accommodating democracies that will give up on the Palestinian problem and let right-wing Israeli government determine the future of the occupied territories without external pressures." "Storm Warnings for a Supply-Side War."

14. For a tongue-in-cheek discussion by a muckraking journalist, see Greg Pallast, "Was the Invasion of Iraq a Jewish Conspiracy?", 2006, available from http://www.gregpalast.com/was-the-invasion-of-iraq-a-jewish-conspiracy/. He thinks that oil corporations were far more important than Jewish intellectuals.

15. France's Chirac succeeded in undermining the U.S. and UK efforts. For interesting meditations on French-U.S. relations, see Simon Serfaty, "Terms of Estrangement," in *Architects of Delusion: Europe, America, and the Iraq War* (Philadelphia: University of Pennsylvania Press, 2008), 13–45.

16. The U.S. mismanagement of the occupation, and its severe difficulties in recognizing and turning to deal with an insurgency, were in fairly stark contrast to the joint European and American interventions in the Balkans, which had their own grotesque moments of incompetence, but in the end halted major violence and successfully blocked the most locally aggressive power, Milosevic's Serbia, and the most brutal of the locals in the region, the Bosnian Serb paramilitaries.

17. For a broad discussion, see Thomas P. M. Barnett, *The Pentagon's New Map: War and Peace in the Twenty-First Century* (New York: Putnam, 2004), 282–94, which embraces a Big Bang strategy for transforming the Middle East and rashly hopes for a *Persia Engulfed* scenario.

18. Charles Tripp, *A History of Iraq*, rev. ed. (Cambridge: Cambridge University Press, 2002), 66 ff., 120 ff.

19. Peter Galbraith, *The End of Iraq*, 124, first made this observation, and this paragraph follows his astute observations.

20. That is so even if one concedes, as I do not, that the Americans and the British pushed Ja'afari out of office; see Chapter 1, note 39.

21. Conversation with the author, Washington, D.C., May 9, 2008.

22. Mo Mowlam, "The Real Goal Is the Seizure of Saudi Oil," *The Guardian*, September 5, 2002. Mowlam was UK Secretary of State for Northern Ireland between 1997 and 2001. I was one of Mo Mowlam's advisors on Northern Ireland before 1997. We lost touch after 1999. I never spoke about Iraq with her.

23. http://www.heritage.org/Research/MiddleEast/bg1594.cfm.

24. Olivier Roy, *The Politics of Chaos in the Middle East*, trans. Ros Schwartz (London: Hurst & CERI, 2007).

25. See, for example, Daniel Yergin, "What Will Happen to Oil After Saddam?" *IEE (Institute of Electrical Engineers) Review* (February 2003).

26. Acknowledged energy expert Daniel Yergin and his colleagues in Cambridge Energy Research Associates have predicted a huge build up of global oil supply between 2004 and 2010, including an increase in the capacity to produce oil of over 16 million barrels a day (to which they expect Iraq to make a modest contribution of 1 million in growth), "It's Not the End of the Oil Age: Technology and Higher Prices Drive a Supply Buildup," *Washington Post*, July 31, 2005, B07.

27. Alan Greenspan, "Excerpt: The Age of Turbulence by Alan Greenspan," *Financial Times*, October 4, 2007.

28. John Mearsheimer and Stephen Walt, "The Israel Lobby," *London Review of Books* 28 (6) (March 23, 2006). The arguments were subsequently expanded in a book, John J. Mearsheimer and Stephen M. Walt, *The Israel Lobby and U.S. Foreign Policy* (New York: Farrar, Straus and Giroux, 2008).

29. See the review of Mearsheimer and Walt by Bill Finan, "Is One Special Interest Special?" *Current History* (December 2007).

30. See the two essays by Jeroen Gunning, "Hamas: Harakat al-Muqawama al-Islamiya," and "Hizballah," in *Terror, Insurgency and the State: Ending Protracted Conflicts*, ed. Marianne Heiberg, Brendan O'Leary, and John Tirman (Philadelphia: University of Pennsylvania Press, 2007), 123–56, 157–88.

31. See Natan Sharansky and Ron Dermer, *The Case for Democracy: The Power of Freedom to Overcome Tyranny and Terror* (New York: Public Affairs, 2004), a book commended by President Bush.

Part II Introduction

Epigraph: Fouad Ajami, "Blind Liberation: Review of Ali A. Allawi, The Occupation of Iraq: Winning the War, Losing the Peace," *The New Republic Online*, April 23, 2007.

1. Bing West, *The Strongest Tribe: War, Politics and the Endgame in Iraq* (New York: Random House, 2008).

2. See "Text of al-Zarqawi Message Threatening More Attacks, April 6, 2004," republished in Robert O. Marlin, ed., *What Does Al-Qaeda Want? Unedited Communiqués, with Commentary by Robert O. Marlin IV*, Terra Nova Series (Berkeley, Calif.: North Atlantic Books, 2004), 78–87, 81.

3. See Tariq Ali, *Bush in Babylon: The Recolonisation of Iraq* (London: Verso, 2004), and "Editorial: Mid-Point in the Middle East," *New Left Review* 38 (March–April 2006): 5–19.

4. The expression is Noam Chomsky's, *The New Military Humanism: Lessons from Kosovo* (London: Pluto Press, 1999).

5. Emmanuel Todd, *After the Empire: The Breakdown of the American Order*, trans. C. J. Delogu. (London: Constable, 2004), xxiii. Todd was not alone in failing to foresee bearish Russian behavior in Georgia despite knowledge of Chechnya that has stalled that "irreversibly forward" movement.

6. Todd, *After the Empire*, 204, 206.

7. Andrew Greeley, *A Stupid, Unjust and Criminal War: Iraq 2001–2007* (Maryknoll, N.Y.: Orbis, 2007).

Chapter 4

1. Economists advise us to ignore sunk costs. That is because they only emphasize future-oriented rationality. They thereby commend amnesia (or minimization of regret) as a way of life. We are probably not hard-wired to discount sunk costs so easily, and that is probably a good thing: the capacity for what the rational deem to be foolish regret may help us to be more cautious in future decisions and to be better people.

2. See http://icasualties.org/oif/ (number of U.S. wounded listed at 30,000); http://www.cnn.com/SPECIALS/2003/iraq/forces/casualties/ (lists wounded at around 30,000); and http://www.globalsecurity.org/military/ops/iraq_casualties. htm (totals around 30,000).

3. See Mike Allen and Sam Coates, "Bush Says U.S. Will Stay and Finish Task," *Washington Post*, August 23, 2005, A10.

4. For morally and politically impressive reflections on Saddam's tyranny, see Kanan Makiya, "The Anfal: Uncovering an Iraqi Campaign to Exterminate the Kurds," *Harper's Magazine* 284 (1704) (1992): 53–61; idem, *Cruelty and Silence: War, Tyranny, Uprising and the Arab World* (New York: W.W. Norton, 1993); and the second edition of his *Republic of Fear: The Politics of Modern Iraq* (Berkeley, Calif.: University of California Press, 1998), which he originally had to publish under a pseudonym. For a sympathetic portrait of Makiya, see George Packer, *The Assassins' Gate: America in Iraq* (New York: Farrar, Straus and Giroux, 2005).

5. See Marion Farouk-Sluglett and Peter Sluglett, *Iraq Since 1958: From Revolution to Dictatorship* (London: I.B. Tauris, 2003), 289.

6. KRG Prime Minister Nechirvan Barzani, "Speech: We Call for International Recognition of Anfal Genocide" (Erbil: Kurdistan Regional Government, January 28, 2008), http://www.krg.org/articles/detail.asp?lngnr=12&smap=02040100&rnr=268&anr=22516.

7. For 2002 the UNHCR *Statistical Yearbook* estimated that there were 421,719 refugees and 51,516 asylum seekers from Iraq, compared with 771,077 and 15,204, respectively, in 1993; see United Nations Refugee Agency, *Statistical Year Book 2002: Trends in Displacement, Protection and Solutions* (Geneva: Office of the UN High Commissioner for Refugees, July 2004), 337, http://www.unhcr.org/cgi-bin/texis/vtx/statistics/opendoc.pdf.

8. Michael E. O'Hanlon and Jason H. Campbell, *Iraq Index: Tracking Variables of Reconstruction & Security in Post-Saddam Iraq* (Washington, D.C.: Brookings Institution, July 31, 2008), http://www.brookings.edu/iraqindex, accessed August 14, 2008, p. 10 of the downloadable pdf.

9. Leading figures in the Western "anti-war movement"—whose members typically confine their campaign to the U.S. intervention—usually deny this judgment, generally in two ways. They add against the United States and its allies the deaths caused by UN-authorized sanctions against Saddam's regime in the 1990s. This is a strange way to allocate responsibility (and its supporters usually forget to note that it implies that wars may be better than sanctions if the relief of suffering is one's priority). Then they rely on controversial estimates of "excess deaths." The estimates of "excess infant mortality" from sanctions are derived in ways similar to those of highly publicized studies highlighted in the British medical journal, *The Lancet*, in 2004 and 2006. These estimate "excess deaths" in relation to a (presumed and controversial) expected baseline. There are reasonable reasons to doubt their validity (see Appendix 1), although not their integrity.

10. The late Frank Wright developed the useful and grim terms "representative violence" (killing people because of whom they are presumed to represent), and "communal deterrence" (representative killing intended to deter another community from trying to resist the domination of another); see Frank Wright, *Northern Ireland: A Comparative Analysis* (Dublin: Gill & Macmillan, 1987).

11. Members of SCIRI or ISCI are often called *majlis* because the Arabic word for council is *majli.*

12. Theo Caldwell, "'I Prefer Messy Democracy to the Stability of Tyrants': An Interview with Iraq's Ambassador to Canada," *National Post*, February 5, 2008.

13. See Joseph Stiglitz and Linda J. Bilmes, *The Three Trillion Dollar War: The True Cost of the Iraq Conflict* (New York: W.W. Norton, 2008).

14. That is $3,000,000,000,000 (in non-American English, 3 billion). That converts to approximately £1,606,700,000,000 or €2,025, 900,000,000 in August 2008.

15. See Stiglitz and Bilmes, *The Three Trillion Dollar War*, 130–31.

16. That said I agree with most of Stiglitz and Bilmes's reform proposals on the economic management of wars, namely, that wars should not be funded (at least beyond their first year) through emergency supplementals but rather, after a year, through levies of war surtaxes; that funding should be linked to strategy reviews by Congress; that there should be comprehensive military accounts across the relevant federal departments; that the Pentagon should supply auditable financial statements to Congress; that there should be regular estimates of the microeconomic and macroeconomic costs of military engagements; that the Freedom of Information Act should be strengthened; that Congress should review the heavy reliance on contractors in wartime; and that limitations should be placed on calling on reserves or the National Guard unless it can be shown that it is not feasible to expand the armed forces. See *The Three Trillion Dollar War*, Chapter 8.

17. Grover G. Norquist and Dov S. Zakheim, "Dollars & Sense," *National Interest* 96 (July–August 2008): 4.

18. Steven J. Davis, Kevin M. Murphy, and Robert H. Topel, "War in Iraq Versus Containment," NBER Working Paper 12092, University of Chicago, 2006. Available from http://faculty.chicagogsb.edu/steven.davis/research/War_in_Iraq_versus_Containment_(15February2006).pdf.

19. They say, "There is no way of answering these questions [those based on counterfactuals] with certainty, but *modern social sciences enable us to provide reasonably reliable estimates*," *The Three Trillion Dollar War*, 267 note 5, my emphasis. Social scientists should be wary of immodesty. In the body of this book I make some claims about what the consequences of a continuation of Saddam's regime might have meant, mostly for Iraqis. These have no greater a priori merit than those of Stiglitz and Bilmes, but at least they are based on detailed historical inquiry into Iraq and its neighborhood.

20. In mid-August 2008, *The Economist* reported that in the second quarter of 2008 Iraqi oil production averaged over 2.4 million barrels of oil per day, the highest level since March 2003; "The Benefits and the Curse of Oil," *The Economist*, August 14, 2008.

21. Paul Collier and Andrew Glyn taught me economics. The first is an admirer of John Maynard Keynes; the second, a neo-Marxist, was an admirer of Michal Kalecki.

22. Stiglitz and Bilmes, *The Three Trillion Dollar War*, 115.

23. Paul Krugman, "The Conscience of a Liberal," *New York Times*, January 29, 2008, http://krugman.blogs.nytimes.com/2008/01/29/an-iraq-recession/.

24. Norquist even claims that, had the United States not intervened in Iraq, the Doha round of trade liberalization would have succeeded, because otherwise Germany and France would not have linked arms against America—the Germans would have pressured France to abandon its agricultural subsidies if there had been no Iraq war—another huge counterfactual claim that seems typical in economic analysis; see Norquist and Zakheim, "Dollars & Sense," 4.

25. The estimate is in purchasing power parity; Stiglitz and Bilmes, *The Three Trillion Dollar War*, 140. Two sentences later they say that "The country had a thriving middle class," statements that are not easy to reconcile. The thriving middle class and the Shia mercantile class had been deeply damaged by nationalization, expulsion, and emigration under the Baathists, and were further damaged under UN sanctions and inflation.

26. See Davis, Murphy, and Topel, "War in Iraq Versus Containment."

27. See Davis, Murphy, and Topel, "War in Iraq Versus Containment."

28. Brendan O'Leary, ed., *The Kurdistan Region: Invest in the Future. An Official Publication of the Kurdistan Region* (London and Washington, D.C.: Newsdesk Publications, 2008).

29. See O'Hanlon and Campbell, "Iraq Index," accessed August 14, 2008, p. 41 of the downloadable pdf.

30. See Anna Bernasek, "An Early Economic Calculation of Iraq's Cost of War," *New York Times*, October 22, 2006.

31. See Davis, Murphy, and Topel, "War in Iraq Versus Containment," quoting the "Executive Summary."

32. See O'Hanlon and Campbell, "Iraq Index," 24.

33. See O'Hanlon and Campbell, "Iraq Index," 40.

34. See Leading Article, "The Iraqi Dustbowl: A Once Fertile Land Is Threatened by Severe Drought," *The Times* (London), July 29, 2008.

35. See http://www.transparency.org/policy_research/surveys_indices/cpi/2007.

36. See "Iraq's Minister of Water Resources Visits Canada, Embassy of Iraq, Ottawa, Media Advisory August 2008.

37. Another Kurdish official bleakly commented to me that "while Dr Rashid works to repair Shia lands, the Shia oil minister, Dr. Shahristani, blackmails oil companies that have signed contracts to work in Kurdish lands! Long live federalization!"

38. U.S. public opinion is more statistically reliable than Iraqi opinion reported here. That is partly because very numerous and reinforcing polls and surveys in the United States, based on reliable representative samples, give significant confidence in what is reported. America is also not internally war-torn, and therefore the conduct of surveys and polls and public responses are more likely to tap authentic views.

39. ABC News/*Washington Post* Poll, July 10–13, 2008. In June 2008, a *Los Angeles Times*/Bloomberg poll found that 67 percent thought the present situation in Iraq meant that going to war had not been worth it, by comparison with 27 percent who thought it had been worth it; http://www.pollingreport.com/iraq.htm.

40. CNN/Opinion Research Corporation Poll, June 26–29, 2008, http://www.pollingreport.com/iraq.htm. Responses had consistently broken in this pattern in 13 previous polls asking the same question since May 2007.

41. CNN Poll.

42. In the relevant *USA Today*/Gallup Poll respondents were asked "In view of the developments since we first sent our troops to Iraq, do you think the United States made a mistake in sending troops to Iraq, or not?" Those defining it as a mistake, 60 percent, significantly outnumbered those who thought otherwise, 37 percent. See http://www.pollingreport.com/iraq.htm.

43. Pew Research Center for the People & the Press Survey, Princeton Survey Research Associates International, http://www.pollingreport.com/iraq.htm.

44. *Time* Poll, conducted by Abt SRBI, http://www.pollingreport.com/iraq.htm.

45. NBC News/*Wall Street Journal* Poll, June 6–9, 2008, http://www.pollingreport.com/iraq.htm.

46. http://www.gallup.com/poll/109294/Exploring-Iraq-Timetable-Issue.aspx.

47. See http://www.gallup.com/poll/109165/Nearly-Half-U.S.-Adults-Now-Applaud-Iraq-Surge.aspx; 109150/Afghan-War-Edges-Iraq-Most-Important-U.S.aspx; 107605/Peoples-Priorities-Economy-Iraq-Gas-Prices.aspx.

48. The low refusal and "don't know" responses in many of the more recent polls and surveys conducted in Iraq raise questions.

49. See Transcript, "Iraqi Public Opinion on the Presence of U.S. Troops," Testimony of Dr. Steven Kull, Director, Program on International Policy Attitudes (PIPA), University of Maryland, and Director, WorldPublicOpinion.org, July 23,

2008, 2:00 PM, Before the House of Representatives Committee on Foreign Affairs, Subcommittee on International Organizations, Human Rights, and Oversight, Washington, D.C.

50. http://www.globalpolicy.org/security/issues/iraq/poll/2008/0308opinion. pdf. The web site of Global Policy Forum from which I extracted the PDF of this survey glosses it with far less care than I have attempted to display in the text.

51. "Ebbing Hope in a Landscape of Loss Marks a National Survey of Iraq," ABC News/ *USA Today*/BBC/ARD Poll, cited in "Iraq: Where Things Stand, Summary Released March 19 2007," at http://abcnews.go.com/International/story?id= 2962206&page=1.

52. Polls in 2006 confirmed strongly negative reactions to the U.S. presence, especially among Arab Iraqis. In a State Department poll, publicized in September 2006, three quarters of the respondents said "they would feel safer if U.S. and other foreign forces left Iraq, with 65 percent...favoring an immediate pullout." In a survey managed by PIPA at the University of Maryland in September 2006, it was reported that "78 percent of Iraqis believe the U.S. military presence causes more conflict than it prevents." See Amit R. Paley, "Most Iraqis Favor Immediate U.S. Pullout, Polls Show," *Washington Post*, September 27, 2006: 22, and David Alexander, "Most Iraqis Favor Withdrawal of U.S. Forces Soon: Poll," *Reuters*, September 27, 2006, available on-line.

53. http://www.globalpolicy.org/security/issues/iraq/poll/2008/0308opinion. pdf; responses to Question 26, p. 15.

54. "Ebbing Hope in a Landscape of Loss Marks a National Survey of Iraq," March 19, 2007. In the special edition of BBC's *Newsnight* for which this poll was commissioned and future scenarios were discussed, I was one of the presenters and interviewees.

55. I am grateful to two opportunities for extensive discussions with Dr. Steven Kull, the Director of the Program on International Policy Attitudes (PIPA) at the University of Maryland and the Director of WorldPublicOpinion.Org in Washington, D.C., in 2006 and 2007. Here I draw upon his recent testimony to the U.S. House of Representatives, "Iraqi Public Opinion on the Presence of U.S. Troops," July 2008.

56. Americans call "nation-building" what the rest of the world calls "state-building." This confusion is partly a matter of wording: American states are units of its federation, and therefore the federation as a whole tends to be called the nation and the federal government the national government. It is also a matter of historical policy. American state-building (the building of all its governmental institutions, federal and state) took place under a policy of building a single nation. Americans therefore equate state- and nation-building, and that makes them less likely to appreciate what is required in multinational states, such as Iraq. American terminological insouciance on the subject can be seen in two books from Francis Fukuyama, *State-Building: Governance and World Order in the 21st Century* (Ithaca, N.Y.: Cornell University Press, 2004), and Francis Fukuyama, ed., *Nation-Building: Beyond Afghanistan and Iraq* (Baltimore: Johns Hopkins University Press, 2006). Both books are in fact mainly about state-building. Fukuyama's verbal carelessness reflects an American blind spot.

57. See Trudy Rubin, *Willful Blindness: The Bush Administration and Iraq* (Philadelphia: *Philadelphia Inquirer*, 2004); James Fallows, *Blind into Baghdad: America's War in Iraq* (New York: Vintage, 2006); and Fouad Ajami, "Blind Liberation: Review of Ali A. Allawi, *The Occupation of Iraq: Winning the War, Losing the Peace*," *New Republic Online*, April 23, 2007.

58. Fouad Ajami laments in a telling anecdote that an American diplomat of considerable sway asked an Iraqi interlocutor what the term *hawza* meant—the

word for a Shia study group and academic circle. "It's amazing," the Iraqi academic answered. "You send a huge army to this country, but you don't know the most rudimentary thing about its life." "Blind Liberation: Review of Ali A. Allawi, *The Occupation of Iraq: Winning the War, Losing the Peace,*" *New Republic Online,* April 23, 2007.

Chapter 5

1. On Muslim political thought see the superb exposition and analysis in Patricia Crone, *God's Rule: Government and Islam: Six Centuries of Medieval Islamic Thought* (New York: Columbia University Press, 2004). Noah Feldman argues that the apparent deference to the absolutist executive in Islamic jurisprudence was designed to maintain the power of Muslim jurists and thereby the rule of law; see *The Fall and Rise of the Islamic State* (Princeton, N.J.: Princeton University Press, 2008), especially Part 1.

2. See Thomas Hobbes, *Leviathan (or The Matter, Forme & Power of a Common-Wealth Ecclesiastical and Civill),* ed. Richard Tuck, Cambridge Texts in the History of Political Thought (Cambridge: Cambridge University Press, 1991[1651]), especially Chapters XIII, XVII, pp. 9, 120–21. Hobbes reversed the symbolic meaning of Leviathan: in the biblical traditions Leviathan represents cosmic chaos; in Hobbes' work, Leviathan is the manmade solution to political chaos.

3. See for example Ian S. Lustick, "Stability in Deeply Divided Societies: Consociationalism Versus Control," *World Politics* 31 (3) (1979): 325–44.

4. See Rudolph J. Rummel, *Death by Government,* with a Foreword by Irving Louis Horowitz (London and New York: Transaction Publishers, 1997).

5. Edward N. Luttwak, "Give War a Chance," *Foreign Affairs* 78 (4) (1999): 36–44. Luttwak thinks letting a civil war conclude is more likely to bring a lasting peace than external interventions, which prevent civil wars from being fought to a conclusion. This viewpoint is expressed in American folk wisdom that I have learned in Philadelphia: "A fire is sometimes the best thing that can happen to a forest; after it has burned out, a new, fresher, and more vigorous forest emerges."

6. See note 4 of Chapter 3 for Daniel Pipes's position on "a democratically-minded strongman to secure the country and eventually move it toward an open political process." He had in mind an Atatürk-style figure, a strongman to pave the way toward long-run democratization—forgetting perhaps that Atatürk had been long dead before Turks had their first moderately free and fair elections in 1950, and that his successors had sought an alliance with the Nazis during Hitler's successes against the Soviet Union.

7. In the 2004, 2005, and 2007 BBC-funded polls, 28, 26, and 34 percent, respectively, of Iraqis polled answered affirmatively to the proposition that the best form of rule would constitute a "strong leader: a government headed by one man for life," a position held, not surprisingly, more by Sunni Arabs than others. See http://news.bbc.co.uk/1/shared/bsp/hi/pdfs/19_03_07_iraqpollnew.pdf.

8. His mother was a Faili Kurd; see Hanna Batatu, *The Old Social Classes and the Revolutionary Movements of Iraq: A Study of Iraq's Old Landed and Commercial Classes and of Its Communists, B'athists and Free Officers* (Princeton, N.J.: Princeton University Press, 3rd ed., 2004), 810–11, Table 42-1. This impressive works remains the most authoritative study of Iraq's Free Officers. See also Dann Uriel, *Iraq Under Qassem: A Political History, 1958–1963* (Tel Aviv: Praeger Publishers, 1969).

9. Nir Rosen, "The Death of Iraq," *Current History* 2007 (December): 412, reports gossip that Allawi is trying to rebuild the Baath party "or some new configuration of

it" with Tariq al-Hashimi, Iraq's Sunni Arab vice-president, and Adnan al Dulami, the leader of the Sunni General Council for the People of Iraq.

10. A variation on this reasoning has been expressed by Barry Posen, "Exit Strategy: How to Disengage from Iraq in 18 Months," *Boston Review*, Jan.–Feb. 2006. He commends actively working for a productive stalemate rather than a winner. That policy would seem to imply either arming all three major communities equally or equally starving them of military resources. Besides being a rather difficult task, it appears not to address what happens if two sides coalesce against one.

11. Barry Posen, "Exit Strategy." This interesting article wrongly states that the "Kurds are trying to drive the Arabs from Kirkuk" and that the Kurds "seem not to have noticed that the export pipelines for the oil of Kirkuk are easily interdicted by Sunni Arabs and by Turkey." See Chapter 7, pp. 147–49.

12. At a reconciliation conference held in Erbil, Kurdistan, in the spring of 2004 I was shocked at the racist contempt displayed by invited Sunni Arab women toward Kurdish women. Some of them called the Kurdish women whores for wearing brightly colored but ankle-length dresses in public.

13. As cited in Jack White, *Minority Report: The Protestant Community in the Irish Republic* (Dublin: Gill & Macmillan, 1975), frontispiece.

14. Such arrangements work well in another largely bilingual federation, Canada, where there is a French-speaking Quebec Regiment. There are many Canadian rather than American federal practices that seem well-suited to Iraq; see John McGarry, "Canadian Lessons for Iraq," in *The Future of Kurdistan in Iraq*, ed. Brendan O'Leary, John McGarry, and Khaled Salih (Philadelphia: University of Pennsylvania Press, 2005), 92–115.

15. See Jack Snyder and Karen Ballentine, "Nationalism and the Marketplace of Ideas," in *Nationalism and Ethnic Conflict*, ed. M. Brown, O. R. Cote, S. Lynn-Jones, and S. E. Miller (Cambridge, Mass.: MIT Press, 1996–97), 61–96. This mode of reasoning resembles that of exponents of the "contact hypothesis" in political and social psychology; for a review see H. D. Forbes, *Ethnic Conflict: Commerce, Culture and the Contact Hypothesis* (New Haven, Conn.: Yale University Press, 1997).

16. The American counterinsurgency planners initially wanted to recruit a third force under the banner of "Concerned Local Citizens," but this expression did not translate well into Arabic, from which comes the preference for the "Sons of Iraq," who are recruited from among both Sunni and Shia Arabs (in a ratio of about 4 to 1, respectively, as of August 2008).

17. Richard A. Oppel, Jr., "Iraq Takes Aim at U.S.-Tied Sunni Groups' Leaders," *New York Times*, August 22, 2008.

18. Peter W. Galbraith, "After Iraq: Picking Up the Pieces," *Current History* (December 2007): 404.

19. Nir Rosen reports that sources in Ramadi say that one of Abu Risha's cousins planted the explosives: "The Death of Iraq," *Current History* (December 2007): 411.

20. Richard A. Oppel, Jr., "Iraq Takes Aim at U.S.-Tied Sunni Groups' Leaders," *New York Times*, August 22, 2008.

21. Erica Goode and Ali Hameed, "Suicide Bomber Kills 15 at a Sunni Mosque in Baghdad," *New York Times*, August 19, 2008.

22. Geographers and political scientists have suggested that sectarian expulsions in Baghdad *before* the surge got under way largely account for the security successes attributed to the surge, i.e., it is sectarian homogenization that has produced calm. They make their case on the basis of a fascinating technique—evaluating the night-time light signatures over districts of Baghdad using data logged in satellites. See John Agnew, Thomas W. Gillespie, Jorge Gonzales and Brian Min, "Commen-

tary," in *Environment and Planning A* 40 (2008): 2285–95. Needless to say, the study is controversial.

23. See Frederick W. Kagan and Kimberly Kagan, "The Patton of Counterinsurgency: With a Sequence of Brilliant Offensives, Raymond Odierno Adapted the Petraeus Doctrine into a Successful Operational Art," *The Weekly Standard* 13 (2008): 25. Since Frederick Kagan was one of the exponents of the surge, he is *parti pris*.

24. See Thomas E. Ricks, *Fiasco: The American Military Adventure in Iraq* (New York: The Penguin Press, 2006), which offers an excellent account of how U.S. military conduct stoked insurgency.

25. In an otherwise revealing account of how the United States tried to operate its military and advisory role in Mosul as late as November 2006, Jonathan Steele (*Defeat*, 235–39) describes the city as one "where the tensions between the two main communities, Kurds and Sunni Arabs, were producing a wave of ethnically based murders as well as frequent attacks on police stations and political parties' headquarters" (235). Had Steele probed further, he would have described the source of responsibility for these murders and attacks, namely, Baathist Sunni Arabs and jihadists rather than "ethnic tensions." This is a regrettable example of how journalists who criticize the U.S. and UK occupation, sadly, have become habituated to treating Kurds as U.S. clients and collaborators, responsible for whatever attacks they suffer from "the resistance" and falsely implicated as equals in ethnic murders. I write with feeling. Sami Abdul Rahman, the deputy Prime Minister of the KRG, whom I was advising, was killed with over a hundred others, including his Londoner son, in a jihadist suicide bombing in February 2004.

26. See Qassim Abdul-Zahra and Robert Burns, "Deal Calls for Troop Pullback in Iraq: U.S. Says Pact Still Needs Final Approvals," *Boston Globe*, August 21, 2008; Karen DeYoung, "U.S., Iraq Near Draft Agreement Regarding U.S. Troops," *Washington Post*, August 21, 2008; Stephen Farrell, "Draft Accord with Iraq Sets Goal of 2011 Pullout," *New York Times*, August 22, 2008.

27. See James Fallows, "Why Iraq Has No Army," in his *Blind into Baghdad: America's War in Iraq* (New York: Vintage Books, 2006), 147–86.

28. For discussions of the PKK see Aliza Marcus, *Blood and Belief: The PKK and the Kurdish Fight for Independence* (New York: New York University Press, 2007); Paul White, *Primitive Rebels or Revolutionary Modernizers? The Kurdish National Movement in Turkey* (London: Zed Books, 2000); David McDowall, *A Modern History of the Kurds*, 3rd revised and updated ed. (London: I.B. Tauris, 2004), 420–54; and Dogu Ergil, "PKK: Partiya Karkaren Kurdistan," in *Terror, Insurgency and the State*, ed. Marianne Heiberg, Brendan O'Leary, and John Tirman (Philadelphia: University of Pennsylvania Press, 2007), 323–58. For discussions of policy approaches toward the PUK, see "Galbraith Says Amnesty Key to End PKK Problem," *Today's Zaman*, September 17, 2007; Karen DeYoung, "Turkish-Kurdish Dispute Tests U.S. Strategic Alliances," *Washington Post*, May 8, 2007; and David L. Phillips, *Disarming, Demobilizing, and Reintegrating the Kurdistan Workers Party* (Washington, D.C., National Committee on American Foreign Policy, October 15, 2007), http://www.ncafp.org/aboutus/pressreleases/articles/PKKFINALReport10-15.pdf.

29. The PKK, which carries out attacks on Turkey, is on the State Department's list of terrorist organizations; the PJAK, which attacks Iran, is not. Conspiracy theorists see design in this fact. They suggest the United States is supporting PJAK to put pressure on Iran. If so, it would be supporting one ally (Turkey) to attack an organization (the PKK), which in its other guise it supports to attack an enemy, Iran (PJAK). It might make a good Hollywood movie, if true, but it would be poor politics, especially if exposed.

30. Amy Zalam, "Kurdish Militants in Iraq Play Dual Role of Terrorists and Allies," *Los Angeles Times*, April 16, 2008.

31. Patrick Cockburn, *Muqtada: Muqtada Al-Sadr, the Shia Revival, and the Struggle for Iraq* (New York: Scribner, 2008), 185.

Part III Introduction

Epigraph: Nir Rosen, "The Death of Iraq," *Current History* (December 2007): 413.

1. See Efraim Karsh, *Islamic Imperialism: A History* (New Haven, Conn.: Yale University Press, 2007), 90.

2. For brief discussions of "the glory that was Baghdad," see, among others, Philip K. Hitti, *The Arabs: A Short History*, with a new introduction by Philip S. Khoury (Washington, D.C: Regnery, 1996 [1943]), 105–21; Albert Hourani, *A History of the Arab Peoples* (London: Faber & Faber, 1991), 32–36. For lengthier treatment see Hugh Kennedy, *When Baghdad Ruled the Muslim World: The Rise and Fall of Islam's Greatest Dynasty* (Cambridge, Mass.: Perseus Books, 2005).

3. See J. J. Saunders, *The History of the Mongol Conquests* (Philadelphia: University of Pennsylvania Press, 2001 [1971]), 231, note 75. He continues, "Chang-te, a Chinese envoy [sent to Hulugu] ... says 'many tens of thousands were killed,' Juzjani, living in India, puts it at 800,000; while Mazkiri, the fourteenth century historian of Egypt, claims that 2,000,000 perished!"

4. See Bernard Lewis, *The Middle East: A Brief History of the Last 2,000 Years* (New York: Scribner, 1995), 97, 99.

5. Rosen's historical ignorance extends to that of the Iraq created in 1920. He writes, "Iraq had no history of civil war or sectarian violence until the Americans arrived" (412). The wars between the Kurds and Baghdad governments seem to have passed him by; so has the Shia intifada of 1991, and Saddam's repression of it. He has also missed the World War II *Farhud* or pogrom against Baghdad Jews; see Charles Tripp, *A History of Iraq*, revised ed. (Cambridge: Cambridge University Press, 2002), 105–6. Rosen's reporting is more convincing. The article I have criticized contains powerful stories about warlordism in Baghdad and elsewhere, but his *The Belly of the Green Bird: The Triumph of the Martyrs in Iraq* (New York: Free Press, 2006) verges on romantic apologetics.

6. Samantha Power, *A Problem from Hell: America and the Age of Genocide* (New York: Basic Books, 2002).

7. Interview with Samantha Power, in Charles Ferguson, *No End in Sight: Iraq's Descent into Chaos* (New York: Public Affairs, 2008), 564.

8. See Ala Bashir, *The Insider: Trapped in Saddam's Brutal Regime* (London: Abacus, 2005), *passim.*

Chapter 6

1. Article 121 recognizes the local rights of Turkomen, Chaldeans, Assyrians, "and others."

2. See Philip G. Kreyenbroek, *Yezidism: Its Background, Observances and Textual Tradition* (Lewiston, N.Y., Edwin Mellen Press, 1995). The Yezidis ("Angelicans") whom I have met in Kurdistan claim to be the exponents of the original religion of the Kurds, which makes some sense because Yezidism seems to be a variation on Zoroastrianism, which the Kurds, speakers of the Iranian branch of languages, were exposed to from the sixth century BCE. Mehrdad R. Izady notes that a Kurdish lit-

erary journal (*Hewár*, 1932–43) championed Yezidism as the native Kurdish faith but comments that the "erroneous supposition was that Yezidism was a direct off-shoot of Zoroastrianism" (championed by Aryanists in the 1930s): *The Kurds: A Concise Handbook* (Washington, D.C.: Taylor & Francis, 1992), 136. He suggests these ideas were part of an attempt to de-Islamize Kurdish identity.

3. For reflections on the fate of Iraq's Jews, see among others Elie Kedourie, "Minorities," in *The Chatham House Version and Other Middle Eastern Studies* (Hanover, N.H.: University Press of New England, 1984 [1952]), 286–317; Esther Meir-Glitzenstein, *Zionism in an Arab Country: Jews in Iraq in the 1940s* (London: Routledge, 2004); Moshe Gat, *The Jewish Exodus from Iraq, 1948–1951* (London: Frank Cass, 1997); Carole Basri, *The Jews of Iraq: The Forgotten Case of Ethnic Cleansing* (Jerusalem: Institute of the World Jewish Congress, 2003); Phil Baum, *The Jews of Iraq* (New York: Commission on International Affairs, American Jewish Congress, 1969); Yåusuf Rizq Allåah Ghanåimah, Reading A. Dallal, and Sheila Dallal, *A Nostalgic Trip into the History of the Jews of Iraq* (Lanham, Md.: University Press of America, 1998); Nissim Rejwan, *The Jews of Iraq: 3000 years of History and Culture* (London: Weidenfeld and Nicolson, 1985); Abbas Shiblak, *The Lure of Zion: The Case of the Iraqi Jews* (London: Al Saqi, 1986); and *Iraqi Jews: A History of Mass Exodus*, updated ed. (London: Saqi, 2005).

4. See John McGarry and Brendan O'Leary, "Iraq's Constitution of 2005: Liberal Consociation as Political Prescription," *International Journal of Constitutional Law* 5 (4) (2007): 670–98, also published in *Constitutional Design for Divided Societies: Integration or Accommodation?*, ed. Sujit Choudhry (Oxford: Oxford University Press, 2008), 342–68.

5. In Lebanon the president must be a Maronite Christian, the prime minister a Sunni Arab, and the speaker of the parliament must be a Shia Arab. Iraq has no such specified requirements. By voluntary agreement Iraq's parties elected a Kurd as president with two vice-presidents, one a Sunni Arab and the other a Shia Arab.

6. Kurdish Muslims are mostly Sunni. Nearly three out of five of all Kurds world-wide follow the Shafi'i school of Islamic jurisprudence (which distinguishes them from most of the Iraqi Sunni Arabs, who mostly follow the Hanafi school). The Shia proportion of the Kurds of Diyala has been estimated at 47.5 percent. By contrast, they constitute 6.5, 8.3, and 6 percent of the Kurds of Dohuk, Kirkuk, and Ninevah, respectively. Christians have been estimated to number 6, 6.5, and 2.5 percent of the Kurdish provinces of Erbil, Dohuk, and Sulaimania, respectively, i.e., within most of the existing KRG, and are estimated at 4.2 and 5.5 percent of the Kurds of Kirkuk and Mosul. (All figures from Mehrdad R. Izady, *The Kurds: A Concise Handbook* [Washington, D.C.: Taylor & Francis, 1992]: 133, Table 5.) There has always been a strong Sufi mystic tradition among the Kurds, and it is part of the less orthodox and more tolerant practice of Islam among the Kurds of Iraq.

7. See note 1 of this chapter. These provisions will need to replicated and improved in regional constitutions to help the targeted minorities; "local rights," we may presume, will include schooling and access to public administration in minority languages.

8. Jim Quilty, "Laughing into the void, making the machine speak Kurdish: Filmmaker Hiner Saleem reflects on art, politics and good vodka," *Daily Star*, October 22, 2004. See Saleem's marvelous memoir, *My Father's Rifle: A Childhood in Kurdistan* (New York: Farrar, Straus and Giroux, 2005).

9. See Khaled Salih, "Kurdistan: From Threatened Entity to Constituent Unit," *Middle East Roundtable*, 3 (39) (October 27, 2005), http://www.bitterlemons-international.org/inside.php?id=427.

10. For typical criticism of the Iraqi constitution-making process, see Andrew Arato, "Post Sovereign Constitution Making and Its Pathology," *New York Law School Review* (2006): 51.

11. The first published history of the drafting process is available from Ashley S. Deeks and Matthew D. Burton, "Iraq's Constitution: A Drafting History," *Cornell International Law Journal*, 40 (1) (Winter 2007): 1–87. I dissent from their generally measured judgments in a few domains, notably on the provisions on natural resources and regional legal supremacy. My views are shaped by my role as one of Kurdistan's advisors and intimate acquaintance with what Kurdistan's leaders and negotiators were seeking—and why. Jonathan Steele argues that the process of drafting Iraq's new Constitution was "largely controlled by American officials…under…Khalilzad" (*Defeat*, 240). His sole source is an article by Herbert Docena, "How the US Got Its Neoliberal Way in Iraq," *Asia Times*, September 1, 2005. Steele's and Docena's analysis mistakes form for substance.

12. This is why Steele's and Docena's parliamentary sources (see note 11) are largely off the point.

13. The ambiguity arose over whether voters should be construed as those who turned out or as those registered (or eligible). Article 61(c) of the Transitional Administrative Law stated that "The general referendum will be successful and the draft constitution ratified if a majority of *the voters* in Iraq approve and if two-thirds of *the voters* in three or more governorates do not reject it" (my italics) (Appendix 2 of O'Leary, McGarry, and Salih, eds., *The Future of Kurdistan in Iraq*, 340). A genuine problem existed because of ambiguous drafting. What was unreasonable was to attempt to read the first reference to mean those who turned out and the second those who were eligible.

14. http://www.theonion.com/content/node/40323.

15. Brendan O'Leary, "A Knitter's Nightmare," *Los Angeles Times* (August 14, 2005): Current, M1.

16. I argued this way in mid-August 2005, during the last days of the negotiations; see Brendan O'Leary, "It Is Past Time to Re-Frame Thinking on the Constitutional Reconstruction of Iraq," *PolitikWissen.de*, August 2005, http://www.politikwissen.de/expertenforum/exp_oleary205.html.

17. Under Article 61(g) of the Transitional Administrative Law, the failure of the National Assembly to write a draft constitution (without having granted itself an extension) would trigger the dissolution of the National Assembly, fresh elections, and the recommencement of constitutional drafting.

18. My friend Jonathan Morrow has argued that Sunni Arab leaders were more malleable and educable in 2005 than I have suggested: *Weak Viability: The Iraqi Federal State and the Constitutional Amendment Process* (Washington, D.C.: Special Report, United States Institute of Peace, July 2006). I respectfully disagree. It may be that the situation is now changed. Morrow is right that the entire process should have been much better managed.

19. The phrase is that of Dr. Jeff Weintraub of the University of Pennsylvania.

20. Syria is not, however, a Sunni Arab regime; see Oded Haklai, "A Minority Rule over a Hostile Majority: The Case of Syria," *Nationalism and Ethnic Politics* 6 (3) (2000): 19–50. It has been a universal norm of Baathist regimes to rest on a dominant sectarian minority.

21. Mowaffak al-Rubaie, "Federalism, Not Partition: A System Devolving Power to the Regions Is the Route to a Viable Iraq," *Washington Post*, February 18, 2008: A19.

22. All preceding citations are from al-Rubaie, "Federalism, Not Partition."

23. International Crisis Group (ICG), "The Next Iraqi War? Sectarianism and Civil Conflict," *Middle East Report 52* (February 27, 2006): ii. The ICG report showed no similar appreciation of Kurdistan's land-locked nature.

24. Kanan Makiya, "Present at the Disintegration," *New York Times*, December 11, 2005. He published the still impressive *The Republic of Fear* under a pseudonym.

25. Yahia Said, "Federal Choices Needed," *Al-Ahram Weekly*, March 2006, http://weekly.ahram.org.eg/print/2006/784/sc6.htm.

26. Donald L. Horowitz, "The Sunni Moment," *Wall Street Journal*, December 14, 2005.

27. "Turkey Wary of Iraqi-Kurd Plans to Export Oil," Nicosia, *Deutsche Presse-Agentur*, June 27, 2006, http://f28.parsimony.net/forum68059/messages/4187.htm.

28. Quotations from the official Constitution given below—and the numbering of sections, articles, and subclauses—follow the UN translation, kindly made available to me by Jonathan Morrow, then of the United States Institute of Peace. This is now the standard translation. I have checked the pertinent meanings with other advisors to Kurdistan's negotiators, including those who have a command of Arabic and Kurdish, and with those whom I advised during the 2005 negotiations. Some articles were negotiated in English before being rendered into Arabic and then back into English. Professor Nicholas Haysom of the United Nations, who was the chief UN advisor during the making of Iraq's Constitution, agreed at the conference in Ottawa in 2006, in which I made these arguments in public, that I had constructed these provisions reasonably.

29. The Bremer dinars were not issued in both Kurdish and Arabic. In the future the currency should respect both languages according to the 2005 Constitution.

30. Article 25(E) of the Transitional Administrative Law made "managing the natural resources of Iraq" one of the exclusive powers of the Iraqi Transitional Government and declared that they belonged "to all the people of all the regions and governorates of Iraq" (see Appendix 2, *The Future of Kurdistan in Iraq*, ed. O'Leary, McGarry, and Salih, 324). The textual contrast with the permanent Constitution is stark and deliberate.

31. Since the clause was negotiated in English and Arabic, it is fair to look at both the English and Arabic wordings.

32. There is no better evidence for the validity of Kurdistan's construction of the key clauses of the Constitution of 2005 than some of the amendments being considered by a subcommittee of the Iraqi Council of Representatives, and that will be emphatically rejected by the KRG. (I have the text from Dr. Khaled Salih, advisor to the KRG's Prime Minister and the Minister for Natural Resources.) The relevant amendments propose modifying the regional supremacy clause to exclude the articles on natural resources and dropping "all regions and governorates" from the ownership clause on oil and natural gas (i.e., Article 111). The only legal reason to propose these amendments is that the current Constitution must mean exactly what Kurdistan's negotiators have said that it means. Deeks and Burton recognize that the implication of Article 112 (pp. 56, 60) is that the KRG has "full ownership and authority over the management and revenue distribution of any 'future' fields," and admit that the "plain language" meaning of Article 115 is what the KRG asserts (and I assert) above; Deeks and Burton, "Iraq's Constitution," p. 57.

33. See, for example, James Glanz, "Iraqi Sunni [Arab] Lands Show New Oil and Gas Promise," *New York Times* (February 19, 2007): A1. This important article brings that newspaper of record's readers up to date on a factual matter misrepresented in many of its opinion pieces. There is nothing "new" about the promise. It has been known for some time.

34. See among others Mahmoud Abdel-Fadil, "Macro Behaviour of Oil Rentier States in the Arab Region," in *The Rentier State*, ed. Hazem Beblawi and Giacomo Luciani (London, New York: Croom Helm, 1987), 83–107, and Terry Lynn Karl, *The Paradox of Plenty: Oil Booms and Petro-States* (Berkeley, Calif.: University of California Press, 1997). Political scientist Michael L. Ross has written an excellent series of articles on the subject. See his "Oil, Islam and Women," *American Political Science Review* 102 (2) (February 2008); "Does Oil Hinder Democracy?" *World Politics* 53 (April 2001); and "The Political Economy of the Resource Curse," *World Politics* 51 (January 1999).

35. Brendan O'Leary, "Multi-National Federalism, Power-Sharing, Federacy & the Kurds of Iraq," Norwegian Foreign Ministry Workshop on Autonomy Arrangements and Internal Territorial Conflict, November 14–15, 2003, Oslo; see also David R. Rezvani, *Federacy: The Dynamics of Semi-Sovereign Territories* (2003, an unpublished manuscript, based on his Oxford University Ph.D. thesis).

36. In his fascinating memoir, Peter Galbraith describes Kurdish leaders in 2003 as thinking merely of devolution rather than of federalism, *The End of Iraq*, 160–61. That was not so of Sami Abdul Rahman, the deputy prime minister of the KRG (Erbil), who would likely have led the KDP's constitutional negotiators had he lived (he was killed in a suicide bombing in February 2004). Dr Khaled Salih and I had several detailed discussions about confederalism, federalism, and federacies with Sami between December 2002 and the end of January 2004. Kurdish knowledge of these matters is much older than this century. The Israeli scholar of Baathist discourse, who works on Arabic sources, observes that Baathists were very angry in the 1970s when Kurds spoke of remaking Iraq as an *ittihad ikhitiyari* (a voluntary union, or a federation with the right of secession); see Ofra Bengio, *Saddam's World: Political Discourse in Iraq* (Oxford: Oxford University Press, 2002), 119.

37. Ronald Watts, however, defines a federacy as an entity that exercises little influence over the actions of the federal government; see Ronald L. Watts, "Models of Federal Power-Sharing," *International Social Science Journal* (March 2001): 23–32. If so, Kurdistan is an exception to Watts's rule: so far Kurdish ministers and a Kurdish president have been key players in the federal executive, and they have not confined their interests to Kurdish regional interests.

38. See Chapter 1, note 30, p. 220.

39. See Deeks and Burton, "Iraq's Constitution," pp. 5–18, for a good discussion.

40. See Peter W. Galbraith, *The End of Iraq: How American Incompetence Created a War Without End* (New York: Simon & Schuster, 2006), 199–200.

41. See the discussion of Articles 115 and 121(2) above, pp. 145–46.

42. Article 43 of the Constitution grants a free choice in personal law for marriage—protecting non-Muslims, although placing Muslim women under jeopardy of having fewer rights than they would have under secular marriage. Article 45(2) forbids tribal customs that are contrary to human rights—so regions that apply these federal provisions, such as Kurdistan, will respect Western secular standards.

Chapter 7

Epigraph: Editorial, "No Hope for Kashmir?" *The Economist* 356 (2000): 18–19.

1. *Al-Iraq al-Arabi* is used in early Islamic sources but most frequently referred to what is now southern and largely Shia Iraq; *al-Jazira*, by contrast, described much of

what is now Anbar, Ninevah, and Syria. The name Iraq is therefore old, but the present state and its boundaries were a British creation in 1920 and cover half as much territory again as medieval "al-Iraq." Kurdistan, the land of the Kurds, had never previously been incorporated within al-Iraq al-Arabi. Often subordinated by Muslim rulers (Arab, Turkish, and Persian), its principalities and places adjoined those that fluctuated in al-Iraq and al-Jazeera, and all were incorporated into Ottoman provinces. The present external borders of Iraq owe almost everything to British strategic and imperial interests. See among others Batatu, *The Old Social Classes and the Revolutionary Movements in Iraq*, 39; Tripp, *A History of Iraq*, 8; Alastair Northedge, "Al-Iraqi al-Arabi: Iraq's Greatest Region in the Pre-Modern Period," in *An Iraq of Its Regions? Cornerstones of a Federal Democracy*, ed. Reidar Visser and Gareth Stansfield (New York: Columbia University Press, 2008), 151–66; and Richard Schofield, "Borders, Regions and Time: Defining the Iraqi Territorial State," in *An Iraq of Its Regions?*, ed. Visser and Stansfield, 167–204. Iraq's border with Iran, modern wars and controversies notwithstanding, is, however, much the same as it has been since the Treaty of Kasr-i-Shirin of 1639, signed by the Ottoman and Safavid Empires of Turkey and Persia—sometimes called the Treaty of Zuhab and known importantly as the "Treaty of Peace and Frontiers"; see Robert Olson, *The Kurdish Question and Turkish-Iranian Relations, From World War I to 1998* (Costa Mesa, Calif.: Mazda Press, 1998), 15, Map 3. The Treaty was reaffirmed in 1746, 1823, and 1847. The text is in J. C. Hurewsitz, *Diplomacy in the Near and Middle East* (Princeton, N.J.: Van Nostrand, 1956), vol. 1, 21–23, and the Ottoman version may be found at http://www.parstimes.com/history/iran_ottoman.html.

2. For an early argument in recent times along these lines, see Shlomo Avineri, "Iraq May Be Wise to Forsake Unity for Democracy," *Financial Times*, November 17, 2003.

3. See Leslie H Gelb, "The Three-State Solution," *New York Times*, November 25, 2003. See also "The Biden-Gelb Plan for Iraq—One Year Later," *All American Patriots*, May 1, 2007, http://www.allamericanpatriots.com/48722178_joe_biden_biden_gelb_plan_iraq_one_year_later.

4. See Peter Galbraith, "Iraq: The Way to Go," *New York Review of Books* 54 (13) (August 16, 2007); "What Are We Holding Together?" *Washington Post*, November 7, 2005; and *The End of Iraq: How American Incompetence Created a War Without End* (New York: Simon and Schuster, 2006). See Christopher Hitchens, "Mesopotamia Split? Considering Peter Galbraith's Proposal for Iraq," *Slate*, March 26, 2007, http://www.slate.com/id/2162656/. See also Edward P. Joseph and Michael E. O'Hanlon, *The Case for Soft Partition in Iraq* (Washington, D.C.: Analysis Paper, The Brookings Institution, June 2007), and David Brooks, "The Road to Partition," *New York Times*, September 11, 2007. For a fanciful remaking and (re-) partitioning of the entire Middle East, see Jeffrey Goldberg, "After Iraq: A Report from the New Middle East—and a Glimpse of Its Possible Future," *The Atlantic* 301 (1) (2008).

5. Thomas L. Friedman, "Watch the Sunni Tribes," *New York Times*, August 29, 2007.

6. In defense of this definition and in elaboration of its significance, see Brendan O'Leary, "Analyzing Partition: Definition, Classification and Explanation," *Political Geography* 26 (8) (2007): 886–908. See also my "Debating Partition: Justifications, Critiques, & Evaluation," *Working Paper in British-Irish Studies, Number 78* (Dublin and Belfast: IBIS, UCD-QUB, 2006). For advocacy of partitions as solutions to civil wars, see Chaim Kaufmann, "Possible and Impossible Solutions to Ethnic Civil Wars," *International Security* 20 (4) (1996): 136–75, and "When All Else Fails: Ethnic Population Transfers and Partitions in the Twentieth Century," *International Security*

23 (2) (Fall 1998): 120–56. My essays just cited were in part replies to Kaufmann but were also a response to one of his critics, namely, Nicholas Sambanis, "Partition as a Solution to Ethnic War: An Empirical Critique of the Theoretical Literature," *World Politics* 52 (July 2000): 437–83.

7. See Brendan O'Leary, "Debating Partition."

8. David Brooks, "The Road to Partition," *New York Times*, September 11, 2007.

9. See the essays of Lehigh University's Chaim Kaufmann cited earlier, "Possible and Impossible Solutions to Ethnic Civil Wars" and "When All Else Fails." See also his discussion of Iraq in Chaim Kaufmann, "Divided and Conquered, Iraq Descends into Civil War," *The Jewish Daily Forward*, April 7, 2006.

10. See Shailagh Murray, "Senate Endorses Plan to Divide Iraq: Action Shows Rare Bipartisan Consensus," *Washington Post*, September 26, 2007; Elana Schor, "Biden's Iraq Plan Scores Senate Win," *The Hill*, September 27, 2007. Reporters confused federalization and partition in a now familiar manner.

11. Vigorous rejection of partitioning Iraq may be found in the writings of the Norwegian Reidar Visser; see, e.g., "Iraq's Partition Fantasy," *openDemocracy* (2006): 1–4, http://www.opendemocracy.net/. A scholar of southern Iraq, Visser is, however, constantly adjusting his views as present-day Shia Arabs surprise him. He is hostile both toward partition and any federation that recognizes ethnicity or sectarian bases for region formation. His central (and correct) empirical claim is the lack of correspondence between the three Ottoman provinces of Basra, Baghdad, and Mosul and the proposed boundaries implied by a "Shiastan," "Sunnistan," and Kurdistan. See his "Basra, the Reluctant Seat of 'Shiastan'," *Middle East Report* (242), http://www.merip.org/mer/mer242/visser.html, and "Unitary State, Federalism or Partition: Poll Data Give Mixed Picture of Iraq South of Baghdad," *Historiae.org*, April 10, 2007, http://historiae.org/poll.asp. For useful discussions of regionalism and provincialism in Iraq, see Visser and Stansfield, eds., *An Iraq of Its Regions?*

12. For a typical Arab nationalist perspective, with myths of his own, see Feisal Amin Rasoul al-Istrabadi, "Rebuilding a Nation: Myths, Realities, and Solutions in Iraq," *Harvard International Review* 29 (1) (2007): 14–19. Istrabadi may imagine his readers are historically illiterate when he writes that "When medieval Islamic geographers referred to 'Iraq,' they meant roughly the same place we mean now" (p. 14). That would be roughly like suggesting that when medieval Latin geographers referred to "England," they meant roughly the same as Great Britain and Ireland.

13. James A. Baker, III, Lee H. Hamilton, Lawrence S. Eagleburger, Vernon E. Jordan Jr., Edwin Meese III, Sandra Day O'Connor, Leon E. Panetta, William J. Perry, Charles S. Robb, and Alan K. Simpson, *The Iraq Study Group Report: The Way Forward—A New Approach* (New York: Vintage, 2006): 39.

14. I leave aside consideration of the disputes between Arab-majority governorates in the South because they are unlikely to lead to major violence; they are not considered to involve major natural resource questions; and they can be decoupled from the management of the territories in dispute between the Kurdistan region neighboring provinces, districts, and sub-districts.

15. See Chapter 6, pp. 127–30.

16. Contrary to the belief of Barry Posen, see Chapter 5, note 11, p. 231.

17. See Peter Sluglett, *Britain in Iraq 1914–1932* (Oxford: The Middle East Centre of St. Anthony's College, Oxford, 1976), and Richard Schofield, "Borders, Regions and Time: Defining the Iraqi Territorial State," in Visser and Stansfield, eds., *An Iraq of Its Regions?*, 167–204.

18. In the plains of Ninevah province there are Christian villages to the East of Mosul that are trying to establish an autonomous entity. Though the idea has some support from Kurds (who would accept its affiliation with the KRG), it is not clear how borders could be drawn to generate a Christian majority entity.

19. The Turkomen, who speak old Ottoman Turkish (unintelligible to the Turks of Turkey) and who write in "administrative Ottoman," have origins that are much debated. Some see them as Ottoman urban settlers, garrison populations spread across the plains of Mosul *vilayat* to hold the major trade routes for the House of Osman. Others trace their origins to the Seljuk Turkic-speaking empire built by Islamized nomads from central Asia before the Ottoman era. And yet others see them as "Ottoman Turkified" elites, i.e., educated Arabs and Kurds who had assimilated into the Ottoman administrative and mercantile upper classes. There is doubtless merit in all of these accounts. Turkomen are both Sunni and Shia—the scale of the latter suggesting both central Asian and Iranian influences.

20. The first translation, by the Associated Press, rendered Article 140 in slightly clearer English, although it refers to a census rather than a referendum, viz., "1st— The executive authority will take the necessary steps to complete implementation of the requirements of Article (58) of the Transitional Administration Law for the Iraqi State, with all its clauses. 2nd— The responsibilities placed on the executive authority provided for in Article (58) of the Transitional Administration Law for the Iraqi State are extended to and will continue for the executive authority until the completion of (normalization, census, ending with a census in Kirkuk and other disputed areas to determine the will of the people) in a period no longer than 12/31/2007."

21. The phrase "correcting nationality" refers to the Baathist practice of forcibly obligating Kurds and Turkomen to define themselves as Arabs, a policy of coercive assimilation, illegal under Iraqi law, and a violation of the International Covenant of Civil and Political Rights (1966), of which Iraq was a signatory.

22. *Law of Administration for the State of Iraq for the Transitional Period (Transitional Law 040308)*, reprinted in *The Future of Kurdistan in Iraq*, ed. Brendan O'Leary, John McGarry, and Khaled Salih (Philadelphia: University of Pennsylvania Press, 2005), 315–40.

23. "Kurdistan President Visits Kirkuk," *Kurdish Globe*, August 14, 2008.

24. See "Professor Brendan O'Leary Interviews Prime Minister Nechirvan Barzani," in Brendan O'Leary, ed., *The Kurdistan Region: Invest in the Future* (Washington, D.C., and London: Newsdesk Publications, 2008), 46–49.

25. Cited in Sumedha Senanayake, "Iraq: Kirkuk Referendum Likely to Be Delayed," September 12, 2007, Radio Free Europe, Radio Free Liberty.

26. The most reasonable reading of Article 140(2) is that the extension of authority to the federal government—handed on from the transitional government— is both time-limited and mandate-limited. Its authority continues only "provided that" it is fulfilling its obligations. It is mandate-limited because it is required only to rectify injustices according to the provisions in Article 58. There is therefore, in my view, no constitutional impediment to other executive authorities in Iraq acting to fulfill the provisions of Article 140, provided they respect the mandate to rectify the relevant injustices and all other provisions of Iraq's Constitution. They could plead necessity.

27. I spoke with them at a conference on the subject in Washington, D.C., in June 2008, held at the International Relations Room in the Rayburn Building of the U.S. Congress.

28. AFP, "Kirkuk 'city of Kurdistan'": Barzani," *Kurdish Globe*, August 9, 2008, http://kurdishglobe.net/displayArticle.jsp?id=87E86DB31934761253CC77510C73CF6D.

Chapter 8

1. Arshak Safrastian, *Kurds and Kurdistan* (The Hague: Mouton & Co, 1948), 97(a).
2. Another translation has this pamphlet as "God should have abstained from creating three things: Persians, Jews and Flies"; Ala Bashir, *The Insider: Trapped in Saddam's Brutal Regime* (London: Abacus, 2005), 285.
3. I borrow the heading for this section from Michael Gunter, "Turkey's New Neighbor, Kurdistan," in *The Future of Kurdistan in Iraq*, ed. Brendan O'Leary, John McGarry, and Khaled Salih (Philadelphia: University of Pennsylvania Press, 2005), 219–34. I draw below on numerous useful treatments of Turkey's Kurdish questions, notably, Henri J. Barkey and Graham Fuller, *Turkey's Kurdish Question* (New York: Rowman & Littlefield, 1998); Michael M. Gunter, *The Kurds in Turkey: A Political Dilemma* (Boulder, Colo: Westview Press, 1990); Kemal Kirisci and Gareth M. Winrow, *The Kurdish Question and Turkey: An Example of a Trans-State Ethnic Conflict* (London: Frank Cass, 1997); Robert W. Olson, *The Emergence of Kurdish Nationalism and the Sheikh Said Rebellion 1880–1925* (Austin: University of Texas, 1989); *The Kurdish Nationalist Movement in the 1990s: Its Impact on Turkey and the Middle East* (Lexington: University Press of Kentucky, 1996); and *The Kurdish Question and Turkish-Iranian Relations: From World War I to 1998* (Costa Mesa, Calif.: Mazda Press, 1998). Robert Olson's epigraph to the last cited of these studies reads, "To the Kurdish peoples: may they live when their existence is no longer defined as a 'question' or a 'problem'." These are my sentiments, too. I have also drawn on the works of David McDowall, notably his *A Modern History of the Kurds*, and the superb wisdom of physicist turned anthropologist and Kurdologist Martin van Bruinessen, notably his *Agha, Shaikh and State: The Social and Political Structure of Kurdistan* (London: Zed Books, 1992); "Multiple Shifting Identities: The Kurds, Turkey, and Europe," Paper read at Conference on Redefining the Nation, State and the Citizen, March 28–29, 1996, Marmara University, Istanbul, Turkey; and "Kurds, States and Tribes," in *Tribes and Power: Nationalism and Ethnicity in the Middle East*, ed. Faleh Jabar and Hosham Dawod (London: Saqi, 2003), 165–84. The sources upon which I have relied for the PKK are listed in note 28 of Chapter 5.
4. Hakan Ozoglu, "Will Turkey Seize Northern Iraq?" *History News Network* (2006), http://hnn.us/articles/32032.html. The writer is the author of an interesting essay entitled "'Nationalism' and Kurdish Notables in the Late Ottoman–Early Republican Era," *International Journal of Middle East Studies* 33 (2001): 383–409, but shows characteristic Turkish reserve in acknowledging the depth of Kurdish nationalism.
5. For a memoir of one of the British policymakers who determined facts on the ground see Cecil J. Edmonds, *Kurds, Turks and Arabs: Politics, Travel and Research in North-Eastern Iraq, 1919–1925* (London: Oxford University Press, 1957), especially Part 4, "The Mosul Commission."
6. Kemal Atatürk mobilized the defeated young Turks after the Ottoman defeat in World War 1, and rebuilt Turkey as a secular ethnic Turkish state. But in the initial stages of the fight against the Greeks, the Armenians, and the European empires he mobilized Kurdish notables behind a neo-Ottoman platform. But once the Kurds had outlived their usefulness they were subjected to the coercive assimilationist rigors of Turkish nation-building—eventually being designated as "mountain Turks" in an infamous public lie (as if the Kurds had forgotten their true ethnic-

ity amid mountain airs). For a sympathetic treatment of Kemalism, see Ernest Gellner's "Kemalism," in *Encounters with Nationalism* (Oxford: Basil Blackwell, 1994), 81–91. On this subject I do not share my Ph.D. examiner's evaluation.

7. After Atatürk reconstructed Turkey out of its Ottoman core, Turkey resembled a rectangle built around Anatolia—an apparently natural shape which enabled many Turks to forget that Atatürk had once hoped to incorporate the Mosul *vilayat* that the British successfully absorbed into Iraq. See Ümit Cizre, "Turkey's Kurdish Problem: Borders, Identity and Hegemony," in *Right-Sizing the State: The Politics of Moving Borders*, ed. Brendan O'Leary, Ian S. Lustick, and Thomas M. Callaghy (Oxford: Oxford University Press, 2001), 222–52.

8. "Turkish Army Flexes Muscles on Iraq, Cyprus," *Washington Post*, January 16, 2004.

9. See Henry A. Kissinger, "Reflections on a Sovereign Iraq," *Washington Post*, February 8, 2004.

10. See Michael Gunter, "Turkey's New Neighbor, Kurdistan," in *The Future of Kurdistan in Iraq*, ed. O'Leary, McGarry, and Salih, 219–34.

11. See Robert W. Olson, Turkish-Kurdish Relations: A Year of Significant Developments," *Insight Turkey* 10 (3) (2008): 23–51.

12. For impressive documentation of the longstanding debates within Islam in which both modernist and fundamentalist positions have been taken, see Mansoor Moaddel, *Islamic Modernism, Nationalism and Fundamentalism: Episode and Discourse* (Chicago: University of Chicago Press, 2005), and Mansoor Moaddel and Kamran Talatoff, eds., *Modernist and Fundamentalist Debates in Islam: A Reader* (New York: Palgrave Macmillan, 2000). See also the writings of the French Islamologist Olivier Roy, especially his *Globalized Islam: The Search for a New Ummah* (New York: Columbia University Press, 2004).

13. Muslims, like Christians, formally place correct religious belief ahead of ethnicity. For a discussion of how Islamists in Turkey treat Kurdish nationalism, see Ümit Cizre, "Kurdish Nationalism from an Islamist Perspective: The Discourses of Turkish Islamist Writers," *Journal of Muslim Minority Affairs* 1 (April 1998): 73–89.

14. See Alfred Stepan, "The World's Religious Systems and Democracy: Crafting the 'Twin Tolerations'," in his *Arguing Comparative Politics* (Oxford: Oxford University Press, 2001), 213–54.

15. For the most succinct statement, see Walker Connor, "Eco- or Ethno-Nationalism?", *Ethnic and Racial Studies* 7 (October 1984): 342–59.

16. See McDowall, *A Modern History of the Kurds*, especially pp. 420–54.

17. Rudolf Rummel, *Death by Government* (London: Transaction, 1997), 209 ff. For a judgment of ethnocide on the crushing of the Dersim rebellion, see Martin van Bruinessen, "Genocide in Kurdistan? The Suppression of the Dersim Rebellion in Turkey (1937–38) and the Chemical War Against the Iraqi Kurds," in *Genocide: Conceptual and Historical Dimensions*, ed. George J. Andreopoulos (Philadelphia: University of Pennsylvania Press, 1994), 141–70. On the genocide of the Armenians, see Donald Bloxham, *The Great Game of Genocide: Imperialism, Nationalism and the Destruction of the Ottoman Armenians* (Oxford: Oxford University Press, 2005), for an insightful comparative analysis that is much better than his book's title. The seminal work by a Turkish author is Taner Akçam, *A Shameful Act: The Armenian Genocide and the Question of Turkish Responsibility*, trans. P. Bessemer (New York: Henry Holt, 2006). It confirms the verdicts long convincingly held by a range of international liberals (notably Arnold Toynbee) and by Armenian and Armenian-American scholars (notably Vahakn N. Dadrian, Richard G. Hovanissian, and Robert Melson). The legal concept of genocide was pioneered by the Polish jurist Raphael Lemkin after

his consideration of the fate of the Armenians—it is a singular irony that the most denied genocide is the one which inspired the concept's formation.

18. See "The Kurdish Rebellions in Turkey," in Jwaideh Wadie, *The Kurdish Nationalist Movement: Its Origins and Development*, with a Foreword by Martin van Bruinessen (Syracuse, N.Y.: Syracuse University Press, 2006), 203–18.

19. McDowall, *A Modern History of the Kurds*, 198. (McDowall's verdict needs only one update: Turkish troops are part of NATO forces in Afghanistan.)

20. See Amir Hassenpour, *Nationalism and Language in Kurdistan, 1918–1985* (San Francisco: Mellen Research University Press, 1992).

21. He is in solitary confinement under twenty-four hour surveillance in the Sea of Marmara. The European Court of Human Rights judged that he did not receive a fair trial. His lawyers and relatives have produced from notes and dictation the first volume of his prison writings. These are not without interest for those familiar with Marxist debates on Oriental despotism and the Asiatic mode of production; see Abdullah Ocalan, *Prison Writings: The Roots of Civilisation*, trans. Klaus Happel (London: Pluto Press, 2007).

22. The Turkish public awaits with interest the outcome of the trials of those charged in "the Ergenekon conspiracy," a clandestine ultranationalist organization with ties to the country's military and security apparatus. It takes its name from a legendary place where Bumin Khan is supposed to have gathered the Turkic people. Prosecutors have charged retired and serving members of the Turkish Armed Forces, politicians, university presidents, and others with illegal efforts to destabilize the AKP government.

23. There are, of course, much deeper obstacles to Turkey's possible membership in the European Union that cannot be fully elaborated here. European liberal and left-wing opinion remains correctly offended by Turkey's continuing public lying in its denial of the Armenian genocide, by the Turkish occupation of Cyprus, and by the formation of the dependent republic, "The Turkish Republic of Northern Cyprus." Turkey's concomitant refusal to recognize Cyprus, a member-state of the Union it wishes to join, is unparalleled diplomatic surquedry. Turkey's continuing maltreatment of its Kurds and Alevis also makes its membership credentials suspect. Turkey's sheer size and pivotality would also affect EU decision making and rule out any excuse to refuse the admission of the Ukraine. Offsetting these obstacles are geopolitical considerations: Turkey's antijihadist nature; its abundant exploitable labor; and its possible role as a bridge across civilizations. The bridge can only be built if Turkey addresses and redresses its maltreatment of its minorities (past and present).

24. See the compelling account of Mark Bowden, *Guests of the Ayatollah: The First Battle in America's War with Militant Islam* (New York: Grove Press, 2007). The hostages were subjected to multiple cruel indignities, including a mock execution (see Tim Wells, *444 Days: The Hostages Remember* (New York: Harcourt Brace Jovanovich, 1985).

25. http://www.youtube.com/watch?v=Xg7r7-R-H2Q. The choice of date by Netanyahu, 1938, is not accidental—it is when European powers appeased Hitler at Munich, to their cost.

26. http://www.youtube.com/watch?v=o-zoPgv_nYg. The candidate, John McCain, fortunately maintains he was just joking, and that we should all "lighten up"; http://www.youtube.com/watch?v=KeThckstKNE&feature=related.

27. Martin Woollacott, "Cyanide on the Table," *The Guardian*, July 10, 2008, 28.

28. There are doubts whether Israel has the aircraft and the bombs to perform such a mission at such a distance; see Pollack, *The Persian Puzzle*, 394–95. It would not have Iraq's permission to overfly its territory on any such enterprise.

29. http://www.parstimes.com/history/algiers_accords.pdf.

30. See Peter Kornbluh and Malcolm Byrne, *The Iran-Contra Scandal: The Declassified History* (New York: W.W. Norton, 1993).

31. Patriotism is loyalty to the state; nationalism is loyalty to a national community. Iran is a multinational and multiethnic state, which commands the loyalty of significant numbers of its large minorities of Azeris and Kurds as well as its Persian (Farsi-speaking) majority.

32. For accounts of the coup d'état, organized by Kermit Roosevelt, the grandson of Teddy Roosevelt, see Stephen Kinzer, *All the Shah's Men: An American Coup and the Roots of Middle East Terror* (New York: Wiley, 2003), and *Overthrow: America's Century of Regime Change, From Hawaii to Iraq* (New York: Henry Holt [Times Books], 2006), 111–28. See also Kermit Roosevelt, *Countercoup: The Struggle for Control of Iran* (New York: McGraw-Hill, 1979). For accounts of Mossadegh, see Sepehr Zabih, *The Mossadegh Era: Roots of the Iranian Revolution* (Chicago: Lake View, 1982); Fakhreddin Azimi, *The Quest for Democracy in Iran: A Century of Struggle Against Authoritarian Rule* (Cambridge, Mass.: Harvard University Press, 2008), 118–53. See especially Roy Mottahedeh's evocative pages in his *The Mantle of the Prophet: Religion and Politics in Iran* (Oxford: Oneworld Publications, 2005 [1985]), Chapter 4. See also the insightful review of the latter by Brian Spooner, "The Mantle of the Prophet: Religion and Politics in Iran (Review Article)," *Iranian Studies* 37 (1) (2004): 109–16.

33. For an excellent exposition of Iranian history between 1906 and 1978, see Ervand Abrahamian, *Iran Between Two Revolutions* (Princeton, N.J.: Princeton University Press, 1982). Curiously, it does not treat Iraq at all.

34. For studies of American-Iranian relations, see James A. Bill, *The Eagle and the Lion: The Tragedy of American-Iranian Relations* (New Haven, Conn.: Yale University Press, 1983); Kenneth M. Pollack, *The Persian Puzzle: The Conflict Between Iran and America* (New York: Random House, 2004); Barry Rubin, *Paved with Good Intentions: The American Experience and Iran* (New York: Penguin, 1981); and Gary Sick, *All Fall Down: America's Fateful Encounter with Iran* (London: I.B. Tauris, 1985).

35. The fascinating details of Israeli-Iranian-U.S. relations since 1948 are conveyed in a realist vein by Trita Parsi, *Treacherous Alliance: The Secret Dealings of Israel, Iran, and the United States* (New Haven, Conn.: Yale University Press, 2007). The above account is taken from pages 243–57 and Appendices A–C, pp. 341ff. See also the review of Parsi's book by Peter W. Galbraith, "The Victor?", *New York Review of Books* 54 (15) (October 11, 2007).

36. Graham E. Fuller, *"The Center of the Universe": The Geopolitics of Iran* (Boulder, Colo.: Westview, 1991).

37. See, e.g., Ken Pollack, *The Persian Puzzle*, 396–98. Had he called his book *The Iranian Imbroglio*, Pollack might have shown more respect without losing an alliterative book title.

38. In the Iraq-Iran war the Baath tried to rename the Persian Gulf as Arab, as *Khaliji Basra* or *al-Khalij al 'Arabi* (the Gulf of Basra or the Arab Gulf); see Bengio, *Saddam's Word*, 140. We should not expect to hear much in this vein from Iraq in the decades ahead.

39. James Glanz and Alyssa Rubin, "U.S. and Iran Find Common Ground in Iraq's Shiite Conflict," *New York Times*, April 21, 2008.

40. Patrick Cockburn, "Iran v. America," *London Review of Books*, 30 (12) (June 6, 2008):7–8.

41. For discussions of possible negotiations over nuclear questions with Iran, see Geoffrey Kemp, *Iran and Iraq: The Shia Connection, Soft Power, and the Nuclear Factor* (Washington, D.C.: Special Report, United States Institute of Peace, November

2005), http://www.usip.org/pubs/specialreports/sr156.pdf; Kenneth M. Pollack, *The Persian Puzzle: The Conflict Between Iran and America* (New York: Random House, 2004); and Ramberg Bennett, John Thomson, Geoffrey Forden, William Luers, Thomas R. Pickering, and Jim Walsh, "Iran and the Bomb: An Exchange," *New York Review of Books* 55 (6) (2008).

42. This is not the place for a digression on the nature of theocracies. Elsewhere I have suggested that theocracies are likely—in the long run—to generate a separation of powers and respect for legality and thereby undermine clerical rule, and that in these respects they differ from one-party totalitarian regimes; see Brendan O'Leary, "Theocracy and the Separation of Powers," in *The Political Economy of Theocracy*, ed. Ron Wintrobe and Mario Ferrero (London and New York: Palgrave, 2009). The argument in here does not depend on the merits of this thesis.

43. See Robert W. Olson, *The Kurdish Question and Turkish-Iranian Relations, From World War I to 1998* (Costa Mesa, Calif.: Mazda Press, 1998).

44. For discussion of the Kurds of Iran, see A. R. Ghassenlou, "Kurdistan in Iran," in *People Without a Country: The Kurds and Kurdistan*, ed. Gérard Chaliand (London: Zed Press, 1980), 95–103. The author, a leader of the KDPI (the Kurdistan Democratic Party of Iran), was assassinated by secret agents from Tehran. See also McDowall, *A Modern History of the Kurds*, especially 214–86, and Farideh Koohi-Kemali, *The Political Development of the Kurds in Iran: Pastoral Nationalism* (New York: Palgrave Macmillan, 2003).

45. Leading Article, "The Iraqi Dustbowl: A Once Fertile Land Is Threatened by Severe Drought," *The Times* (London), July 29, 2008.

46. In his *Reflections on Exile and Other Essays* (Cambridge, Mass.: Harvard University Press, 2002), Edward Said defined Iraq as "an Arab country" (397). He referred later in the same collection to the fact that "the Iraqi Baath was universally condemned for its oppression of the Kurdish people" (429). He did not use the term genocide or expulsion or reflect, as far as I know, on the fact that the Baath killed extraordinarily far more Kurds than Israelis have killed Palestinians. Said used the fact of universal condemnation of the Baath (which he did not explicitly join in the essay from which I have taken the phrasing above) to reflect on the fact that were was no similar condemnation of Saudi Arabia's expulsion of 800,000 Yemeni—because of Yemen's votes in the United Nations in 1990–91, or of the Kuwaiti collective punishment of Palestinians after the 1991 Gulf War, "because, it was argued, the PLO had supported Iraq." Well, Arafat did; and so did many Palestinians, not that these facts justify their collective punishment. Said's evasive references to the maltreatment of the Kurds at the hands of Arab nationalists is a sad blot on his proclaimed universalism. One of Kanan Makiya's most impressive engagements with Said and other Arab intellectuals on their responses to Saddam and the Baath is contained in his "New Nationalist Myths," in *Cruelty and Silence: War, Tyranny, Uprising and the Arab World* (New York: W.W. Norton, 1993). There he rebukes Said for casting doubt on whether the Iraqi regime ever gassed its own citizens (256) and for failing to address Saddam's culpabilities in his first response in English to the invasion of Kuwait, (278).

47. Sageman, *Leaderless Jihad.*

48. Roula Khalaf, "Why Arab States Must Embrace Iraq," *Financial Times*, August 19, 2008.

49. For a Muslim critique of Wahhabism, see Hamid Algar, *Wahhabism: A Critical Essay* (Oneonta, N.Y.: Islamic Publications International, 2002).

50. For an essay that has mostly withstood the passage of time, see Fred Halliday, "Saudi Arabia 1997: A Family Business in Trouble," in his *Nation and Religion in the Middle East* (Boulder, Colo.: Lynne Rienner, 2000), 169–76.

51. Robert Vitalis, *America's Kingdom: Mythmaking on the Saudi Oil Frontier*, Stanford Studies in Middle Eastern and Islamic Studies (Stanford, Calif.: Stanford University Press, 2006).

52. See, for example, Minister of Foreign Affairs Prince Saud Al-Faisal's statement to the 62nd session of the UN General Assembly, September 28, 2007, http://www.saudiembassy.net/2007News/Statements/StateDetail.asp?cIndex=700. Of interest, this speech gently raised the issue of placing Israel's nuclear weapons capabilities into a general discussion of peace and disarmament in the region; it also shows (in the stress on the word "unity") mildly worded opposition to federalism in Iraq.

53. See Gabrielle Rifkind et al., *From the Swamp to Terra Firma: The Regional Role in the Stabilization of Iraq* (London: Oxford Research Group, King Faisal Center, and Diplomatic Institute Riyadh, April 2008), http://www.oxfordresearchgroup.org.uk/publications/briefing_papers/fromtheswamp.php.

54. Reliable brief discussions of the Golan Heights may be found throughout William B. Quandt, *Peace Process: American Diplomacy and the Arab-Israeli Conflict Since 1967* (Washington, D.C.: Brookings Institution/University of California Press, 2001), and Mark Tessler, *A History of the Israeli-Palestinian Conflict* (Bloomington: Indiana University Press, 1994).

Chapter 9

Epigraphs: Barzani quotation from "A Talk with Kurdish President Massoud Barzani," Interview by Ma'ad Fayad, *Asharq Alawsat*, September 1, 2008, http://www.asharq-e.com/news.asp?section=3&id=13920. Kennan quotation from http://hnn.us/articles/997.html.

1. http://www.youtube.com/watch?v=rw2nkoGLhrE.

2. "A Talk with Kurdish President Massoud Barzani."

3. See, notably, Noah Feldman, *What We Owe Iraq: War and the Ethics of Nation Building* (Princeton, N.J.: Princeton University Press, 2004), and Kenneth M. Pollack, *The Threatening Storm: The Case for Invading Iraq* (New York: Random House, 2002).

4. Some have started to think about these matters—including those who see an enhanced role for the U.S. Air Force during and after disengagement from Iraq; see Clint "Q" Hinote, "The Drawdown Asymmetry: Why Ground Forces Will Depart Iraq But Air Forces Will Stay," *Strategic Studies Quarterly* 2 (2) (2008): 31–62.

5. John Kenneth Galbraith, *How to Get Out of Vietnam* (New York: Signet Books, 1967).

6. For a collection which I find unreliable on Iraq although not on Vietnam, see Lloyd C. Gardner and Marilyn B. Young, eds., *Iraq and the Lessons of Vietnam: Or, How Not to Learn from the Past* (New York: New Press, 2007).

7. Max Boot, "How Not to Get Out of Iraq," *Commentary*, September 2007.

Appendix 1

1. For their critical commentary see Hamit Dardagan, John Sloboda, and Josh Dougherty, "Reality Checks: Some Responses to the Latest Lancet Estimates," Press Release, October 16, 2006, *Iraq Body Count*, http://www.iraqbodycount.org/analysis/beyond/reality-checks/. The latest *Lancet* study details may be found in Gilbert Burnham, Riyadh Laftah, Shannon Doocy, and Les Roberts, "Mortality After the

2003 Invasion of Iraq: A Cross-Sectional Cluster Sample Survey," *The Lancet* 368 (October 2006): 1421–28.

2. See Iraq Family Health Survey Study Group, "Violence-Related Mortality in Iraq from 2002 to 2006," *New England Journal of Medicine* 358 (5) (January 31, 2008): 484–93.

3. For a sensible commentary see Catherine A. Brownstein and John S. Brownstein, "Perspective: Estimating Excess Mortality in Post-Invasion Iraq," *New England Journal of Medicine* 358 (5) (January 31, 2008): 445–57.

4. John Sloboda, *Can There Be Any "Just War" If We Do Not Document the Dead and Injured?* (Oxford: Oxford Research Group, April 2008), http://www.oxfordresearchgroup.org.uk/publications/briefing_papers/pdf/justwar.pdf.

5. David McKittrick, Seamus Kelters, Brian Feeney, and Chris Thornton, *Lost Lives: The Stories of the Men, Women and Children Who Died as a Result of the Northern Ireland Troubles* (Edinburgh: Mainstream Publishing, 2001). See my review, Brendan O'Leary, "3,636 So Far, and Counting," *Times Higher Education Supplement*, March 3, 2000.

6. *Le Livre noir de Saddam Hussein*, ed. Chris Kutchera (Paris: OH Éditions, 2005), has not been published in English. His own summary in French may be found at http://www.chris-kutschera.com/livre_noir.htm. For some commentaries on the text in English, see the web site of Jeff Weintraub: http://jeffweintraub.blogspot.com/2006/05/mass-murder-political-atrocity.html.

Appendix 2

1. Ronald Inglehart, Mansoor Moaddel, and Mark Tessler, "Xenophobia and In-Group Solidarity in Iraq: A Natural Experiment on the Impact of Insecurity," in *Values and Perceptions of the Islamic and Middle Eastern Publics*, ed. Mansoor Moaddel (New York: Palgrave Macmillan, 2007), 298–322.

Index

Information presented in tables and figures is indicated by *t* and *f*, respectively. Information in the Notes section is indicated by an "n" between the page number and the note number.

Acknowledgments and Sources

This book was written rapidly in August 2008. Bill Finan, of the University of Pennsylvania Press, Lori Salem, Director of Temple University's Writing Center, and Diarmuid Ó Mathúna of the Institute of Advanced Study Dublin, provided expert editorial assistance, but are responsible for none of the remaining faults of logic or fact. I sincerely thank Leonard Lauder, who endowed my chair at Penn, and the Dean of the School of Arts and Sciences at Penn, Rebecca Bushnell, for her support for the Penn Program in Ethnic Conflict (PPEC), where David Bateman, Stephan Stohler, Joanne McEvoy and Zulal Neyzi provided intellectual and moral support. Jena Laske organized my electronic and paper files on Iraq from 2002. Emily Toops provided entirely voluntary, very fast and reliable bibliographical and source-checking research assistance, for which I am deeply indebted. David Bateman drew the map of the Saddam-ander, and of Iraq's regions (as advocated by Mowaffak al-Rubaie), and provided critical comments on the manuscript.

I have reflected on the questions addressed here since advising the Kurdistan Regional Government in Iraq in the making of the Transitional Administrative Law in 2004, and the Constitution of Iraq in 2005. I have made presentations to U.S. government officials since 2004, and contributed to public debates on the American Iraq Study Group, and the British Iraq Commission (organized by Channel 4 and the Foreign Policy Centre). Many of the ideas here were first presented in public lectures in Great Britain, at the Universities of Exeter and Sheffield, and at Chatham House and LSE; in Ireland, at the Queen's University Belfast, Northern Ireland, and the National University of Ireland, Galway; and in North America at the University of Western Ontario, Canada, New York University, Dartmouth College, and the Universities of California (Irvine), Chicago, and Pennsylvania. I am grateful to all who invited me and who posed difficult questions. The Sawyer-Mellon funded grant on "Power-Sharing in Deeply Divided Places" (2006–8) enabled me to learn from academics and practitioners in ways that might otherwise have taken decades. I have also been one of the international beneficiaries of the Ethnicity and Democratic Governance Project, funded by Canada's SSHRCC and co-held by Professor John McGarry, who provided invaluable commentary and counsel.

I have taught on Iraq at the University of Pennsylvania since 2005, and on power-sharing in deeply divided places at the University of Pennsylvania since 2002 and before that at the London School of Economics and Political Science. I thank the numerous students who have questioned my evolving thoughts and brought materials to my attention that I might otherwise have missed. At the University of Pennsylvania I especially wish to thank Alyssa Casey, Jonathan Friedman, Niall O'Donnell, Kyle Pickett, Emily Toops, and Michael Zubrow.

The sources used here are mostly acknowledged in the footnotes. The factual materials are derived almost entirely from open-source materials in the English language. I have also regularly used Juan Cole's web site *Informed Comment* at http://www.juancole.com/. Though I rarely agree with his political views Professor Cole's translations of key materials in Arabic and Farsi sources provide an invaluable public service. Where I have forgotten the origins of an argument or piece of evidence I apologize and plead the legendary professorial defense, "if you steal from one author, it's plagiarism; if you steal from many, it's research." I have a substantial library of books and articles published on Iraq and its neighbors since 1920. The University of Pennsylvania has superb collections on Middle Eastern politics. I speak merely a few words of Arabic, derived from my adolescence, when my father worked for the United Nations Development Program in Khartoum, Sudan, between 1969 and 1976. I have an equally small vocabulary in Kurdish, derived from my work for the Kurdistan Regional Government since 2003. That I have no serious reading capacity in either of Iraq's official languages puts me on a par with most U.S. public officials who have managed Iraq since 2003. I have no Farsi and no Turkish. Since 2002 I have kept abreast of Kurdish, Arabic, Turkish and Lebanese web sites which publish in English, especially the official web sites of the Iraqi government and of the KRG. The *New York Times*, the *Washington Post*, and the *BBC* are to be commended for operating major news-gathering operations since 2003, and I am grateful to their correspondents, some of whom I know. I do not always agree with them, especially with their Baghdad focus, but they have individually and collectively performed remarkable work in extremely adverse conditions.

My times in Iraq have given me regular access, on a confidential basis, to senior Kurdish politicians and officials, and a smaller number of Arab intellectuals and politicians. My close friend, Khaled Salih, who is fluent in Kurdish, Arabic, Farsi, English, Swedish, Danish and German, and whose PhD is in political science, has regularly pointed me toward multiple materials that I might otherwise have missed. He should not be presumed to agree with what I write here but I am grateful to him for being a truly extraordinary friend in deeply difficult times for both of us, personally and politically. This book is dedicated to him. I would also like to thank Sinje Stoyke, the Director of Archaeologists for Human Rights, who proved with her colleagues how intrepid German pacifists with forensic skills could help document Saddam's genocide, and who allowed me to become a member of her organization, which facilitated my travel in and out of Iraq in 2003–4.

I am especially grateful to Dr. Najmaldin Karim, and Dr. Kendal Nezan, the heads of the Kurdish Institutes in Washington and Paris, respectively. For numerous forms of help too numerous to particularize here I would like to record my thanks to Peter Agree, Shanaz Ahmed, Katharine Adeney, Alex Anderson, Liam Anderson, Harriet Arnold, Andrew Apostolou, Amatzia Baram, Minister Taha Barwary, Minister Falah Mustafa Bakir, Henri J. Barkey, Anny and Brian Barry, Prime Minister Nechirvan Barzani, Ali Al Bayati, Alan and Liz Beattie, Sharon L. Burke, Hamit Bozarslan, Stafford Clarry, Eric Clemons, Paddy and Delia Close, Andrew Cockburn, Patrick Cockburn, Cathie Connor, Walker and Mary Connor, Pat Conway, Shelley Deane, Mohsin Dizayee, Elizabeth Doering, Patrick Dunleavy, David Edgerton, Roy J. Eidelson, Nader Entessar, Geoff Evans, Brian Feeney, Chuck Feeney, George Freimarck, Ambassador Peter Galbraith, David Gardner, David Gellner, Eleanor Gibson, Michelle Grajek, Bernie Grofman, Michael Gunter, John A. Hall, Michael Howard, Jim Hughes, Fuad Hussein, Michael Ignatieff, Sam Issaccaroff, Burhan Jaf, George W. Jones, Melik Kaylan, Kemal Kerkuki, Sherko Kermanj, Bill Kissane, Janet Klein, Steve Kull, Roula Khalaf, Quil Lawrence, Simone Lewis, Marc Liberman, Arend Lijphart, Michael Lind, Robert Lowe, Ian S. Lustick, Tristan Mabry, Carolyn Marvin, John McGarry, Chris and Caroline McCrudden, Katherine McDermott, Paud and Marie McGuone, Joe and Trisha McKenna, Cindie McLemore, Molly McNulty,

Nicola Meyrick, Mansoor Moaddel, Jonathan Morrow, Lokman Muhamad, Jack H. Nagel, Fionnula Ni Aolain, Sima Noznisky, Carole A. O'Leary (no relation), Donal O'Leary Sr., Donal O'Leary Jr., Anne O'Leary, Lynda O'Leary, Raymond O'Leary, Christine O'Leary and Mary O'Leary (all relations), Robert Olson, Shane O'Neill, Gratia Pelliciotti, Ted Perlmutter, Sam Preston, Monroe Price, Bob Rae, Vian Rahman, High Representative Bayan Sami Abdul Rahman, Adolph Reed, Safia Rizvi, David Romano, Trudy Rubin, Marc Sageman, Waria Salhi, Deputy Prime Minister Barham A. Salih, Gwen Sasse, Holli Semetko, Greg Shapland, Minister Karim Sinjari, Alan and Jane Sleator, Karol Soltan, Dan Smith, R. Jeffrey and Lola Smith, Rogers Smith, Gary Spieker, Gareth Stansfield, Al Stepan, High Representative Qubad J. Talabani, Nisar Talabany, Holly Temple, Bob Vitalis, Karin von Hippel, Lorelei Watson, Jeff Weintraub, Marc Weller, Ed Webb, April Wells, Ali Willmore, Ron Wintrobe, Stefan Wolff, Martin Woollacott, Oren Yiftachel, Bob Young, Shwan Ziad, and Ambassador Howar Ziad.